Buffalo Niagara:
Diagnosis
& Prescription
for Change

by Lawrence Brooks

RPSS
BUFFALO, NEW YORK

Cover:

In my mind, the cover photo symbolizes the state of the region: It is in pieces, broken down. The many pieces represent the mosaic of cities, towns, and villages that have yet to be assembled into a single whole. Maybe we're doing well, but we could do so much better. This book diagnoses what is wrong and prescribes the change that will help us realize our potential.

Text and design by Mark D. Donnelly, Ph.D.

ISBN 978-0-9908997-4-7
Printed in the United States of America

14 15 16 9 8 7 6 5 4 3 2 1

www.rpsspublishing.com

Contents

Part III: Reconstructing Buffalo Niagara: Prescriptions

PREFACE

Buffalo Niagara was flooded by good news recently:

- The Census Bureau estimated that in 2013 the region's long-declining population actually rose;
- The city and state turned the former Republic Steel brownfield into a brand-new industrial park that lured two high-tech solar firms to open business in Buffalo;
- Crime and unemployment were down;
- Construction at Canalside continued and received a substantial contribution from the new HarborCenter hockey and entertainment center;
- New hotels are popping up in the cities of Buffalo and Niagara Falls;
- The Community Foundation for Greater Buffalo (CFGB) was able to attract investment capital from national charitable foundations intrigued by a new sense of public and private sector teamwork in the city;
- Consolidation of medical facilities continued in newly constructed buildings on the Buffalo Niagara Medical Campus;
- The $50 million cleanup of toxic sediment in the Buffalo River was nearly complete;
- And more.

The spate of good news had residents buzzing about "renaissance," "resurgence," and "revival" and thinking the region is on the comeback trail. There's been a lift in spirit, which is a good thing. But is it justified? Are we really on the comeback trail, or have we been down so long we set our sights low?

Positive changes have been happening: Our adult native sons and daughters have been returning, and a new awareness has been growing among transplants and visitors about the strengths of the region. There is unprecedented support from the governor and a level of construction activity not seen in decades. But has it been enough to reverse decades of decline? Thomas DeSantis, senior planner for the City of Niagara Falls, thinks that it's a "sense that we're on the cusp, that we're on this kind of trajectory where we're on the upward as opposed to flat or declining.... I think it's the waning of pessimism and the ascendance of optimism. While it may be a current trend, whether it's sustainable is the question."[1]

Cara Matteliano, vice president of community impact at the Community Foundation of Greater Buffalo, thinks the area is at the tipping point with "a lot of energy and resources to push us over."[2]

I remain skeptical. For almost all my life, my city's been on a downward slide. Yet despite having my hopes and expectations dashed numerous times—remember Wide Right? No Goal?—I remain cautiously optimistic about the region because I keep picturing the city that could be.

What I know is this: We have been declining for decades; despite all the attractions and amenities that are right about our region, they are not enough to attract people here; whatever public sector leaders, private entrepreneurs, nonprofit leaders, and outstanding citizens are doing, it's not enough. The region lags so far behind other communities that there may be few other places in the country with a bigger gap between potential and reality. To say that our region underperforms is an understatement. We should be mindful of what urban planners Luis Bettencourt and Geoffrey West write, "Cities tend to stay remarkably close to their overperforming or underperforming histories."[3]

What's the real story? Much of what I listed above consists of developments that have little to do with the human and social capital of the region and haven't even scratched the surface of some of the fundamental forces that keep this region from thriving, such as fractured governance, sprawl, and segregation. There is more to a region than economic development. While some pieces show significant and promising improvement, what's the whole picture?

You won't get the real story from our elected leaders. They don't want to tell you the bad news because that would make them look bad, and they want you to think well of them so you reelect them the next time around. And very often the good news that they report consists of their spending one million here on this and several hundred thousand there on that. This is a confusion of efforts and results: The expenditure of money does not measure results. Also, their annual messages, the states of the city, the county, and the region tend to ignore other important aspects of the community such as voter engagement, the health of the population, and the increase in toxic waste dumps, to name a few.

Right now the real story is missing two important considerations: The first is the need to put such measurements in context. For instance, while crime rates are dropping locally, they're also dropping across the nation and around the globe. The city of Buffalo still ranks among the top twenty most crime-ridden cities. Unemployment is dropping locally, but it is also dropping across the nation, and our metro area's rate is rising more slowly than the rest of the nation. The drop in the unemployment rate here is caused more by people dropping out of the workforce than it is caused by new job creation.

The second major consideration literally missing from the real story is the issues we don't talk about. The public conversations—in media, during political campaigns, in groups of people—omit unpleasant truths. Clearly, for all the uniqueness of the "best designed city in the world," people aren't rushing to move here. Most instruments of the local media celebrate our cultural roles and architectural heritage, yet the majority of the best and brightest of our children leave town for other places. It is true that there are books and articles in the alternative press, but I don't see many reports that think about our region critically and are based on evidence and reasoning I can trust. There are a few, most notably the work of UB's Regional Institute and its multi-year planning initiative One Region Forward and the reports from the Partnership for the Public

Good (PPG).

Consider that it is never wise to ignore physical symptoms of disease. The same holds for issues that afflict our community. The issues listed in the following chapters will not fix themselves or go away by ignoring them; they must be addressed. Sam Magavern, co-director of the Partnership for the Public Good, said, "We would never say, 'don't talk about the negative' because there's a lot of work to do."[4]

Some people deny negative issues with reactions such as, "It's not all that bad!" or echoes of the wicked witch in the musical The Wiz who sings, "Don't nobody bring me no bad news." When I told a successful businessman and community leader about the book I was writing which would mention some of the problems, his reply was, "You're writing the wrong damn book! Don't write anything negative! We're on the upswing." Denial is a refusal or rejection of unpleasant or painful facts, realities, feelings, or situations, and we all have expressed it. But denial can be dangerous. It is an obstacle standing in the way of those who are working toward solutions. To paraphrase the 1960s call to action, "If you're not part of the solution, you're part of the problem."

What's wrong with celebrating a little, enjoying the good news? One of my concerns is that we will ease up on the gas, decrease our efforts. It's happened before. Attorney Paul Wolf of the Center for Reinventing Government was in the audience when Congressman Brian Higgins told the story about a twelve page feature in *Fortune* magazine in the late 50s proclaiming Buffalo a city on the rise. Unknown to the writers of that feature, the city had only just crested the first hill of a roller coaster. Higgins attributed the subsequent decline partly to the fact that the community "put its feet up on the table."[5] That is, satisfied with the way things were going, it relaxed. That is my concern today. Some residents of the region may feel as though recent developments are sufficient to return us to good fortune. Take RiverBend, for example: It is truly good news that two new high-tech companies will create some 1700 jobs at a site that was formerly a steel plant. At one time, however, there were 3500 good-paying jobs at that site. Today, the region falls below the national average of high-tech STEM (Science, Technology, Engineering, and Math) jobs by at least eight to ten thousand. So instead of a celebratory, "Yay, we did it!", we should be saying, "Good start, but where are the next jobs and businesses coming from?" Community leaders don't say.

So why another book about the region? Many fine local writers—Mark Donnelly, Francis Kowsky, Lynda Schneekloth, Maria Scrivani, Robert Shibley, Thomas Yots, and others; many fine local publications—ArtVoice, The Buffalo News, Buffalo Spree; and many websites of fine local organizations—Buffalo By Choice, Citybration, Buffalo Rising—write eloquently and entertainingly about what's right with our region. There is a need for that, but not many people are willing to talk about what's wrong with our region, except perhaps political candidates opposing incumbents in an election campaign. There is a natural reluctance to confront the unpleasant. That, in part, is what this book attempts.

I have lived in Buffalo, New York, all the years of my life. I have traveled to forty states, three continents, twenty countries, and eight of the top twenty globally significant cities, yet I choose to live here. I have had chances to move elsewhere to advance my career but turned them all down, remembering a homily I heard once during months of unemployment: "Bloom where you're planted." I believe that, but more importantly, I am here because I love this place. I know it well. In the past year, I have visited family, friends, and businesses, or attended events in almost all the towns, villages, and cities of the two counties. Some people may know this region better than I do, but I know it better than most.

I have made an effort to contribute, to do my part: I raised a family here, invested here, I volunteer for several organizations, and, since my 18th birthday, never missed a vote and have campaigned for some candidates. I hope this book is one more contribution.

I don't wish to appear a cranky old curmudgeon, cynical and negative. I certainly don't want to discourage those who are making progress in our community. On the contrary, I want to encourage more people to get involved, because, as Chapter 2 shows, our rate of civic engagement is below average. Imagine what we could do if more people in our community were involved.

ACKNOWLEDGMENTS

I'm deeply grateful to the following community experts for giving to me so freely of their time: Jay Burney, communications coordinator for the Global Justice Ecology Project; Richard Deitz, assistant vice president, regional analysis function, Federal Reserve Bank of New York, Buffalo branch; Thomas DeSantis, senior planner, City of Niagara Falls; Martin Doster, regional engineer, New York State Department of Environmental Conservation; Philip Haberstro, founder and executive director, Wellness Institute of Greater Buffalo and WNY Inc.; Erin Heaney, director, Clean Air Coalition of Western New York; Jill Jedlicka, executive director, Buffalo Niagara Riverkeeper; Sam Magavern, codirector, Partnership for the Public Good; Cara Matteliano, vice president, community impact, Community Foundation for Greater Buffalo; Lynda Schneekloth, chair, Sierra Club Niagara Group; Robert Shibley, dean, University at Buffalo, School of Architecture and Planning; Loren Smith, executive director, Buffalo Audubon Society; Marlies Wesolowski, executive director, Lt. Col. Matt Urban Human Services Center; Paul Wolf, Esq., founder, Center for Reinventing Government; and Dale Zuchlewski, executive director, Homeless Alliance of Western New York.

John Slenker, economist, New York State Department of Labor, helped me by answering many questions via email. I also drew from community activist Kevin Gaughan's campaign to consolidate government and from his website.

Robert Hochberg of REH Designs made this a more pleasant book to read with his graphic artistry.

Kary Clark, my editor, made this book much better with her good work.

Publisher Mark Donnelly has been a good friend and supporter of my work. I am grateful for his friendship and enthusiasm for this project.

Lastly, my muse, supporter, and best friend, Carrie, who helped me throughout this and all of life's labors.

INTRODUCTION

On November 15, 1896, in Niagara Falls, the switch was thrown on an important scientific experiment that settled the debate of direct versus alternating current and created the world's first modern utility. In the process, Buffalo became the world's first city to be lit with electricity. Six years later, a local man, Willis Havilland Carrier, invented air conditioning while working for Buffalo Forge.

The region played a pivotal role in the lives and careers of three U.S. Presidents, all in a span of four years: Former Buffalo Mayor and Erie County Sheriff Grover Cleveland finished his second term in the White House in 1897. Four years later, Cleveland's successor, President William McKinley, while visiting Buffalo, was assassinated. His vice president, Theodore Roosevelt, came to Buffalo to take the oath of office as 26th president of the United States.

In the middle of all that was a World's Fair, the Pan-American Exposition, which featured a dazzling illuminated array of buildings by Thomas Edison. This is how a Buffalo visitors guide described the area then:

> The City of Buffalo has, by the census of 1900, a population of 352,387, standing eighth among the cities of the United States. It leads the world in its commerce in flour, wheat, coal, fresh fish, and sheep, and stands second only to Chicago in lumber. In cattle and hogs, only Chicago and Kansas City exceed it....Its railroad yard facilities are the greatest in the world, and are being increased rapidly...In marine commerce, although the season is limited to six months, Buffalo is exceeded in tonnage only by London, Liverpool, Hamburg, New York, and Chicago...The climate in summer is delightful, and it is one of the healthiest cities in the country, with a limitless supply of pure water...Coal and food supplies are so low in price it is one of the cheapest of the large cities in which to live.....in flour, grain, and coal alone equals ten percent of the yearly foreign trade of the entire United States.[1]

In the late 19th century, the area's largest newspaper was run by one of America's greatest writers, Mark Twain. Twain arrived in Buffalo in 1869 a bachelor and left in 1871 married and a father. In 1874, the Chautauqua Institute was founded and, since then, has hosted a constellation of luminaries including Presidents Grant through Clinton. Elbert Hubbard founded the utopian Roycroft community of arts and crafts in East Aurora. In 1898 Edmund Fitzgerald moved his family, including son "Scotty"—that's F. Scott Fitzgerald—to Buffalo. The Fitzgeralds lived in Allentown and young Scotty attended Nardin Academy.

It was here in 1883 that one of the towering figures of the 20th century was born and lived, the most decorated soldier of WWI, the father of the CIA and American intelligence agencies, and the "Last American Hero" according to President Dwight Eisenhower—William Donovan.

Frederick Law Olmsted, one of the greatest landscape architects of all time, spent much time here between 1868 and 1896, leaving behind his masterpiece park and parkway system and also the nation's first state park, the Niagara Reservation, in 1885. He would be followed by a number of the nation's most famous architects. Louis Sullivan designed and in 1895 built one of the world's first true skyscrapers. Ellsworth Statler built the world's first hotel to have a bathroom in every room. In 1896 the Ellicott Square Building was the world's largest office building and housed what is believed to be the earliest known dedicated movie theater in the world, the Vitascope Theater. Frank Lloyd Wright came shortly thereafter and designed numerous buildings for the Larkin Soap Company and its executives.

In 1908 the *New York Times* sponsored an around-the-world auto race to demonstrate to Europeans the advancements of the fledgling U.S. auto industry. Until they contacted tiny Thomas Flyer in Buffalo, one auto company after another had turned down the Times invitation to represent the United States. Thomas Flyer would send a car and team that won the Great Race.

At the turn of the twentieth century, Buffalo Niagara was one of the most successful settlements and exciting regions of the United States, if not the world.

Flash forward 113 years: I am standing in Larkinville with hundreds of other people awaiting the premiere of John Paget's film *Best Designed City*. In it, Paget lovingly created a lavish vision of the city that showcased water, the parks and parkway system designed by America's best landscape architect, historic architecture, the award-winning Elmwood Village, and told a proud, hopeful story narrated by some of the region's most accomplished activists, people such as Jill Jedlicka, Robert Shibley, and Tim Tielman. I had never seen the city look so good. However, the film begged the question: Why aren't we swarmed by people wanting to move here? How could someone outside this region who watches this film not decide to put their house up for sale, pack up, and move to Buffalo Niagara?

How did the exciting metropolis of 1901 fall to the current state? Our once "happenin' place" is a world-class city no longer. The Global Cities Index, for years produced by the management consulting firm A. T. Kearney, ranks New York City number one on the list and our neighbor to the north, Toronto, number fourteen.[2] Don't bother looking for Buffalo on their 2014 list of 84 global cities, nor on their list of 34 emerging cities, despite this region's globally significant assets—Great Lakes, Niagara Falls, and a globally important bird corridor, the Niagara River. Could Buffalo be a world-class city again? Should it be? If so, what would it take?

Is it a matter of increasing the population? Some people don't think so. Urban expert Edward Glaeser thinks we should be "shrinking to greatness."[3] Sam Magavern, writer, public interest lawyer, and codirector of the Partnership for the Public Good (PPG), a local nonprofit that provides research and advocacy support to a broad array of partners that share a community-oriented vision of a revitalized Buffalo Niagara, doesn't think size matters; "it's quality of life that matters."[4]

Many aspects of community life rank below average when compared to our state and our nation. Many community quality of life indicators are subpar or negative and trending downward, and some of the upward-trending indicators lag behind the state and the nation. Assets and resources exist—such as our geography, our climate, a blank urban slate, a wealth of successful and active nonprofits and their leaders, etc.—to affect considerable improvement in the human, social, economic and environmental capital of our region. Forces are brewing nationally and globally—such as climate change, a disadvantage to other regions but a possible advantage for ours—that will make this region ripe for growth—not the negative kind, like sprawl, but increased quality of life.

We could be, and should be a globally important city again.

The goal of this book is to tell the real story, to give a true and accurate measure of where we are historically—the arc from past to present to future—and globally, compared to other New Yorkers and to our countrymen; to analyze the forces at play to see what is moving us up and what is pulling us down; to write a new narrative about what we could be and to propose some steps to get us there.

Throughout, I refer to this region as Buffalo Niagara, and I have chosen to limit this study to two counties—Erie and Niagara—of the eight-county Western New York where most of the population is concentrated. For practical purposes, the majority of data for the region are collected for the Buffalo Niagara Falls metropolitan statistical area. Additionally, the people of the region tend to identify this way. Sam Magavern says, "Compared to [a place] like a Detroit, people in this region really do identify as Buffalonians. People living outside Detroit don't even say they're from Detroit. They say, 'I'm from Southeastern Michigan' or whatever. People in Cheektowaga, Amherst, if you met them on an airplane, they would say, 'I'm from Buffalo'. So we still have pretty good cohesion in that way."[5]

This book is divided into three parts, each attempting to answer the questions asked above.

Part One is descriptive, a problem statement called "How are We Doing?" because it measures the current state of the region. Such stark contrasts exist in the region that it is much like a tale of two cities:

- Buffalo, the core of the region, is labeled the fourth poorest city in the country, while the region as a whole is about average for poverty;

- On the edge of the world's largest supply of surface freshwater in a world facing increasing water scarcity, the region pollutes and threatens that supply of water;

- With a geography that features one of the natural wonders of the world, the region is also home to a disproportionate share of toxic waste sites;

- Our special geography offers us a spectacular waterfront, yet the trend is for new homes to be built and people to move farther inland;

- Despite an abundance of rich agricultural land and a favorable growing climate, our agricultural industry cannot provide sufficient fruits, vegetables, and grains for the region's residents, a condition that worsens with the annual loss of farmland;

- For all of our Olmsted parks and historic architecture and affordable housing and award-winning neighborhoods such as Elmwood Village, this is one of the last places in the United States that people want to move to.

Many factors comprise our community life and have experienced no growth or decline over the past few decades. It seems as though, as Kevin Gaughan expressed it in a Buffalo News article, "While Western New York stands still, the world passes us by."[6] Buffalo Niagara is neither the "best kept secret in America" that Buffalo boosters boast, nor is it the armpit that callous critics claim. What do the data tell us? Solid, objective indicators will provide answers to how well our community and region are doing.

Part Two is analytic and will attempt to analyze the forces that have, for the past fifty years, been at play and gotten us to this point. What must we understand before we know what to do? In addition to research online and in print, I interviewed sixteen of this region's most accomplished individuals from nonprofits, government agencies, and the private sector, who have contributed improvements to the various capital indicators of the region. Relying on their experience and expertise, I use their words, as much as possible, to help explain the forces at work.

Part Three is prescriptive, containing a new narrative for the way to go forward and for this region to realize its potential. It is the most subjective and includes ideas both untried and, collectively, undiscussed. I am inspired by something Sam Magavern tells me about his work, "What I try and do is capture a sense of hope, because I think if people don't have hope they don't do stuff. People have to be motivated and hope has to be part of the motivation."[7] That's what I want to do: motivate and inspire. I am also inspired by this quote from the book of Isaiah (50:4), "that I might know how to speak to the weary a word that will rouse."

Why we are failing to fulfill our potential? Why don't people want to move to the "best designed city"? Why are our sons and daughters—some of whom are the best and brightest of their generation—moving elsewhere to make their life's contributions?

Fitting the status and future of our region into a larger context, this book will compare and contrast with similar works on this topic by asking new questions and reframing old questions by putting the topic into a new context, by exploring questions that other researchers have not asked, and by seeking answers to questions that others have posed but do not answer. My intention is to modify, clarify, and expand what we know about the subject and, in the end, persuade others what actions we, as members of the community, must take to realize our potential.

PART ONE:

HOW ARE WE DOING?

Professor Mike Brill of the University at Buffalo (UB) School of Architecture in the 1970s taught his students that a well-defined statement of a problem is ninety percent of the solution. Defining what is wrong with our region is crucial to determining a solution.

In 1998 UB's Institute for Local Governance and Regional Growth under director John B. Sheffer II produced a report titled "State of the Region: Performance Indicators for the Buffalo Niagara Region in the 21st Century," which focused on eleven areas of regional life, with eight to ten performance indicators in each area. Community leaders chaired task forces for each of the areas, and within those task forces each chair appointed between twelve and twenty community experts to contribute to the effort. Unfortunately, after a few years, funding ran out and the project ended.

A similar structure is attempted in this book. The number of issue areas and the number of indicators for each issue area have been reduced. Through personal interviews, I have gathered the opinions of a number of local experts with knowledge of the issues and years of experience with the selected indicators. However, practicality also obviated so comprehensive a report as UB's and as far as is known, no effort since their state of the region, including this book, is as comprehensive, complete, and objective, nor is there a one-stop resource with information about the health of this region:

• The Institute for Local Governance and Regional Growth's successor, the UB Regional Institute, and its program One Region Forward have undertaken similar work, collecting data and researching issue areas such as Housing and Neighborhoods, Food Access and Justice, but they have not followed up on issue areas such as health of the population and education, which were covered in the original report;

• The Partnership for the Public Good (PPG) has reported on regional population, poverty, jobs, education, environment, and good government;

• The Western New York Regional Economic Development Corporation (REDC), the state's public-private partnership made up of local experts and stakeholders from business, academia, local government and non-governmental organizations to transform economic development, has an annual report that focuses mainly on economic capital and only recently, due to the initiative of Buffalo Niagara Riverkeeper, addresses environmental capital;

Narrate mo

• The John R. Oishei Foundation's (Oishei) Mobile Safety Net Team has conducted assessments of neighborhoods and communities throughout the region over the last three years. Although they include indicators for human, social, and economic capital, they do not yet cover the whole region;

• The 2011–12 Community Needs Assessment Executive Summary by the United Way of Buffalo and Erie County, is one of the more comprehensive reports. Conducted in partnership with Fiat Evaluation, a local research and evaluation firm, and graduate students from the University at Buffalo School of Social Work, the assessment utilized a variety of data collection techniques in order to obtain data on the demographic, social, and economic conditions of the area. Data was collected on more than 100 measures of community well-being related to education, income, and health and wellness.

Beyond omission of certain indicators these reports have other limitations. Marlies Wesolowski, executive director of the Lt. Col. Matt Urban Social Services Center, a multifaceted agency providing a variety of housing and work skills services to youth, crime victims, seniors, the homeless, and others in need, participated in the United Way's Community Needs Assessment. She said this, "I don't think any one study really tells you everything you need to know about what's going on, and I think you need to be paying attention to a lot of different voices." She adds that these studies are put together by well-meaning individuals who may or may not have walked in the shoes of the individuals on whom they are reporting, "so it's really hard to get the emotion or the recognition of some of the underlying reasons why people find themselves where they are in life." With some studies there's a disconnect between what is thought to be the need and what the need actually is. The United Way and other organizations, she said, "try very, very hard not to have that happen, But I think sometimes it does happen because people who are in positions similar to mine usually come from economic backgrounds where they're a little bit better off than, say, the clients that they're serving."[1]

Still, she acknowledges that there are good reports with errors nonetheless. For instance, she explained, regarding the Oishei Foundation Mobile Safety Net Team, which assesses community-based human services, addresses access barriers, and identifies areas of unmet need, the Matt Urban Center is listed in the report but not credited for all of the things that they do.

When elected officials offer an annual "state of" report, which, for the most part, is nothing but a recitation of that official's economic "successes" in the previous year, it seldom, if ever, mentions human, social, and environmental capital. Take, for example, Mayor Byron Brown's 2013 State of the City address.

* Mayor Brown is not alone in this practice; his address follows a template that all such reports follow. A good part of the mayor's address is occupied by recognition of attendees and applause, some of which is reasonable: By recognizing individual contributions, the mayor gives credit where credit is due. Generally speaking, however, the address is full of self-congratulation and includes not a discouraging word (except for a brief allusion to how bad things were when he took over). He touts "progress" and "the state of the city [as] the strongest it's been in years," ignoring the fact that during his administration, the population has declined. If you believe that the best part

of the city is its people, that decline means the loss of the city's strength. Statements about the expenditure of taxpayer monies outnumber the few statements about results. For instance, the mayor mentions $10 million to repave sixty miles of roadway; $27 million for two dozen housing development projects; and $30 million to improve city parks, including a $4.5 million splash pool at Martin Luther King Park and paving and landscaping at that park. He also cites $1.5 million in upgrades to Broderick Park and $750,000 in upgrades to Coca-Cola Field. This is not news, however, nor is it exceptional, as deterioration of capital assets requires repair, renovation, or replacement over time. One expects such expenses as the cost of doing the business of running the city.

In terms of results, the mayor mentions improvements in financial rating and a drop in taxes, which really indicate progress. He also talks about a "safer Buffalo" and his zero tolerance crime policy which has resulted in a 6.5% one-year drop, as well as a 19% drop since 2005 in crime and a 45% decrease in arson since 2006. As presented, the mayor takes full credit for these decreases, failing to mention that crime has not only been dropping all across the United States of America but also across the globe. Generally speaking, the mayor's address is absent any recognition of challenges or problems.[**]

Look for improvement in the future. Cara Matteliano, vice president for community impact, the Community Foundation of Greater Buffalo, a 501(c)3 public charity holding different charitable funds established by individuals, families, nonprofit organizations and businesses to benefit Western New York, said they have a position in the foundation called a knowledge management officer. They hired a new person, a sociologist, "who will be collecting data on our focus areas and keeping us informed." Understanding how things are, what progress has been made, and what progress needs to be made is something they pay attention to through that position. There is also a similar person at United Way and Oishei, "so now the three of them work together," she said.[2] The new organization, Open Buffalo, a collaborative civic initiative to make long-term improvements in justice and equity, will also be developing that capacity.

Numerous city ranking reports exist which rank Buffalo in various ways. One such example is Sperling's Best Places to Live[3], accessed in 2014, which ranks us as follows:

- #2 for The Best Cities to Relocate to in America
- #6 of the Most Energetic Cities and of the Most Secure Places to Live 2011 (Large Metros)
- #7 as a Hypertension Hot Spots
- #12 America's Manliest Sports Cities,
- #31 America's Least Manly Cities and, at the same time strangely, #35 America's Manliest Cities
- #18 Most Romantic Cities for Boomers
- #19 Most Secure Places to Live in the U.S. (Large Metro Areas)
- #28 The Most Single Cities
- #32 America's Migraine Hot Spots and #86 America's Most (and Least) Stressful Cities (100 Largest Metro Areas)
- #32 Cities on the Edge of Greatness
- #47 Most Irritation Prone Cities
- #49 Most and Least Risky Places for Identity Theft
- #53 Drought-Riskiest Cities
- #181 Best Green Cities

The National Civic League has links to all sorts of rankings by specific topics such as best places to raise children and families. Forbes also has numerous lists, and we have fared both well and poorly on them. For instance, in 2009 we were the eighth most miserable city in the country, but now we're out of the top twenty.

These lists may be fun or frustrating to read, but they are not very useful. They usually focus narrowly and do not include the wide range of data covered by local reports. It is interesting, however, to see what these analysts consider important for each of the topic areas, and those factors should be considered while planning our public policy if we intend to attract others to the region.

The template for this state of the region report is written in the context of the concept of healthy cities or communities. According to the World Health Organization (WHO), "A healthy city is one that is continually creating and improving those physical and social environments and expanding those community resources which enable people to mutually support each other in performing all the functions of life and in developing to their maximum potential."[4]

Phil Haberstro, founder and executive director of the Wellness Institute of Greater Buffalo and Western New York, which has a mission of creating healthy communities, credits the healthy communities concept to Drs. Trevor Hancock and Leonard Duhl. stemming from a 1985 seminal meeting in Toronto, when Duhl and Hancock were working with the WHO. The concept crossed the ocean to the WHO in Europe and back stateside where the National Civic League launched the U.S. movement. The same year, Haberstro and John Giardino incorporated the Wellness Institute of Greater Buffalo as a not-for-profit.[5]

"Experts in 'alternative economics' have long suggested that wealth consists of four types of capital. That view is increasingly accepted among others, the World Bank, the World Economic Forum, even (parts of) Wall Street....The new capitalism for the 21st century must simultaneously increase ecological capital, social capital, economic capital, and human capital."[6]

So, how are we doing? How "well" is our region? These questions are addressed in Chapter One that follows.

Footnotes:

* At this writing, the 2014 State of the City address was not available online except for a brief press release summary. The 2013 State of the City address is available as a video on YouTube.

** Mayor Byron Brown's 2013 State of the City address video on You Tube drew 473 views. On the same YouTube page there is a link to "The Dying Buffalo-a documentary" posted May 2013 by jacobjrrwt, which has 1672 views. On that page are links to: "Niagara Falls, a Tale of Two Cities" with 12,259 views; "Ghosts of Buffalo,

NY: City of Lackawanna" with 5972 views; and Buffalo USA – City of No Illusions" 4256 views, all of them a complete contrast to the mayor's report on the region.

There are exceptions to this style of reporting, of course. Erie County Executive Mark Poloncarz's 2014 State of the County address recognized the failure of the Buffalo public schools and committed county resources to the Say Yes program, along with a recognition that poverty is spreading into the suburbs.

BUFFALO/NIAGARA TIMELINE

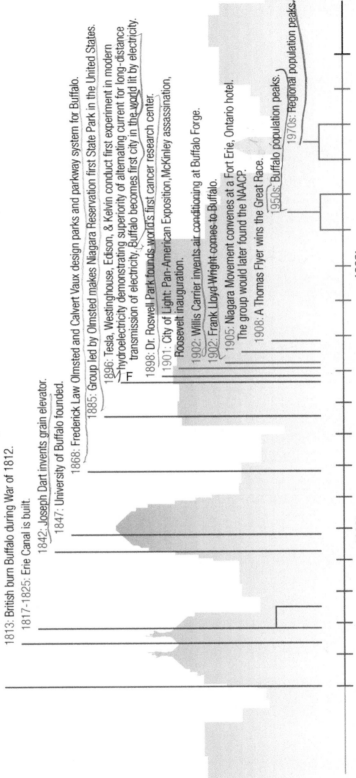

12,000-10,000 BP CLIMATE CHANGE: Last glacial maximum of the Wisconsinan glacial period. Laurentide ice sheet retreats northward over central North America scouring bedrock forming depressions which then fill with glacial meltwater forming present-day Great Lakes and Niagara River.

12th or 15th century: FIVE NATIONS CONFEDERACY: Five nations of Native Americans convene after solar eclipse to form a Confederacy known as the Haudenosaunee which is said to have influenced the U.S. Articles of Confederation and Constitution.

1678-1679: Robert de la Salle and Father Louis Hennepin explore region. Hennepin's writings introduce Niagara Falls to the world.

1800-1821: Holland Land Company & Joseph Ellicott survey Western New York, Ellicott designs Buffalo, Buffalo named.

1813: British burn Buffalo during War of 1812.

1817-1825: Erie Canal is built.

1842: Joseph Dart invents grain elevator.

1847: University of Buffalo founded.

1868: Frederick Law Olmsted and Calvert Vaux design parks and parkway system for Buffalo.

1885: Group led by Olmsted makes Niagara Reservation first State Park in the United States.

1896: Tesla, Westinghouse, Edison, & Kelvin conduct first experiment in modern hydroelectricity demonstrating superiority of alternating current for long-distance transmission of electricity. Buffalo becomes first city in the world lit by electricity.

1898: Dr. Roswell Park founds world's first cancer research center.

1901: City of Light: Pan-American Exposition, McKinley assassination, Roosevelt inauguration.

1902: Willis Carrier invents air conditioning at Buffalo Forge.

1902: Frank Lloyd Wright comes to Buffalo.

1905: Niagara Movement convenes at a Fort Erie, Ontario hotel. The group would later found the NAACP.

1908: A Thomas Flyer wins the Great Race.

1950s: Buffalo population peaks.

1970s: Regional population peaks.

1800's

1900's

A. Burning of Buffalo B. Joseph Dart's grain elevator C. Niagara Movement
D. Nikola Tesla E. Pan-American Exposition F. Thomas Flyer

CHAPTER ONE

HUMAN CAPITAL

"Human capital—the end: educated, innovative, creative people; participatory governance and civil rights; healthy people. Human development means ensuring that every human being attains their fullest possible human potential."[1]

It has been said and written many times that the best thing about Buffalo Niagara is its people. So how well, in terms of quality, are the people of Buffalo Niagara? I can think of three major ways to measure that.

Population

There is no better indication of the direction in which a community is headed than its population trajectory, which indicates either growth or decline. It is well-known that the population of this region has been in decline for decades.

What that graph shows are the population trends for the country, the state, the largest subdivision of the region, and the largest municipality in the region, from 1900 until 2010. It also shows the population for the metropolitan statistical area from 1940

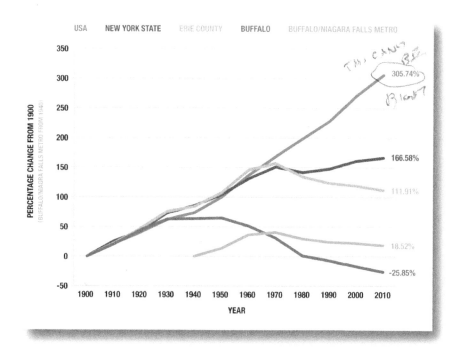

Figure 1.1: Population trajectories for the nation, state, and region

Source: U. S. Census Bureau, census.gov.

on. The graph clearly indicates that for the first half of the 20th century, growth occurred in all four geographical areas. But sometime in the 1950s, the population of the city of Buffalo began to decline. In the 1970s, the population for the County of Erie began to decline. In the 1990s, the metro population began to decline. All the while, the population for New York State and the rest of the United States continued to increase.

Regardless of how you feel about population growth, the fact is that population increased in most places in the United States and even within our own state. Good or bad, it is the norm for population to increase. But not here. This is the first and, perhaps, most important indicator of problems here.

There were indications long ago that Buffalo was falling behind the norm for the rest of the country:

Figure 1.2: City of Buffalo ranking among U.S. cities

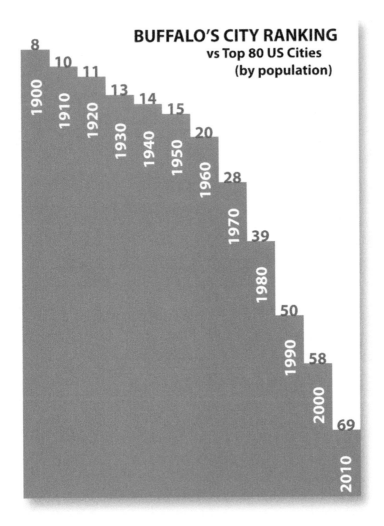

BUFFALO'S CITY RANKING
vs Top 80 US Cities
(by population)

Source: U.S. Census Bureau, Statistical Abstracts, census.gov

That graph charts the trajectory of Buffalo's population relative to the populations of the other cities in the United States. While the population of the city of Buffalo did in fact increase in the first half of the 20th century, that increase lagged behind the increase of other cities. For instance, in the first decade of the 20th century, the city of

Pittsburgh leapfrogged Buffalo in the city ranking chart. From 1910 to 1920, Los Angeles leapfrogged Buffalo. In the next decade, Milwaukee and San Francisco surpassed Buffalo.[2] One decade, perhaps, would not be sufficient information for local leaders to sense that something was wrong. But over several decades, the trajectory of Buffalo's population continued to slip behind that of other cities.

From 2000 to 2010, of the top 100 metro areas in the U.S., only eight had lost population. All but one—New Orleans—were in the Great Lakes region. Of those eight, Buffalo Niagara was sixth from the bottom.[3]

The situation is actually worse than at first glance. For instance, in 2009 the Census Bureau estimated Buffalo's population at 270,240 and in 2010 the actual census count was 261,000. It would seem that in one year 9240 more people moved out of the area than moved in. But that doesn't take into account, however, the fact that in 2009 there was a surplus of 1241 births over deaths.[4] Thus, if no one moved out of the area, then the 2010 population would be 271,481. But the Census Bureau reported 261,000, a difference of 10,481 people. Policymakers seldom mention that total numbers of how many people move out of this area start with the difference in population between the two years, then add the surplus of births over deaths.

A bit of seemingly bright and hopeful news concerns recent census data showing that the rate of population decline is slowing for Erie County but not Niagara County and, in 2013, the Census Bureau estimated a slight increase of a few hundred people, which is not something to become excited about as yet: it's merely an estimate, and a short-term uptick does not signify a trend. Is the slowing rate of decline a sign that our population loss is reversing? Jan Vink, a research specialist for Cornell University's Program on Applied Demographics says, "I find it very hard to read anything into it,".[5]

Another dimension to consider is which segment of the population shows the greater loss. According to the Federal Reserve Bank of New York report, "A Brain Drain or an Insufficient Brain Gain?", upstate New York's weak population labor force growth is partly been the result of a lower rate of in-migration to the region versus an average rate of out-migration by college-educated people, hence the title "insufficient brain gain."[6] The upstate New York out-migration rate is roughly equivalent to the median across all the United States. The report concludes that sluggish regional economies do not necessarily have high out-migration rates; "[i]n fact, better performing economies had higher out-migration rates than poor performing ones."[7] The in-migration rate—the number of college-educated people moving into the area as a percentage of the entire college-educated resident population—is the problem. According to the report, "if upstate New York were a state, it would have the nation's lowest in-migration rate, 9.3%."[8] With the net migration rate explained as the difference between the in- and the out-migration rates, the report states, "Upstate New York, along with 12 states, experienced a net outflow of college-educated workers between 1995 and 2000."[9] Upstate's net loss was 4.1%, the second worst in the nation if the region were a state. The in-migration rates of New York State as a whole are the second lowest in the nation at 10.0%, and upstate New York's rate is 9.3%.

Recent data show, however, that New York State has the highest number of out-migrations. A USA Today article that analyzed census data for twelve months ending July 1, 2013 counted 104,470 people moving out of New York, a number considerably larger than the next worst state, Illinois, and more than double the out-migration rate of California.[10] A study on Americans' interstate moves by the Center on Budget and Policy Priorities indicates that, from 1993 to 2011, New York State had the lowest share, 68.3%, of departing households replaced by new arrivals, a statistic confirmed by an annual study performed by the Atlas Van Lines moving company, which since 1993, has tracked by origin and destination of interstate moves undertaken in the previous year. In 2013, New York State clearly registered the most outbound moves.[11,12] In a USA Today analysis, "Bright lights, big cities win new grads," Buffalo ranks 68th out of the top 100 metros for attracting new grads, gaining only 8.8% of them between 2006 and 2011, versus a 17% gain for all areas.[13]

Sam Magavern points out another dimension: "The most striking thing is that foreign-born population is very small here compared to other major metros. Latin Americans and Asian-Americans aren't settling in Buffalo. The only exception is the refugee population, which is booming, but it's a pretty small sliver when compared to a city that has a big Mexican-American population. So that's quite different from how people are thinking about why everyone's fleeing."[14] According to the Census Bureau,

12.9% of the U.S. population is foreign-born versus 22.0% of New York State and only 6.0% of Buffalo Niagara.[15]

We do receive immigrants and refugees, yet the population loss occurs in spite of an increase of people from other countries to the region. New York State is the fourth-largest recipient of refugees in the U.S. A large percentage (32%) of these refugees—more than 14,000 over the past seven years—have settled in Erie County.[16] But they are concentrated in a small area of Buffalo's West Side where immigrants and refugees of 29 ethnicities make their home.

Age is another dimension. Compared to New York State and national age distributions, Erie County has slightly lower percentages of young people and a higher percentage of people 65 and older. According to the United Way's Community Needs Assessment:

> Of special concern is the fact that Erie County is now home to the nation's 9th oldest population. In 2010, the area included 197,365 individuals sixty years of age and older. This equates to one out of every five Erie County residents—an increase of 3.9% from 2000. The vast majority of these individuals (95% in Erie County and 98% in City of Buffalo) are living in the community outside a formal care setting (i.e., nursing home, skilled nursing facility). Consistent with shifting national trends, the area is seeing growing concentrations of aging populations in rural and suburban locations.[17]

The report goes on to say, "Embedded in these aging populations are growing concentrations of need."[18] Many elderly individuals live on small incomes in modest houses that are their primary asset. In many cases, their relatives and other supports have left the region or remaining relatives face challenges managing their own lives and children while simultaneously addressing the needs of their older family members. The assessment predicts a possible decline by 2015 in the number of individuals aged 20 to 65 available to give support to the number of individuals aged 65+ years. Likewise, the number of adults on pension (85+years) vs. the number of working adults 45 to 65 years old will likely reduce from a rate of 20.7 in 1980 to 10.1 by 2015.[19] The report concludes,

"This means that there will be fewer caregivers directly available to provide assistance to aging family members, as well as diminished societal capacity to do so."[20] Disability of the population is an issue as well. The metro area has a larger disabled population (12.9%) than New York State (10.8%) and the nation (12.2%).[21]

The bottom line is this: More people leave this area than move in to this area. This is not normal in most places in the United States of America. Population growth is the norm. So why is our population in decline? This population decline is a sign that many of these people feel that the grass is greener elsewhere. That they are better off somewhere else. Why do so many think the grass is greener elsewhere? These people feel that whatever assets there are about Buffalo Niagara, other things outweigh them.

Not everyone agrees that population decline is a problem. Sam Magavern said, "Who cares about how many people live here? I sure don't. Whether it's 50,000 more or 50,000 less it's not going to affect quality of life that much. So I care much more about how are the people who live here are doing." He suggests shifting how we measure success. "We could be shrinking, staying the same, or growing but let's see how we're actually doing," he said, "not how many of us there are."[22] Urbanist Edward Glaeser's article "Can Buffalo Ever Come Back?" calls for "...Buffalo to become a much smaller but more vibrant community, shrinking to greatness."[23] Magavern responded to that: " I do like the idea that you don't have to equate quality with growth." He doesn't believe in measuring quality by new buildings and new developments, and concludes, "it may be that the number of people who want to live in cold weather, Northeastern, postindustrial city, is not going to be that huge."[24]

Health

Although the January 2014 Buffalo News Prospectus featured an entire section on healthcare, it contains not a single word on the actual health of the population. The section covers just the business—economic capital—of the healthcare sector: jobs, etc., not how well it's performing vis-à-vis the health of the population. Is all this investment making us healthier? Not answered, not even asked. And you won't find the mayors, the supervisors, or the county executives discussing the topic, either.

It is true that the health of the population is very difficult to measure. There is no one number, no one letter grade and there are many indicators for health: physical, emotional, and mental. A comparison of two nationwide surveys measuring the health of populations underscores this difficulty: The first, the Gallup Healthways Well Being Index, ranks New York State 35th in the country overall for health.[25] Contrast that with the United Health Foundation's America's Health Rankings which ranks New York State 15th in the U.S.[26] Obviously, they are examining different factors (these differences are far too numerous and complicated to detail here; the reader is encouraged to visit the links cited in the endnotes and explore this for themselves); still it goes to show how difficult it is to formulate one measure of how healthy a population is. Nonetheless, they can be useful. Philip Haberstro of the Wellness Institute says, "I think those become reasonable tools for baseline metrics." But they are seldom talked about by our leaders. Said Haberstro, "There is a lack of consciousness as to what really creates health [because] there's a dependence on the sickness care system to bail you out."[27] *(More about that in Chapter 3, "Eds and Meds the Business".)*

Here is how we stand in a sampling of health care rankings:

- In 2013, the six-year old Gallup Healthways Well-Being poll conducted 178,000 interviews across America and ranked the Buffalo Niagara Falls metro area 92nd overall (out of 189 metro areas) for overall well-being and 122nd for physical health despite being ranked 23rd for basic access—thirteen items measuring residents' access to food, shelter, healthcare, and a safe and satisfying place to live. New York State ranks 35th for well being overall and 23rd for physical health.[28]

- Some good news here: The United Health Foundation, in its 24th year, ranks New York State 15th in the USA, above the national average, for most health indicators. This study includes some infrastructure (such as public health funding) and non-disease indicators (crime rates, exercise) in its findings.[29]

- The Robert Wood Johnson Foundation, which lists health status rankings for all

Table 1.1: Comparison of selected health indicators for Erie and Niagara counties

Health Indicator Rates per 100,000 population	Erie County	Niagara County	New York State	USA
Total deaths	776.5	802.8	658.1	740.6
1. Diseases of the heart	192.0	248.9	198.6	173.7
2. All cancers (mortality)	184.2	177.3	162.5	168.6
Lung cancer mortality (total)	52.4	53.8	42.3	45.9
Breast cancer mortality (female)	25.2	23.1	21.6	12.0
3. Chronic lower respiratory diseases	38.5	50.2	31.0	42.7
4. Cerebrovascular disease (stroke)	41.6	37.6	26.9	37.9
5. Unintentional injury	26.3	30.6	22.7	38.0
Motor vehicle	6.0	9.0	6.0	10.9
Non-motor vehicle	20.2	21.7	16.8	26.2
7. Diabetes (mortality)	22.1	19.9	17.0	21.5
10. Suicides	10.1	10.7	7.2	12.0
Homicides	6.5	2.5	4.3	5.2
12. Cirrhosis (liver)	8.1	7.9	6.4	9.7

Data: County & State: New York State Community Health Indicator Reports (CHIRS), 2008-2010 age-adjusted data, http://www.health.ny.gov/statistics/chac/indicators/, accessed 6/30/14;
USA: National Vital Statistics Report, V. 61, No. 6, October 10, 2012, http://www.cdc.gov/nchs/data/nvsr/nvsr61/nvsr61_06.pdf, accessed 6/30/14. Later data are available but this report is closer in time to the NYS DOH data.

the counties in the U.S., ranks Erie County 53rd and Niagara County 59th out of 62 New York State counties.[30]

- The Commonwealth Fund, a nonprofit that studies healthcare issues and collects healthcare data on the nation, states, and local areas, in 2012 ranked the Buffalo region 54th of 306 regions they study. Nationally we ranked 11th for access to healthcare but 100th for healthy lives. Rochester ranks 27th.[31]

- The American College of Sports Medicine's annual American Fitness Index ranks the top 50 metros. In the 2014 version, Buffalo Niagara ranks 29th out of 50. It would seem that the region is just about average. The index, however, includes indicators such as number of farmers' markets and sports activity infrastructure (such as playgrounds, tennis courts, golf courses, swimming pools and ballparks per capita), indicators for which the area is above average. Offsetting that, when it comes to health behaviors and chronic health problems, the region is below average in more categories than it is above average.[32]

There is no more accurate or comprehensive measure of the health of Erie County's population than the 2014–2017 Community Health Assessment for Erie County, New York. A similar health assessment was done for Niagara County. [33]

Some of the findings are summarized in Table 1.1.

Health Indicator

The annual birth rates in Erie County (10.6) and Niagara County (10.2) are lower than NYS (12.3), and the two counties have higher rates of infant deaths, neonatal deaths, and post neonatal deaths than the state. The number of infant deaths per thousand in Erie County (7.8) is worse than in New York State (5.5) and the U.S. (6.15). Erie County (72.4%) lags behind the state (75.4%) and the nation (83.3%) for early prenatal care (within the first trimester), which is a strong indicator for health outcomes in later life. The newborn drug related discharge rate per 10,000 newborns was 134.0 in Erie County for 2005–2007, well over double the NYS rate of 58.1.

The 2014-2017 Erie County Community Health Assessment (CHA) reports the

Centers for Disease Control (CDC) national goal of decreasing the rate of teenage pregnancies to 43 per 1,000 females aged 15 to 19 years by 2010. A two-year average (2008-10) of teenage pregnancy rates from the New York State Department of Health (NYS DOH) showed that Buffalo zip codes 14201–14216, and 14222 average 105.4 pregnancies per 1,000 females aged 15 to 19 years, and 100.7 within Niagara Falls zipcodes 14301–14305. With teenage pregnancy rates in the two urban areas nearly 2.5 times the national goal, the results, the CHA says, "are nothing short of epidemic."[34]

Erie County's incidence rate for elevated blood levels in children is more than double the statewide rate and 7th highest in the state. The Matt Urban Center offers services to residents of the East Side where the homes are very old and many contain lead and asbestos. According to executive director Marlies Wesolowski, the Erie County Department of Health has found that many school-age children in Buffalo have high blood lead levels because of the city's older housing stock where growing children are exposed to or inadvertently ingest paint containing lead. Wesolowski believes that "one of the reasons why many Buffalo kids don't perform well in school is, in part, because of high lead levels. Instinctively I know that, whether there's a study out there that proves it or not," she said, "but I suspect that is the case because older homes have got a lot of lead."[35]

The CHA also shows that homicide rates are higher here than the state or the country; the suicide death rate is lower than in NYS but higher than in the U.S. as a whole. In addition, it indicates a decline in the overall death rate from all cancers from the period 1989 to 2002 and a decline in the death rate in each of the individual types of cancer examined over the same time period. However, Erie County still has higher rates than those set in Healthy People 2010, a national health promotion and disease prevention initiative, in all the cancers examined except for cervical and prostate cancers. Locally, cancer rates, while declining, are still substantially higher than in New York State and the U.S., led by lung cancer.[36]

Other statistics reveal the following:

- Prostate cancer rates are less than U.S. but greater than NYS.

- Breast cancer rates are greater than USA & greater than NYS but the death rate has been declining.

- Oral cancer death rates are higher here.

- The death rate for diabetes is greater than NYS but less than U.S.

- The death rate for strokes is greater than NYS but less than U.S.

- The death rate for diseases of the heart is less than NYS but greater than U.S.

- Tobacco use has slightly declined since 2008 but was still an unacceptable rate of 11.9% of mothers who smoked during last three months of pregnancy. 35% of HS students continued smoking.

- 87.7% of all 2008 emergency room visits were non-emergent, primary care treatable, or emergency department care needed but preventable/avoidable.

Not all is bad news. Erie County's rates of AIDS, syphilis, and tuberculosis are lower than the state's. Teen pregnancy rates for both the 10 to 14 and 15 to 17 age groups have been falling in Erie County and New York State. Motor vehicle death rates per 100,000 are better here (5.6) than NYS (7.6). The unintentional death rate per 100,000 is lower than in NYS & the U.S. but has changed little over the years 1992 to 2005. Rates from Salmonella and Campylobacter are lower than NYS & USA. Asthma death rates are lower than in NYS & the U.S. but on the rise, whereas falling in the state and country. Cervical cancer death rates are lower than in NYS & the U.S. Colorectal cancer rates declined from higher than in NYS & the U.S. in 1989 to less than in NYS & the U.S. in 2006. Erie County had the highest rate of coronary heart disease in 1989–1990 but twelve years later posted the greatest decline.

In Erie County, the number of children experiencing abuse or maltreatment increased from 14.7 per thousand in 2005 to 17.1 per thousand in 2010. Elder abuse is also a concern, with 1500 cases of abuse and neglect reported each year locally. Domestic violence is the largest category of family violence: Since 2008, there have been twenty-eight reported domestic violence homicides in Erie County, and in 2011 nearly 8800 calls were made to domestic-violence-related hotlines. All of these forms of family violence exact long-term physical and psychological consequences on their victims.[37]

A Community Health Needs Assessment for Charitable Hospitals was conducted in 2014 by the Niagara Falls Memorial Medical Center.[38] Here is one of their key findings:

> The shortage of health professionals serving the City of Niagara Falls, coupled with the city's poverty indicators, have led the federal government to designate most of the city's territory as a Health Professional Shortage Area (HPSA) and as a Medically Underserved Area. The City of Niagara Falls has 43 percent fewer primary care physicians than the federal government's target and the city has only one community-based psychiatrist. The core of Memorial's service area…suffers from population loss, high unemployment, widespread poverty, high rates of crime and a low rate of higher education. The health status indicators for Niagara County are extremely poor.[39]

In the face of above-average illness, there is a shortage of health professionals in the area overall. According to the Health Resources and Services Administration (HRSA), a branch of the Department of Health and Human Services, the Buffalo service area is considered a medically underserved area/population. These are areas or populations designated by HRSA as having too few primary care providers, high infant mortality, high poverty and/or high elderly population, with shortages of primary care, dental care, and mental health professionals. What's interesting to note is that New York State's Medicaid spending in 2012 was the highest of any state in the union at $53,305,797,436 even surpassing California—$50,165,335,340—which has twice the population. Both states receive 50% federal assistance in funding.[40]

The health of the region's population is a complex picture lacking a single, comprehensive measure to determine it. Whether the people of Buffalo Niagara are average or slightly above or below average, it's safe to say that this region is not one of the healthiest in the United States. The answer to "why?" is complicated as well. But consider these quotes from two studies:

> "The health care system has less impact on public health [because it centers on] patients' lifestyle choices at home, work, and in the broader community."[41]

"Because the roots of the chronic conditions that are the leading causes of morbidity and mortality can be traced to lifestyle factors — principally smoking, diet, and physical activity..."[42]

So the primary cause is our lifestyle, but other clues can be found in the various sources quoted in the CHA:

- Lead paint and lead pipe in Buffalo's older housing stock is one significant cause of lead poisoning in children.

- The percentage of smokers in Erie and Niagara County is higher than that of the state or the country.

- Residents consume unhealthy snacks such as deep-fried chicken wings dipped in dressing high in saturated fat.

- We are sports spectators more often than participants.

- And more. But that would fill a whole other book.

Education

An article in *Current Issues in Economics and Finance* underscores the contribution of human capital to an individual's economic success, adding that a college degree represents a significant, quantifiable block of human capital. The writers point to research showing a positive relationship between the share of a metro area's working-age population holding at least a four-year college degree (the most common measure of a region's human capital stock) and its GDP per capita (a standard measure of economic activity).[43]

As the table below shows, while the Buffalo Niagara Falls metro area exceeds the New York State and U.S. average for high school graduates, it does not do as well for four-year college degrees. However, the high school graduation rate increased 3.3% versus a .3% decline in New York State from 2011 to 2012.

High school graduation rate mirror assessment scores, with a four-year graduation rate in Buffalo in 2010–11 (54%) significantly lower than the overall New York State graduation rate (74%)....It is estimated that in the future, 80% of

	USA	New York State	Buffalo-Niagara Falls metro area
High School or higher	86.4%	84.8%	89.2%
Bachelor's degree or higher	29.1%	32.6%	28.5%

Table 1.2: Educational attainment

job openings will require postsecondary training or education....People with lower educational attainment are more likely to be unemployed. In Erie County, only 51.5% of individuals without a high school education were employed; that figure jumped to 86.5% for those with a bachelor's degree or higher.[44]

For the performance of individual school districts, the reader can go to "New York State Report Cards," issued by the New York State Education Department, at reportcards.nysed.gov.

The area is fortunate to have many colleges and universities. The metro region's thirteen have an enrollment of approximately 82,000 and an estimated economic impact of approximately $3.8 billion. According to regional economist Richard Deitz of the Federal Reserve Bank of New York's Buffalo branch and co-author of the article on human capital cited above, "Local colleges and universities are a strength these days for regional economic growth. The strength is that we have a lot of local colleges and universities, the research universities can really be a driver of growth."[45]

But the fact that the top four in enrollment locally are all branches of the State University of New York system [46]—University of Buffalo, Erie Community College, Buffalo State College, and Niagara County Community College (the area's largest private college, Canisius, breaks in at number five)—presents a strength and a weakness in educational opportunities because it is generally held that private universities are better than public ones. They are more market oriented and flexible, and there's often more money, especially with prestigious universities. As evidence of this, explore the *U.S. News & World Report* rankings of colleges and universities.[47] Though this ranking system has its critics, and some of that criticism is valid, it is probably the most popular and widely used ranking system in the country. On their list of top national universities, the top twenty are all private except for the University of California at Berkeley which is tied for number twenty. In their rankings for liberal arts colleges, only two public institutions, the Naval Academy at number twelve and the Military Academy at West Point at number seventeen, rank in the top twenty. Down the university list is the University of Rochester at number thirty-two and it isn't until number 82 that a SUNY school, Stony Brook, is listed. Following is the SUNY College of Environmental Science and Forestry at 86, and SUNY Binghamton at 97. The University at Buffalo is ranked number 109.

Looking ahead, there's hope. Cara Matteliano describes the Community Foundation's initiative Say Yes to Education, which in collaboration with other local leaders incentivizes graduation rates from the Buffalo Public Schools by committing 100% of the tuition needed to attend participating collegiate and post-secondary institutions through a scholarship fund:

> The long-term goal is that Buffalo students will graduate from high school, be prepared to have a whole secondary experience that gives them a credential that they can use to have a job that pays family-sustaining wages…. In the last two school years the graduation rate has increased by 7 to 9% depending on how you calculate it. The percentage of kids matriculating to college has increased by about 9%. We're hoping to take kids who have been in poverty, have lived in distressed neighborhoods, have had all kinds of issues that come along with that, [and] take their place in a working life that pays them enough to be able to have a family. We want to position people for good jobs.[48]

The regional education system is surely an asset, but does it compete favorably with other regions at the national level?

CHAPTER TWO

SOCIAL CAPITAL

According to the World Health Organization,

> Social capital represents the degree of social cohesion which exists in
> communities. It refers to the processes between people which establish
> networks, norms, and social trust, and facilitate co-ordination and co-
> operation for mutual benefit....Social capital is created from the myriad of
> everyday interactions between people, and is embodied in such structures as
> civic and religious groups, family membership, informal community
> networks, and in norms of voluntarism, altruism and trust. The stronger
> these networks and bonds, the more likely it is that members of a
> community will co-operate for mutual benefit. In this way social capital
> creates health, and may enhance the benefits of investments for health.[1]

For Dr. Trevor Hancock, one of the founders of the healthy communities movement,
social capital is "The glue: high cohesion and civicness; safe, livable built environments;
equitable access to the basic determinants of health."[2] He describes three aspects of
social capital: social cohesion and civicness; public investment in the soft social
infrastructure; and the judicial, political and constitutional infrastructure of society. He
says, "Social capital is distinguished from human capital in that it does not exist within
any single individual but instead is concerned with the structure of relationships

between and among individuals."[3] Social capital is equally as important as human capital.

The World Bank contends that, traditionally, natural capital, physical or produced capital, and human capital constituted the wealth of nations and formed the basis of economic development and growth. Today, however, according to the bank, these three types of capital only partially determine economic growth because they do not include the way in which the economic factors interact and organize themselves to generate growth and development. That interaction and self-organization is social capital.[4]

For Phil Haberstro, "Social capital is the critical piece." It also means "bridging—across divides: race, gender, class and bonding—friends and family relations." In addition he says, "When you look at the business of trust, social capital is one of the elements in that framework of trust. There's a spiritual dimension to communities."[5]

Our social capital, however, is declining. In his pioneering book on social capital, *Bowling Alone*, sociologist Robert Putnam[6] shows how we have become increasingly disconnected from family, friends, neighbors, and our democratic structures. Putnam warns that our stock of social capital has plummeted, impoverishing our lives and communities. Putnam draws on evidence including nearly 500,000 interviews over a quarter century to show that we sign fewer petitions, belong to fewer organizations that meet, know our neighbors less, meet with friends less frequently, and even socialize with our families less often. We're even bowling alone—hence the title. More Americans are bowling than ever before, but they are not bowling in leagues. Putnam shows how changes in work, family structure, age, suburban life, television, computers, women's roles, and other factors have contributed to this decline. He points particularly at baby boomers, the largest core of our population, as doing less volunteering and having less philanthropy, less trust, less share of responsibility for community life, than older generations. This is a national problem, not strictly a regional problem.

For Putnam, expressions of social capital include political participation—voting, working for a political party or campaign, attending public meetings, signing a petition, etc.; civic participation—membership in organizations such as unions, PTAs, youth groups, charities, church groups, fraternal and veterans organizations, etc.; and religious participation—attendance at religious services and volunteering for religious activity. Altruism, volunteering, and philanthropy are also informal social connections, but these are hard to measure.

Putnam measures civic engagement by using indicators such as reading a newspaper daily, attending a religious service weekly, signing petitions, being a member of a union, attending public meetings, writing elected officials, being an officer or committee member of a local organization, writing letters to the newspaper, working for a political party, running for or holding public office, working on a community project, or any combination of the above.

Activist and filmmaker Annie Leonard, best known for her film *The Story of Stuff*, describes social capital in a different way: "Each of us has two parts. We have a consumer part and a citizen part, a consumer muscle and a citizen muscle…. We have this other part of ourselves, our citizen muscle that we are not called upon to use as much as our consumer muscle. That citizen muscle has atrophied."[7]

So how do we measure the region's social capital? Because it's a relatively new concept, there are not a lot of tools and data. But the Wellness Institute's Haberstro has been working on this issue for years now, using parts of the national reporting. Wellness Institute has a project to measure the social capital of Buffalo Niagara. He said that the National Civic League's civic index is "…another tool I would marry alongside with Putnam's work on measuring social capital,"[8] and that a good set of tools for baseline measurements seems to be evolving in this area.

"I don't think we've ever tried to measure [social capital] with numbers," is PPG's Sam Magavern's take. "When the new Open Buffalo (a collaboration to increase Buffalo's capacity to effect systemic change through strategies such as original research) project is underway there's going to be a lot more measurement of things like that so we kind of get into some of the aspects of that."[9] He has a sense of the level of social capital from the work they are doing, but is it strong or weak in a particular area? He follows voter turnout and the number of people show up for various hearings, but they currently don't have a structured way to measure that.

Cara Matteliano says the Community Foundation has a number of ways to measure.

In their collaborative leadership initiatives such as the Say Yes and the Healthy Homes Initiative, there's generally a set of indicators about how people are served. The CFGB's staff of 23 also does it less formally with their ear to the ground and they have a lot of networks and grantees; and they're always trying to find out what's going on.

The United Way's useful Community Needs Assessment measures mostly human capital—such as population characteristics, health and wellness, and education; and economic capital—such as poverty, which will be discussed in further detail in chapter 3 under economic capital, rather than social capital.

The following are some indicators of the region's social capital:

Voting and Political Engagement

Contrary to Putnam's assertion that voter participation is declining over time, turnout for presidential elections has risen since 1996, which was the lowest point since World War II. Election data primarily includes the voting eligible population (VEP) but neither those ineligible to vote such as noncitizens, felons, and the mentally incapacitated, nor voter registration. The United States Elections Project at George Mason University[10] contends that "comparing state turnout rates based on voter registration is not informative" because "voter registration rolls contain 'deadwood'—people who are registered at an address but no longer reside there, for whatever reason."[11]

	USA	New York State	Erie County	Niagara County
Voting age population	240,203,630	15,314,401	726,117	170,748
Turnout for 2012 presidential election	54.1%	46.6%	57.5%	52.1%

Table 2.1: Voter engagement
Source: "America goes to the polls 2012", nonprofit vote,
http://www.nonprofitvote.org/documents/2013/03/america-goes-to-the-polls-2012.pdf, accessed

7/30/14; Erie County Board of elections; Niagara County Board of elections.

Unfortunately, voting eligible population figures are not available at the county or metro level. The table below substitutes voting age population so that county data can be compared with the state and the nation.

In the presidential election of 2012, New York State's voter turnout was 44th in the nation and showed an 8.9% decline from the 2008 presidential election. According to data compiled in Corporation for National & Community Service, Volunteering and Civic Life in America, only 9% of the nation's residents, 8.5% of the New York State residents, and only 8% of Metro Buffalo's residents participate in public meetings.[12] Once again, the region is below average.

Church Attendance

The Census Bureau does a survey of religious affiliation—but not attendance — for the entire nation and not at the state, county, or metropolitan area level. Likewise most surveys on religious attendance are at the national or state level. However, as measured in a survey by the American Church Research Project in 2000,[13] the Buffalo Niagara area, of the 55 largest metropolitan areas, had the second highest church attendance at 26.1%.

Other statistics from the Religion Facts website[14] rank New York State 39th in the country with a 33% religious attendance figure, and a Pew Research Center survey finds religious attendance declining across the nation,[15] further evidence of the decline in social capital in the larger context.

Volunteering and Philanthropy

Putnam describes these aspects, "Altruism, volunteering, and philanthropy—our readiness to help others—are by some interpretations a central measure of social capital."[9] While philanthropy is admirable, personal interaction is more important. Putnam says, "A check in the envelope, no matter how generous, cannot have that same effect. Social capital refers to networks of social connection—doing with. Doing good for other people, however laudable, is not part of the definition of social capital."[16]

Putnam explains how social networks provide the channels through which we recruit one another for good deeds, and also foster reciprocity that encourages attention to others' welfare. Volunteering and philanthropy and even spontaneous "helping" all coincide with civic engagement. Putnam says, "Any assessment of trends in social capital must include an examination of trends in volunteering, philanthropy, and altruism."

Our society has a tradition of philanthropy and volunteering dating to the very beginning of. Americans donate and volunteer more than the citizens of most other countries. For the first few centuries, these activities sprouted from religious activity, but "during the 20th century both volunteering and philanthropy became more organized and professionalized.... While the church remained the single most important locus of volunteering and philanthropy, it was joined by new institutions for organized altruism – the foundation, the corporation, and community organizations of all sorts."[17]

In terms of social capital, as seen in the table below, the Buffalo area has a higher rate of volunteering than New York State but lower than the nation as a whole.

Table 2.2a: Volunteerism, an overview

Buffalo

- 24.7% of residents volunteer, ranking them 36th among the 51 largest Metropolitan Statistical Areas.
- 215,200 volunteers.
- 60.9% of residents donate to charity.
- 8.0% of residents participate in public meetings.
- 26.5% of residents over age 55 volunteer.

New York State

- 20.6% of residents volunteer, ranking them 50th among the 50 states and Washington, DC.
- 24.7 volunteer hours per resident.
- 3.06 million volunteers.
- 384.3 million hours of service.
- $11.0 billion of service contributed.

- 44.9% of residents donate to charity.
- 8.5% of residents participate in public meetings.
- 19.7% of residents over age 55 volunteer

USA

- 26.5% of residents volunteer.
- 32.4 volunteer hours per resident per year.
- 64.5 million volunteers.
- 7.9 billion hours of service.
- $175 billion of service contributed.
- 51.0% of residents donate to charity.
- 9.0% of residents participate in public meetings.
- 25.8% of residents over age 55 volunteer.

From: Volunteering and Civic Life in America 2013,
http://www.volunteeringinamerica.gov accessed January 6, 2014

Table 2.2b: Volunteering Specifics

	USA	New York State	Metro Buffalo
Donates to charity	51.0%	44.9%	60.9%
Attends meetings	9.0%	8.5%	8.0%
Active in neighborhood	8.3%	6.5%	4.7%
Volunteer rate 2004	28.8%	21.1%	29.9%
Volunteer rate 2012	26.5%	19.6%	25.8%
Change from '04-'12	-2.3%	-1.5%	-4.1%

Source: Corporation for National And Community Service,
http://www.volunteeringinamerica.gov/export.cfm, accessed 8/19/14.

While we have higher rates of donating to charity, which is a good thing, writing a check is easier than attending meetings and neighborhood engagement, where we fare poorly compared to the national and state averages. The column "Active in neighborhood" is a result of a survey which asked this question, "Have you worked with other people in your neighborhood to fix a problem or improve the condition in your community or elsewhere?" Here, we are significantly below national rates.

The executive directors of some local nonprofits that run volunteer programs spoke about the volunteer trends they have experienced. The Buffalo Audubon Society's Loren Smith reported that their number of volunteers and volunteer hours have been "flat to declining."[18] Some of the reasons for the decline, he said, are specific to Buffalo Audubon, such as the fact that their headquarters is 40–45 minutes outside the urban and suburban core, resulting in fewer volunteers convenient to where the majority of Audubon's work takes place. "On top of that, [the population of] the region is getting older and fewer younger people are in the volunteering pipeline."[19]

For Buffalo Niagara Riverkeeper, the numbers are up. "We have more requests for participation and volunteering than we have the capacity to sustain," said BNR's director, Jill Jedlicka. "We're at 1500 to 2000 people every year."[20] She explained that their expanding restoration projects along the Buffalo and Niagara Rivers, the field-based River Academy, and River Watch, a volunteer water-quality-monitoring program, bring out volunteers who want to "want to get their hands dirty and their feet wet" as well as learn and understand. "That's a huge cultural shift,"[21] she said, adding that BNR's volunteers range from high school age to retirees who all care about the water.

Volunteerism at the Matt Urban Center runs in cycles, according to Marlies Wesolowski. Numbers tend to be higher during the Christmas season and New Year. Wesolowski cited the center's location on the city's East Side as a reason for the lower numbers at other times. "When we tell people where we're located, oftentimes they don't want to come here. So I think the neighborhood, the demographics, and the economic issues surrounding our neighborhood will sometimes put people off."[22] Negative media coverage of the neighborhood is also a factor, she said, perpetuating feelings of unease about safety and security.

Cara Matteliano of the Community Foundation explained that not every community has very wealthy families who can put a lot of dollars into philanthropy. The Community Foundation makes it possible for individuals and families who don't have great wealth to contribute to a philanthropy whose dollars create an endowment that progresses forever. Matteliano explained the Community Foundation's role as providing a place where donors—average residents, government, not-for-profits, faith communities—have the opportunity to leave a legacy in perpetuity through their personal giving.   Matteliano explains that donors can decide for themselves what it is that they want to do with their funds. "One of the choices they can make is to assign their funds for the changing needs of the community over time." For example, someone who made a gift in 1935, who wasn't aware then that lead poisoning was going to be a big issue will have his dollars used toward education and abatement because we know it is an issue now. Because the CFGB is at the crossroads of so many different agencies, Matteliano says, "We're in the position of figuring out what the really important issues are and what we can do to help."[23] The foundation also sees its job as acquiring additional resources, increasingly from outside the community, because the extent of resources needed is far greater than what is available.

Data collected by the Chronicle of Philanthropy and Pew Trust indicate that metro Buffalo is below the national average in percentage of household income given to philanthropy, which raises two questions: Is Buffalo's level of poverty to blame? Or is it a sign that our social capital isn't as high as it is in other communities?

Matteliano points to the lack of big corporate foundations here. Unlike Cincinnati, for example, which has the giant Procter & Gamble foundation and other corporate foundations, Buffalo, she said, has a "big three," the John R. Oishei Foundation, the Margaret L. Wendt Foundation, and the Community Foundation, plus smaller foundations that are quite specific about what they fund. "We really need a fuller complement of that bigger philanthropy."[24]

Regarding individual giving, Matteliano thinks that numbers alone don't tell the whole story: "One of the things that I cherish about this community is that people will pull together… in ways that are really moving, helping their neighbors, coming together. There's a lot of social capital that happens outside the numbers."[25]

Loren Smith's take on philanthropy is influenced by demographics. "Millennials aren't accumulating wealth like older generations did," he said. Instead, younger generations are giving in ^other ways than money. The Volunteering and Civic Life in America website tracks activities that are formal and involve record-keeping. What Smith describes doesn't involve record-keeping, so it's hard to get a handle on that. Matteliano said, "It is hard to keep track of because so much of it is informal."[26]

It is likely, however, that our informal activity is in line with the formal. Putnam points out, "Amid the pressures of everyday life, giving time and giving money often seem alternative avenues for generosity. If we lack one, we can give the other. Generally speaking, however, volunteering and philanthropy are complements not substitutes. Some of us give lots of both, while others give little of either.... Volunteering is among the strongest predictors of philanthropy, and vice versa. Altruistic behaviors tend to go together."[27]

Audubon's Smith commented on recent trends and forecast for the future in light of a declining population and declining incomes. "Philanthropy is slowly rebounding from a low we saw with the fiscal crisis in '08 and '09," which isn't unique to Western New York. He goes on to say historically "there's a generation that grew up in the Depression and was very frugal and accumulated significant wealth," but, "the newer generations are not accumulating that wealth and are being philanthropic in different ways,"[28] such as supporting their kids' sports teams.

In terms of philanthropy, one of the best gifts an individual can give is the donation of an organ or tissue. Here, too, the region is substantially behind the national average. In Western New York only 33% of adults are registered organ and tissue donors, compared to 48% of the adults across the nation.[29] We are, however, better than the state average of 22% which is the third-lowest donor registration rate in the United States despite being third-highest among all states for the number of residents in need of transplants, nearly 10% of all those on the nationwide waiting list.

In other dimensions of volunteering, Putnam's book points out that well-to-do, highly educated people are more likely to volunteer, to donate money, and to give blood, making education a powerful predictor of virtually all forms of altruistic behavior. On the other hand, material resources are not the most important predictor of altruism.

"As a matter of fact, because of their relatively active church involvement, the poor give no less a fraction of their income than the wealthy," the author says.[30]

Formal volunteering and informal helping behavior are all more common in small towns than big cities. Putnam again:

> Age makes a difference: volunteering and blood donation generally follow an inverted U-shaped life cycle pattern, reaching a peak in one's late 30s or early 40s. Volunteering is especially common among parents of school-age children. Philanthropy typically accelerates with age, as disposable wealth accumulates.

> More important than wealth, education, community size, age, family status, and employment, however, by far the most consistent predictor of getting time and money is involvement in community life. Social recluses are rarely major donors or active volunteers.

> Social capital is a more powerful predictor of philanthropy is financial capital.[31]

Whatever the reasons, Buffalo Niagara's stock of social capital seems to be below average and, if it follows the national trends, is on the decline.

Marriage and Family

There is a considerable body of evidence to show that marriage is good for health and longevity. But does marriage affect social capital? Over the past half-century, the decline in marriage correlates with the decline in social capital.

Robert Putnam argues that marriage can crimp social capital. He finds that civic involvement declines with marriage and kids. The traditional role of housewife, and now househusband, is particularly socially isolating. Still, a happy marriage is one of the most popular values sought after by respondents to polls on the elements of the good life. But the trajectory of the American family structure over the last few decades has resulted in fewer marriages, more divorces, and more people living alone. So Putnam asks the question, "To what extent [have these changes] contributed to the decline of civic engagement?"[32]   His surprising answer is "probably not much." He does acknowledge that married adults and those with children are much more likely to be involved activites such as school and youth groups. But, he says, "On other hand, neither marital nor parental status boosts membership in other sorts of groups."

In his book *Coming Apart*, sociologist Charles Murray argues that marriage is one of the most important values of social life. He writes, "Trends in marriage are important...because they are associated with large effects on the socialization of the next generation. No matter what the outcome being examined," such as the quality of the mother-infant relationship, delinquency and adolescence, criminality as adults, illness and injury in childhood, sexual decision-making in adolescence, school problems and dropping out, emotional health, or any other measure of how well or poorly children do in life, he states "the family structure that produces the best outcomes for children, on average, are two biological parents who remain married."[33]

Regardless of how you feel about marriage, it is arguably one of the most difficult social relationships, and rates of marriage are a fair indicator of the level and success of social capital. Looking at that indicator, it's interesting to see how the region measures up.

Table 2.3: Family and marriage indicators

	United States	New York State	Buffalo Niagara Falls Metro
Family households (families)	66.5%	64.3%	61.4%
Married-couple family	48.8%	44.5%	43.1%
Nonfamily households	33.5%	35.7%	38.6%
Average household size	2.62	2.60	2.36
Average family size	3.21	3.26	3.02

Source: American Fact Finder, custom data table DP 02, Selected Social Characteristics in the United States, 2009-2011 American Community Survey Three-Year Estimates, accessed 6/26/14.

The United Way's Community Needs Assessment describes the need for and importance of families:

> All members of a family—children, youth, adults, and seniors—need safe, nurturing relationships to promote good health and well-being. Increasingly, local families are turning to informal caregiving relationships—for example, adult children caring for aging parents or other relatives, grandparents assuming parental responsibilities for their grandchildren, and children in foster care. These relationships and responsibilities can take a toll on the physical and mental health of caregivers and care recipients alike.[34]

The Matt Urban Center delivers services to families as well as individuals. Director Marlies Wesolowski has this perspective: "I think that the breakdown in family has not helped. As a society, in policies, we don't do anything to drive the message home that kids are going to be more successful when they have a Mom and a Dad in a home all working together."[35] She talks about lots of single heads of household (the data in table 2.3 back her up), and "a lot of girls getting pregnant before they really should be getting pregnant." In the absence of a significant other or two-person household, she feels "a single mom trying to raise kids trying to do the best [she] can, it doesn't help. We've actually got a whole culture where it's acceptable." Wesolowski is not suggesting we go back in time; rather she laments that "there is no emphasis on the importance of the family staying together."[36] She believes that needed are more policies, more programs, and more educational opportunities that help kids understand that they and their children are going to be more successful if they build a family structure.

With statistics showing that the region has smaller families and households, fewer families, and lower rates of marriage than average, what does this say about the region's social capital?

CHAPTER THREE

ECONOMIC CAPITAL

Economic capital means creation of adequate wealth and healthy jobs;
equitable distribution of wealth and income; ecologically sustainable
development. economic development means: development of the economy
to provide the means of ensuring that the basic determinants of health are
adequately met, thus avoiding absolute material deprivation.[1]

—*Dr. Trevor Hancock*

In their 2014 Prospectus edition of the *Buffalo News*, the editors declare "a lot to like in 21st century Buffalo....a city whose outlook has radically changed from one of glum acceptance to one anticipating better days that have already begun to arrive... .The evidence is all around....The best of what has occurred here over the past couple of years [is] not just that things are looking up, but that the region's expectations have risen."[2] Are better days here? Are outlook and expectations enough?

Reporter David Robinson injects a healthy dose of caution.

> But is it for real?...This spark in the Buffalo Niagara region's economy faces threats—economic and political. But challenges aside, the change is astounding by Buffalo standards, where for the past sixty years, economic growth has pretty much been something that happens someplace else.... What could go wrong? There's no guarantee that any of this will provide

enough of a jolt to jump-start the local economy and turn it from a laggard to a leader. Dozens of things could go wrong.[3]

As someone who's lived here for over six decades, I would agree. We've had our hopes raised before. The paper's business and finance editor Grover Potter suggests there are differences now. "So what's different this time? First, this time the state is firmly behind the effort....Second, there is solid planning behind the effort....And third, a new crop of leaders are filling spots across the economic spectrum, from college campuses to factories to start-ups....And finally, and perhaps most importantly, young people are digging in."[4]

To know for sure, we need more data and information

The overall economy

How are we really doing?

The Brookings Institution ranked the top one hundred metros in the United States on four indicators (jobs, employment, output (gross product), and house prices) during three time periods (the recession, the recovery, and the combination of the two).[5] During the recession, the Buffalo metro area was sixth best in the country; for the recovery we ranked 89th; for the combined recession and recovery, we ranked 32nd. In terms of jobs, the metro area roughly follows the national trend but is not growing as fast. In 2014, the region was .3% behind its peak in the third quarter of 2008. In terms of unemployment, we kept pace with the national average. In terms of output—gross product—our recovery lags behind the national average, 91st out of 100. Our best performance indicator is for house prices. During the recession, we had the second lowest drop; for combined recession and recovery, our metro area had the third-best performance of the top 100 metros.

The Federal Reserve's Richard Deitz sums it up thus: "There's been no overall economic growth on a gross basis for twenty-five years basically at this point.... The region is not growing very rapidly, and we're starting to fall behind again relative to the rest of the country after the last business cycle." We are not alone, however, and he goes on to say, "This is not just a Buffalo issue either, it's the whole Northeast, especially around the Great Lakes."[6] Why this is will be explored in chapter 7 when we look at causes.

The Western New York Regional Economic Development Council (REDC)'s 2013 state of the region report7 includes indicators on the state of economic capital. The report shows results for the years 2011 to 2012. Its jobs indicator shows a .4% increase for Western New York, lagging behind New York State (1.4%) and the U.S. (1.6%). For total wages, it shows the region's 2.3% increase lagging behind New York State, 2.9%. Other indicators show

- Percent change in total number of firms; the region's increase of 1.2% was exactly half that of New York State's 2.4% increase.

- Percentage of minorities in the workforce increased 1.6% versus .9% for New York State and .5% for the US but, as will be discussed in further detail in chapter 7, the region has more work to do in this regard. Still it is significant, moving in the right direction, and worth celebrating.

- Western New York's average annual wage increase of 1.9% outpaced New York State's 1.5% and the nation's 1.2%.

The U.S. Bureau of Economic Analysis issues a regional fact sheet on income and GDP.8 In 2012, the per capita personal income of the metro area ranked 100th in the U.S. and was 98% of the national average. Per capita personal income had increased 3.1% from 2011 but the national increase was 3.4%. For the ten-year period from 2002 to 2012, the metro's compound annual growth rate of per capita personal income was 4.0%, outperforming the nation's rate of 3.2%. Total personal income for the region's population ranked 49th in the United States in 2012, down from 47th in 2002. Worth noting is that the percentage contribution by personal current transfer receipts (i.e. benefits, payments by governments and businesses to individuals and nonprofit institutions for which no services are performed) stand significantly higher for the region versus the ten-year national average (21% versus 17%). For total personal income, the compound annual growth rate over 2002 to 2012 was 3.8%, lagging slightly behind the national average of 4.1%.

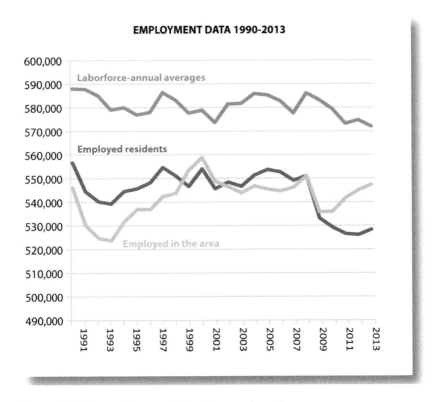

Figure 3.1: Metropolitan area labor force and employment.

From: New York State Department of Labor, Historical Employment by Industry and the Local Area Unemployment Statistics Program, for the Buffalo Niagara Falls Metropolitan statistical area, accessed 7/7/14.

Employment

Jobs are the most important indicator of how well the regional economy is doing, measured several ways. Unemployment numbers are common but can be deceiving because they're the result of several factors. Recently, the state Labor Department reported good news on the local unemployment rate: It had dropped to a six-year low, and the number of jobs had been growing. This drop in unemployment, however, is due in part to a shrinking labor force, and the addition of jobs is at a rate less than the national rate. The decline of workers in the region's labor pool follows a national trend, partly due to the fact that our aging local workforce has many baby boomers retiring.

How much is this shrinking labor pool due to baby boomers getting older, and how much of it is because unemployed people are getting discouraged and dropping out of the labor force? The numbers are attributable to discouraged workers as much as anything. When the *Buffalo News* wrote about the June 2014 unemployment report, they concluded, "The big drop in the unemployment rate was caused entirely by a steep decline in the number of workers who were considered to be unemployed."9 But there's more to it than that. From 1992 to 2013, the labor force declined by 2.6% while the number of employed residents dropped by 4.9%.

Figure 3.1 plots three sets of data. "Labor force" measures the total number of people in the metropolitan region who are working or looking for work. The trend over this period of time roughly parallels that of the trend in the United States as a whole: a declining labor force resulting from many factors such as the retirement of the baby boomers and the discouragement of the unemployed. The second line, "Employed residents", represents the number of residents of the metropolitan region that are working. But these data include residents who are working outside the metropolitan area, for instance, people who live in Alden but work at Darien Lake. The third line, "Employed in the area", plots the results of a survey of local firms reporting the number of jobs available in the metropolitan area, but some of these jobs are held by people who live outside the metropolitan area.

Looking at the chart, one of the most striking points is that the number of jobs within the region has been pretty much flat for the last quarter century. The total number of jobs during 2013, 547,900, is almost the same as it was in 1990, 546,800. This reinforces Deitz's quote above.

The number of employed residents in the region has declined 4.9% from 1990 to 2013, but the number of people working in the region has increased slightly, by .02%. This discrepancy is caused by an increase in the number of people who reside outside the metro area but called the metro area their workplace. Marlies Wesolowski observed, "Even though the people who live in the community are not very well off, there are some high-paying jobs within [it], but very few people who live in the community actually have access to those jobs. So people from other communities are coming in filling those positions and there's [less] opportunity for people who live [here]."10

What kind of jobs are they? Regarding the nature of jobs and employment, Richard Deitz reflects on the question of the quality of jobs. He asks, "Are they better paying jobs, are they worse paying jobs, what kind of jobs are they? Those are big questions too." Regarding ways of measuring the quality of jobs he says, "the knowledge content of jobs and the skill level of jobs," is a factor to consider.[11]

The Community Health Assessment offers this historical perspective:

> Buffalo Niagara, like many of the Great Lakes metros had long been a blue collar community with the steel, auto and aviation industries dominating the region. During the 1980's many companies including Bethlehem Steel and Republic Steel, two of the largest employers in the County, closed the majority of their operations and laid off a preponderance of their workforce. As those factories/facilities closed, people took lower paying jobs or left the area altogether. The primary industries in Erie County have since shifted from blue collar manufacturing industries to service industries. The number of manufacturing jobs fell from over 67,742 in 2000 to 47,681 in 2011. Conversely, in 1975 there were approximately 67,000 jobs in the service industry compared to over 200,000 service industry jobs in 2011.[12]

UB's Regional Institute did an analysis in 2010 of the breakdown of the Western New York economy by industry.[13] They found that health services was the largest sector at 15%. In their 2014 Prospectus on healthcare, the *Buffalo News* reported that health care and social assistance provided 13.8% of all jobs of Buffalo Niagara, followed by retail, professional and business services, and education. Interestingly, health services, manufacturing, and education contribute larger percentages of the local economy than they do in the U.S. economy.

The bad news is that the percentage of manufacturing jobs in the metro area declined by almost 44 percentage points from 2000 to 2012, a drop of 16,200 jobs. That was offset somewhat by the increase of 3600 in the number of professional, scientific, and technical services jobs over the same span.

STEM is the buzzword in jobs. STEM is an acronym that stands for "science, technology, engineering, and math." These jobs are high skill, high knowledge content, and usually high-paying. In 2011 STEM jobs accounted for 18.5% of the regional jobs (nationwide it's 20.1%), ranking Buffalo 73rd out of the top 100 metros. Albany and Rochester have much higher rankings—26th and 30th in the country—and even Syracuse has a higher percentage.[14]

The New York Fed reports this national trend which further complicates things:

> Since the 1980s, employment opportunities in both the United States and the New York–northern New Jersey region have become increasingly polarized. While technological advances and globalization have created new jobs for workers at the high end of the skill spectrum and largely spared the service jobs of workers at the low end, these forces have displaced many jobs involving routine tasks—traditionally the sphere of middle-skill workers. Moreover, these same forces have pushed up wages for high-skill workers disproportionately, contributing to increased wage inequality.[15]

Not a postive sign for economic capital.

Looking to the future, the New York State Department of Labor projects for 2010 to 2020, for the five-county Western New York region, that there will be an eight percent growth in total employment over the decade, a net change of 56,070 jobs.[16] But this will trail their projected growth rate for New York State of 9% and for the U.S. of 14.3%. While almost three-quarters of the annual openings will be replacement jobs, they actually project growth of about 6000 jobs per year.

- The largest growth for occupational categories will occur in business and financial operations, computer and mathematical occupations, community and social service occupations, healthcare practitioners and technical occupations, and food preparation and serving-related occupations.

- The biggest reductions will be in farming, fishing and forestry occupations and production occupations.

- The five fastest growing occupations in terms of percentage increase will be service unit operators in oil, gas and mining; software developers and system software; personal care aides; meeting, convention and event planner; and veterinary technicians and technologists.

• In terms of absolute numbers, the five fastest growing occupations will be home health aides; personal care aides; software developers and system software; market research analysts and marketing specialists; and information security analysts and web developers.[17]

Infrastructure

Infrastructure represents the major publicly-owned capital assets. They are in bad shape and seldom maintained to stay ahead of deterioration. There is no accounting of the region's infrastructure either comprehensively or by municipality. Niagara Falls planner Tom DeSantis, when asked if public works or some other department does an accounting on public assets measuring depreciation and overall condition, replied, "No. Basically they track where our streets get fixed, what year, what they do. There's really not a financial accounting."[18] It may not represent all the municipalities of the region, but it does seem to be typical.

The American Society of Civil Engineers does do a rough survey of the state of New York's (but not local) infrastructure.[19] They conclude 60% of the major roads are poor or mediocre quality, there are 2169 structurally deficient bridges, and there are 403 high-hazard dams. They estimate that, to maintain and upgrade systems over the next twenty years, it will take $27 billion for drinking water infrastructure and $29.7 billion for wastewater infrastructure statewide. One could safely assume that the Buffalo Niagara region has its share of these problems.

In the past twenty years, the region added 525 miles of roads costing $26 million to maintain. If we stay on our current trajectory, from 2010 to 2050 we will add an additional 660 miles more, despite the region's declining population.[20]

As an example, a July 2014 Investigative Post report revealed a two-year-old consultant's report that concluded Buffalo's buildings and parks would need over $600 million in repairs over the coming decade.[21] These assets fell into disrepair because of deferred maintenance, a problem common among public entities, and mismanagement of capital funds allocated to routine maintenance. Quite simply, the executive department did not put enough funds in the budget and the legislature let that slide. Although this is the most extreme case in the region, similar problems could be found in other municipalities and at other levels of government.

Housing

For an individual household, real estate is the most important economic asset. For a region, too, it is one of the most important economic capital assets, one of the region's strengths or disadvantages.

The National Association of Homebuilders develops a survey called the Housing Opportunity Index, counting homes sold in that area that would have been affordable to a family earning the local median income.[22] Buffalo has a housing opportunity index of 92.2 (100 being the national median, anything under that is good) ranking number two in the region and number nine in the nation for the first quarter of 2014. Sperling's Best Places Index ranks the cost of housing in the metro region below the national average.[23] In March 2014, Forbes declared Buffalo America's most affordable city of 2014.[24]

Is it affordable? Looking at the policy papers on the Partnership for the Public Good website, under 'Assets', the metro is third-best in the country in affordable housing. In other briefs such as 'Housing', the metro is ninth worst in the country.[25] Dale Zuchlewski, executive director of the Western New York Homeless Alliance, the non-profit that coordinates community-wide efforts to mitigate homelessness, says lack of affordable housing is the number one reason for homelessness. A very large portion of the county population falls under the federal guidelines for affordable housing. How to reconcile these two faces?[26]

PPG's Sam Magavern explains that we have low housing prices and low median rents, so we score high on affordability indexes that look at those two things but we have low median income and high utility costs so the percent of your income you end up paying for housing is high. "That's how you end up on both indexes, we're so affordable and we're so unaffordable." People in the human services sector would call it a problem, but somebody on the Western New York Regional Economic

Development Council would say this is wonderful. Magavern said, "It's both true." How do we bring both parties together in agreement? He replied, "I don't think they have to agree because both are telling the truth. It's different contexts. So if you're recruiting someone to move here, from Brooklyn, absolutely you should be marketing highly affordable rents and home prices. If you're worried about homelessness you should be calling attention to the fact that rents and home prices are affordable but many residents can't afford them."[27]

Housing prices may be changing though: a recent *Buffalo News* feature reported a hot seller's market with bidding wars and steep jump in prices. "Bidding wars and big prices" detailed a sharp rise in prices per square foot in some Buffalo city neighborhoods—more than double the previous year's figures on the West Side, and nearly double in Allentown and University Heights. Interviews with sellers and realtors revealed that a shrinking number of homes for sale is the big cause: the number of homes for sale declined in 28 of the 30 months since November 2011.[28]

Table 3.1: Housing stock characteristics

	Buffalo	Buffalo Niagara MSA	New York State	USA
% of total units occupied	84.3	91.3	90.3	88.6
% of occupied units owner occupied	40.7	65.6	53.3	65.1
% vacant units 2000	15.7	8.7	9.7	11.4
% built before 1950	74.7	42.5	42.4	19.3
Median year structure built	1939	1954	1955	1975

Source: American Fact Finder, tables DP-01, DP-04, QT-H1, B25034, and B25035.

An analysis of 2012 Census data by Business Journals revealed Buffalo Niagara has the second oldest housing stock in the top 100 metros, with roughly two out of fiveexisting homes (42.45% to be exact) built before 1950.[29]

The 2010 census counts 45,374 vacant housing units in the metro, nearly half—20,908—in the city of Buffalo alone.[30] From 1972 to 2010, new housing increased 22% while vacant or abandoned housing units increased 204%. If we stay on our current path, by 2050, vacant or abandoned housing units will more than double.[31]

Table 3.1 compares local, state and national data. Some significant things stand out: the region has better occupancy rates than the state and nation and fewer vacant units and the age of the housing stock is on par with the state. But the city of Buffalo is a special case and its statistics skew the perception of the region.

As mentioned in chapter 1, one of the more serious health issues is lead contamination. One of the major sources is lead paint in homes, one of the downsides of the older housing stock. The Matt Urban Center offers services to homeowners with very old homes. Marlies Wesolowski works with the Erie County Department of Health, which cites homeowners for having high levels of lead. She says, "We actually train welfare-to-work people to encapsulate the lead paint to prevent kids from becoming lead poisoned." The center takes low income community residents through a six- to eight-week program, teaches them how to remediate the issue, and then gives them some hands-on experience. At the end of the training period, these individuals get their OSHA (a federal work safety program) cards and rehab certificate which they can then take to an employer. "I think we've got about 50% of them employed." Wesolowski says, but the great thing is "it's kind of a win-win because the homeowner who has been cited, gets the work done [even if they] can't afford to get the paint encapsulated, and has a safer home environment for themselves and their kids. The welfare-to-work individual gets the training and the skills and the certificate that goes along with it."[32]

The Matt Urban Center has rehabbed old homes and built new residences. Is it worth the effort to put resources into old houses or is it better to build brand-new homes?

For Wesolowski, it's a tough question. "It does cost a lot to fix up old homes. Some of the homes are just too far gone to warrant doing anything for. It has to be case-by-case based on a thorough examination of the home and the cost-benefit analysis. The problem is that right now we have too much housing stock for the population. We can't save everything." The majority of their new building is multi-unit. The center also provides grants and loans to low-income families to fix up and repair the homes that they are living in. Another big problem is a lot of renters in this neighborhood because people can't afford to buy. Some of the owners—absentee landlords—don't even live in Buffalo; some live out of state, which contributes to the decline of the neighborhood. Wesolowski knows of people going to the City's foreclosure auction not really knowing or understanding the amount of work that has to go into an auctioned property or having the wherewithal to do it. "They have no concept on how bad a shape the house is in. Some of the houses in the foreclosure sale really should be demolitioned."[33]

Tom DeSantis has similar sentiments. The city of Niagara Falls has a unique program for urban pioneers—Live NF—in which encourages young people to live in targeted neighborhoods in return for which the city will help pay for their student loans.[34] How is it doing? He says, " 'Slow' I guess would be the adjective that you would apply. One of the problems we found out very quickly," because it's limited geographically, "is that there are not a lot of available housing units. So even if you wanted to live here, your potential places to rent or buy are tiny. Unless you are ready to buy something ready for the wrecker's ball and put $80,000 into it to fix it up. The housing supply of units that you or I would live in is just tiny."[35]

DeSantis says the top major problem that Niagara Falls faces now is "the housing market. The housing problem is really an intractable one. I don't think we really have devoted enough attention or brainpower to just how serious it is." DeSantis describes the typical processes of the last two decades, such as using federal housing and urban development money, as having little impact. " For a while somebody gets a little better house to live in or a better apartment to live in. But in terms of stemming the tide, no, it hasn't stemmed any tide." The economic and population decline leads, eventually, to demolitions." So you look around, you think wow, where'd all the houses go on that street?" One gets knocked down, then two, and before you know it, "there's only two houses left on the block." He describes the demolition process as "managed triage, it's cutting limbs off as you go along. Pretty soon you're not going to have anything left."[36]

Poverty and Homelessness

The quotation at the top of this chapter included the element "equitable distribution of wealth and income." Reports such as the *Buffalo News* Prospectus, seldom discuss these topics and they remain serious challenges to the region.

The Wellness Institute's Phil Haberstro said, "Some of the Wall Street people have said is we figured out how to create a lot of wealth, we just haven't figured out how to share it."[37]

Poverty is connected to a number of factors, including gender, race, disability, veteran status, and educational attainment. Poverty also has implications for educational status, health status, and access to employment based on transportation concerns, all of which make it difficult for those living in poverty to change their status.

The Community Foundation's Cara Matteliano says that the top critical problems facing our region include, "economic inequity and embedded in that is racial inequity, educational inequity, and all sorts of opportunity."[38]

The Gini index, a measure of income inequality, shows that New York State has the highest income inequality of any state and is second only to Washington, D.C.[39]

A *Business First* analysis of the Census Bureau's American Community Survey shows that Buffalo Niagara metro has the 19th worst disparity in per capita income between whites and blacks of the top metros in the United States; for every $1000 in income for whites, it's only $524 in income for blacks.[40]

Buffalo has long been near the top of the poorest large cities in the U.S. The Census Bureau's American Community Survey in 2012 found the city to have the fourth-highest rate of families, 26.36%, living in poverty.[41] What is interesting is that the poverty rate for the surrounding county, Erie, is only 14.2%, which is below that for New York State and the U.S. The concentration of poverty in the region's central city gives the entire region a negative image.

But poverty is not confined to the cities. Suburban poverty is on the rise, increasing

Characteristic	USA	New York State	Buffalo Niagara Metro	City of Buffalo
Median Household Income	51,914	55,603	49,572	30,043
Per Capita Income	27 334	30,948	27,280	19,409
% Families Below Poverty Level	10.1%	10.8%	10.4%	25.2%
% Individuals Below Poverty	13.8%	14.2%	14.0%	29.6%
% Children Below Poverty	19.2%	19.9%	20.0%	43.1%
% with food stamp/snap benefits (last 12 months)	9.3%	11.2%	Not available	26.5%

Table 3.2: Poverty: national, state, and regional comparisons.

From: American Fact Finder, tables DP-03, B17026, and B19301, 2010 census data, census.gov.

33% nationally from 2000 to 2012. Poverty in the metro region increased 41% from 2000 to 2011.[42]

Concentrated poverty (defined as census tracts where 40% or more of residents have incomes below the federal poverty threshold) is of particular concern. Between 2005 and 2009, the metropolitan area had a concentrated poverty rate of 15.7%, with a significant disparity between city (26.2%) and suburbs (4.9%). Buffalo is now home to twenty concentrated poverty census tracts including four neighborhoods clustered on Buffalo's East Side (Broadway-Fillmore), three in the Black Rock-Riverside area, and three on Buffalo's West Side (astride Niagara Street near downtown).

Poverty is a significant issue for local families and individuals, particularly in Buffalo where 55% of the population has an income at or below 200% of the federal poverty line. People in financial crisis often turn to community resources for assistance with basic needs such as food and clothing, rent and utilities, and connections to other resources. These services are critically important given the lack of affordable housing: 50% of renters and 25% of homeowners pay more than 30% of their income on housing in both the city of Buffalo and county of Erie.

Homelessness

Homelessness can be seen as an indicator of social capital but is placed here as a measure of economic inequity. Has homelessness increased? Dale Zuchlewski, executive director of the WNY Homeless Alliance, replied, "No." Not all shelters provide data and a lot of data still uses estimates, but he thinks "we're at the point where we have pretty good data from the people that are reporting."[43]

How does this area's homeless population compare with the rest of New York State and the U.S.? Zuchlewski replied, "We're proportionally sort of equal to Rochester and Syracuse. Certainly nobody compares to New York City. And you see that the warmer parts of the country have higher numbers also." He says that New York State has better safety nets, especially so for families, than for individuals. "If you go out west to California or in the south, you'll see families that are living out on the streets. Here in Erie County, even Niagara County, you do not see families living out on the streets. If you do it's for a very short period of time. The Department of Social Services (DSS) makes sure that there are no families out on the streets."[44] DSS gets them services and, at least at a minimum, into a shelter immediately.

Zuchlewski explains that poverty and affordable housing are the bigger picture when it comes to homelessness. "Seems to be common knowledge, but nobody seems to be able to figure out what to do about it."

He reports, "There have been $1.3 million worth of cuts in the last two years to homelessness [programs] mostly in Buffalo, Erie County and some in Niagara County also. Apparently those haven't been increased in 25 years. That's part of the problem."[45] The New York State Office of Temporary and Disability Assistance is responsible for that, but they need state legislation to increase budgets. But that's another problem, as

Dale explained, "Nobody gets reelected advocating for increased welfare for people, which is sad. Curbs, trees, and sidewalks. That's what people want. They're more interested in what's in front of their houses and what affects them on a daily basis."[46] (This same point will be reinforced in chapter 6.)

Zuchlewski speaks from experience—he was on the Buffalo Common Council for eight years. The Department of Housing and Urban Development (HUD) has targets for reducing or eliminating homelessness. Zuchlewski thinks they're realistic and achievable. HUD wants to end chronic homelessness by the end of 2015. If the Homeless Alliance gets all the money they applied for, they should come close to it. Some services locally should be able to at least come close to ending veterans' homelessness. Ending family homelessness in 2020 might be difficult just because people are always going to fall off the edges at some point, making a bad decision after getting laid off from work, not having sick days, and getting the flu for a week or two and missing a paycheck. Zuchlewski paraphrases the president of the National Alliance to End Homelessness who says, "When we talk about ending homelessness we're not ending all types of homelessness. But creating a system to rapidly rehouse people when they do become homeless," he says, "That's achievable."[47]

The New York State Department of Education tracks homeless and at-risk homeless children. When parents register for school in September, the schools have somebody during the registration process telling parents what services are available. Principals, social workers, guidance counselors, and teachers are looking throughout the course of the year for families that need help. Zuchlewski says they've done a much better job identifying people in need, and their definition of homeless is broader than his. They take people that are "doubled up": living with friends or family or couch surfing—as homeless. Zuchlewski says, "Our statistics show that you're one step away from being homeless when you're doubled up." Other studies have shown when children are unstably housed, it affects a child's schoolwork. Zuchlewski believes that is more of a determining factor of these children's success in school than any Common Core standards. He referred to research regarding the incidence of sexual and physical violence to women and children in shelters: Studies show something like 75% of the women in shelters had been physically abused and half have been sexually abused. "If you have this kid who is being physically or sexually abused, when they go home at night, they're not doing their homework. That's the furthest thing from their mind."[48]

Establishing a temporary shelter or permanent shelter in a neighborhood sometimes encounters opposition. Zuchlewski says, "Lakeshore took four years to open [a facility] because of political and neighborhood opposition. So if you're trying to open up [a] facility, you face some opposition." Not always: Depaul just opened up a facility in Riverside with no opposition. But, he continues, "I know you go into some of the suburban communities and people there have fought senior citizen housing,"[49] which is less threatening.

Philosophically, Zuchlewski thinks, "for the most part people don't see homelessness." Some people may see some downtown, but the panhandlers downtown aren't necessarily homeless "and it's easier for people to ignore them or to think they choose to be homeless, because it relieves them of any moral responsibility to try to help."[50] Rarely do they think of a victim of domestic violence or a child as being homeless. A lot of times people think that the homeless are lazy but a single mom with a couple of children who aren't school age yet, has difficulty finding daycare or a decent paying job with health care. How can they work themselves out of that? Couples make up only 25% of the homeless families while single mothers account for 75%."[51] It's easier to think that people choose to live like this. People are living on the streets aren't making a rational decision, it's usually a mental illness and people start to self-medicate. You can say 'people choose to be homeless, my responsibility is over because they want to live like that.' "[52]

The Matt Urban Center is building Hope Gardens for chronically homeless women. Wesolowski reinforces Zuchlewski when describing the residents her organization serves:

> Chronically homeless individuals have two or more episodes of long-term homelessness within a two to three-year period....A lot of stigma surrounds individuals who are homeless. There's a train of thought that people consciously make a choice to be homeless....Often we find the people we work with don't necessarily have the mental capacity to make the choice.

They're on the street because they don't know any better. Some of this happens when some of the safety nets are not there anymore for the people who have suffered from significant mental health issues. Those individuals find themselves increasingly alone with no family support because the family's not around or available, or the family has divorced themselves of these individuals because they are too high maintenance for them to take care of.[53]

Another problem is that, "Some of the women that we serve have had multiple abuses and rapes," says Wesolowski. "They came from domestic violence situations where their husbands or partners have thrown them out in the street where often they become victimized again by some other individual that is on the street with them."

The state of the region's economic capital is a mixed and complex one.

....

CHAPTER FOUR

ENVIRONMENTAL CAPITAL

Natural capital is the land, air, water, living organisms and all formations of the Earth's biosphere that provide us with ecosystem goods and services imperative for survival and well-being. Furthermore, it is the basis for all human economic activity.

—*International Institute for Sustainable Development*[1]

People depend utterly on nature to sustain and fulfill human life, yet the values of nature are typically ignored in decisions. If properly managed, Earth's lands, waters and their biodiversity yield a flow of "ecosystem services," including: the production of goods such as food and timber, life-support processes such as water purification and coastal protection, life-fulfilling benefits such as beautiful places to recreate…. Despite their vital importance, ecosystem services are generally taken for granted, scarcely monitored, and, in many cases, undergoing rapid degradation and depletion. This has serious—and potentially catastrophic— consequences for human well-being.

—*Natural Capital Project*[2]

A brand-new multidisciplinary science called ecological economics marries traditional economic accounting to valuing ecosystem services. The people in that movement refer to 'natural capital' but the people in the healthy communities movement refer to "environmental capital", which is how it will be referred to in this book.

Erie County's Environmental Management Council issues a state of the environment report.[3] Jay Burney, Chair of the Habitat and Natural Resources Workgroup of the Western New York Environmental Alliance and communications coordinator for the Global Justice Ecology Project, was on the Environmental Management Council and has worked on those reports. Regarding these reports he says they're "driven by how the county engages and sells itself as environmentally concerned and it's got a very traditional base. In other words, it focuses on economic development, and that means externalities are not as recognized as they should be." The reports look at traditional land-use models and are constrained by budgets and the kinds of work that participating agencies can do, and who is working in the county. "So it's not as good a work as it could and should be." The people on the environmental management council are appointed by towns and villages and "they bring their own sets of concerns which often are very often budget-driven." How do they conserve a tree, a forest, or water resource if they don't have the money? Burney says it may improve this year because they made progress to broaden the scope despite a tremendous amount of resistance due to budget and staffing concerns.[4]

Audubon's Loren Smith comments on the state of Buffalo Niagara's environment: "From Buffalo Audubon's point of view [the environment] has been subject to 100, 150, 200 years of environmental degradation. In the 1950s, 1960s, when Buffalo was at its economic, industrial, and demographic peak, that also resulted in the greatest insults to the environment." Some of those insults were in the past, "but right now Buffalo Audubon views the region as turning the corner and improving, partly because of demographic shifts: there are fewer people having a negative impact on the environment. But we still have that legacy of insults to the environment. So, cautious optimism would be a phrase that I would suggest."[5]

Buffalo Audubon sees an increasing number of environmental organizations and individuals who care about the environment and greater coordination among those. They also see national attention on the Great Lakes and our region, specifically Great Lakes restoration. Smith says, "Personally, I think that the region still suffers from a 'we've always done it this way' and isn't good at reinventing itself and is still suffering from the contraction from our heyday and not adequately addressing what that means for the future of the region."[6]

Air

The American Lung Association's State of the Air 2013 Report states, "Thanks to the Clean Air Act, the United States continues to make progress providing healthier air." The region is not represented on their numerous lists of "cleanest" or "most polluted" in various categories except that Niagara County is one of the cleanest counties for short-term particulate pollution. They grade the Buffalo Niagara region a "C" for high ozone days, a "B" for 24 hour particulate pollution, and a "pass" for annual particulate pollution.[7]

Scorecard the Pollution Info Site states Erie County is fourth highest and Niagara County is eleventh highest in New York State for health risks from air pollutants.[8]

Erie County's State of the Environment report has an air quality section which focuses on just two pollutants, sulfur dioxide and ozone. They show measurements under the acceptable limit of the national ambient air quality standards (NAAQS). They also state:

> Air in Western New York enters the state principally through the prevailing westerly winds blowing across the heavily industrial Midwestern states. When it arrives, it already contains significant contamination.
>
> Sulfur dioxide levels within Erie County have remained consistently below NAAQS recommendations. However, levels for Tonawanda exceed those of Buffalo, suggesting that people residing in areas close to Tonawanda are at a higher health risk. These findings may be a product of the fact that the point source that emits the greatest amount of sulfur dioxide in Erie County is located in Tonawanda. C. R. Huntley, a coal-fired powerplant, emits 48,484 tons of sulfur dioxide per year. This figure is nearly ten times greater than the next highest emission facility... and is greater than the next top 25 emission facilities in Erie County combined.[9]

Only two groups in the region monitor air quality, the New York State Department of Environmental Conservation (DEC) and the Clean Air Coalition of Western New York (CAC). Erin Heaney, executive director of the CAC, comments on the county's state of the environment report that air entering the region already contains significant contamination. She said, "I get a little nervous when I hear that because often I hear many elected officials and people in power use that as an excuse to not have to do things here."[10]

Do we know how much of the pollutants come from outside the region? Heaney replied, "We know best in Tonawanda. One of the amazing things that the DEC did when they did their Tonawanda air quality study, the study broke down what percentage of pollution in Tonawanda came from Tonawanda versus outside background." While a lot of coal-burning power plants west of us send their pollution to Western New York, Heaney says, "The DEC's report actually showed that while there was some background pollution, [a] pretty significant part of air pollution [comes from] right here at home and that the vast majority of air pollution challenges come from right here in Western New York."[11]

Regarding overall air quality, she said, "We have a pretty grave air quality issue in the region in general but it is getting better. There are positive stories too but I don't want us to shy away from the fact that there are serious challenges."

What positive stories? Heaney says, "The enforcement action at Tonawanda Coke was really important. It reduced benzene omissions in the town by 86% within a year and a half, which is a tangible reduction. We're also seeing better compliance from other companies in Tonawanda, as a result of seeing Tonawanda Coke get into a lot of trouble."[12]

How does the CAC monitor air quality? "Our monitoring is not really as sophisticated or as comprehensive [as the DEC's], but we have trained a team of residents to use a number of different air monitoring devices. Most rudimentary is the bucket, which is a three-minute grab sample of volatile organic compounds. On the lower West Side we've trained residents to be able to use a monitor for ultrafine particulates."[13]

NYS DEC has a website for their air testing quality data, and they look at carbon monoxide, lead, nitrogen dioxide, particulates, ozone, sulfur dioxide, and hydrocarbons. Are these all the pollutants in the EPA's National Ambient Air Quality Standard or are there more? Heaney thinks, "the DEC and EPA should be monitoring for much more than that. I think the reason that they monitor for only those is that there are national standards." As an example, Heaney says, "We were looking at air pollution down by the [Peace] Bridge; we wanted them to look at ultrafine particulates. There is no national standard for that yet, even though there's a growing and robust body of literature that shows that ultrafines are extremely harmful."[14]

Is the DEC doing a good job? Heaney thinks "it's hard to say, on the whole, when an agency is doing well." CAC has had really good experiences. She says, "There are great people inside DEC who want to do the right thing and there are amazing scientists and their hearts are totally with the community and in protecting public health. On the other hand, they're subject to political pressures that are very great." CAC observes a tug between those two things. "I think the DEC has done a pretty good job in Tonawanda on the monitoring side; the scientific team there has just been just incredible, very communicative with the community, and they've used that data to do some enforcement action with a lot of pushing from us. On the lower West Side, I would say they're not doing a very great job. They did this study really only after there was an enormous community pressure, and they haven't really worked with us or with the community to disseminate that information and educate folks. So it's kind of a mixed bag."[15]

The DEC has an air quality index (AQI) but no comprehensive report. The New York State Department of Health is more concerned with indoor air quality but does point to resources such as those at the EPA. EPA has an air quality index report which is very simplistic.

Besides the Peace Bridge neighborhood, Covanta at Niagara Falls (one of the state's largest emitters of mercury), and Tonawanda Coke, are there more pollution sources? Heaney said, "Yes. Tonawanda has the highest concentration of air permitted facilities in all of New York State. There are 53 plants within a two-mile radius. That includes the coal burning power plant; Tonawanda Coke; FMC; 3M, which is the world's largest sponge making plant, DuPont plant which makes Corian countertops; NOCO's petroleum distribution terminal–those are some of the big ones." The EPA's Toxic Release Inventory lists the biggest air polluters. "Then there's all the mobile sources of pollution. We've done a really good job of encircling our city with highways. Some of the other hotspots we worked with are folks who live in neighborhoods that have school bus terminals in their backyards."[16]

Water

Abundant water doesn't seem to matter for population growth. The five driest major cities in the country—Las Vegas, Phoenix, El Paso, Albuquerque, and San Diego—are all growing in size despite being water-constrained. As mentioned in chapter 1, of the top 100 metros only eight are losing population and seven of those are on the Great Lakes.

Buffalo Niagara Riverkeeper has a goal of drinkable, swimmable, fishable for the Buffalo and Niagara Rivers, and Lake Erie. How are we doing? Executive director Jill Jedlicka replies, "We have certainly made significant progress. As a community we have taken what were literally liabilities and barriers to our advancement and identified the problems, identified the solutions, and started to implement changes."[17] She thinks that fishable, swimmable, drinkable are important metrics but not the only ones because there are nuances with each one of them. Can we ever reach that those three things? Jedlicka says Riverkeeper believes "our region is defined by its water, by our location on the water, and it's going to define our future. We have to be able to use that resource, we have to be able to drink that water, we have to be able to swim without worry about getting a rash or getting sick, and we have to be able to eat the fish. That's going to take time and we have to be realistic about that time frame; it's not overnight, it could be another generation until all the species of fish are safe to eat."[18]

Is there a report card on the region's waters? Jedlicka said that report cards were good communication tools maybe five, eight years ago, but because things are moving so quickly and communication happens in real time, whether it's through social media, their website, or through individual engagement on a daily basis, they really haven't produced a report card in a few years. Is there one place where a citizen go to find out how the lakes are doing, now and over time? Jedlicka said, "I don't think you could say one place."[18] She lists sources such as the Great Lakes Commission, the Environmental Protection Agency, and the International Joint Commission, which oversees and manages the water quality of the Great Lakes. She singles out the Healing Our Waters coalition because "they've got their finger on the pulse of what's happening in the Great Lakes basin from a science, policy, and economic perspective and they are starting to become more of a clearinghouse for that information."[19]

A lot of agencies, non-profits, and individuals are collecting data, generating many data sets, but there really hasn't been a synthesis of all these data sets. Jedlicka replied, "It's very difficult to house everything in one place. You can find it more on a regional level. We do try to be that clearinghouse or at least have the most up-to-date information in terms of the Niagara River watershed and some of the Lake Erie stuff."[20]

Jedlicka is optimistic because of the awareness, the number of individuals and groups that are involved is growing, and tangible progress that is beginning to be seen. When she does presentations and talks with people about what's going on, it's no longer the silver bullet solution and it's not just one person that everybody's relying on and looking to. "Yes, there are certain elected leaders and developers that are kind of being elevated in the media because everybody wants a hero, right? For us, when we look at the hero, it's the community because it's been driven by the community, people demand it because they are aware of it now. At the end of the day, we're all responsible for this, and I would hope that message comes through."[21]

Jay Burney considers our location unique on the planet and the water of the Great Lakes our greatest asset. The Great Lakes hold about 20% of the Earth's total surface fresh water. Burney emphasizes, "If climate changes, water becomes more of an issue and we have access to this incredible resource. It's obviously a threatened resource."[22]

The Great Lakes are currently threatened by five major sources: climate change, diversion, pollution, loss of habitat, and invasive species. Burney added, "Development is the main culprit and that covers a lot of territory: agricultural, urban, and industrial development."[23] Burney explains that economics traditionally treats the environment and other social issues as externalities, a concept which means that the effects on the environment and to society are not part of economic accounting. They're written out so when pollution occurs it is generally not the responsibility of the profit taker. The consequences of pollution, including public health impacts and loss of ecological resources, becomes the responsibility of individuals and citizens and communities. He believes how we develop the economy is probably the greatest threat to the resources of the Great Lakes.[24]

Agriculture and Farms

The number of farms and farmed/cultivated land in the region is declining. One Region Forward calculates from 1969 to 2007, 160 square miles of farmland were lost. If we stay on our present trajectory, by 2050 we will lose 8000 more acres or 12.5 square miles.[25]

The Western New York Regional Economic Development Council (REDC) recognizes this problem:

> WNY is a rich agricultural region within one of the nation's top producing states. Its moderate climate, fertile soils, entrepreneurial farmers and solid infrastructure give the region a competitive edge. The industry is primed for diversification and expansion in food processing, value-added products, tourism and untapped local and external markets. These opportunities are particularly important with growing concerns over local food system sustainability and community health. Meanwhile, rising costs, outdated and cumbersome state regulatory policies and global competition challenge farm sustainability, inhibit growth and threaten next-generation farming.[26]

Figure 4.1: Declining Acres of Farmland

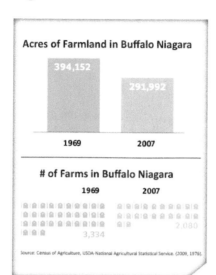

From: One Region Forward, http://www.oneregionforward.org/datastory/how-much-agricultural-land-have-we-been-losing/, accessed 11/7/13.

This, in part, has led to a situation where the population of the region needs to be fed from somewhere beyond our boundaries. It wasn't always so.

Figure 4.2: Agricultural production vs. area population needs

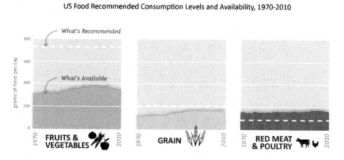

From: One Region Forward, http://www.oneregionforward.org/datastory/arewegrowing-enough-food-in-our-region/, accessed 11/7/13.

What this means is that the region is becoming less self-sufficient and less secure, food-wise. This leads to higher prices, cash flows out of the region, a higher carbon footprint for all consumers, and vulnerability to supply disruptions.

Figure 4.3: Regional production of population's needs

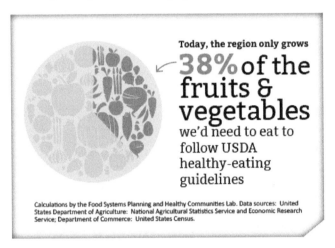

Today, the region only grows

38% of the fruits & vegetables
we'd need to eat to follow USDA healthy-eating guidelines

Calculations by the Food Systems Planning and Healthy Communities Lab. Data sources: United States Department of Agriculture: National Agricultural Statistics Service and Economic Research Service; Department of Commerce: United States Census.

From: One Region Forward, http://www.oneregionforward.org/datastory/arewegrowing-enough-food-in-our-region/, accessed 11/7/13.

Parkland and Trees

Data for Buffalo show the city's park acreage below the national averages but right on the median for US cities.[26] For all the glorious Olmsted parks, parkways, and other parklands, we still have less than half the parkland versus total city acreage than New York City, Minneapolis, Virginia Beach, El Paso, New Orleans, Austin, San Diego, and San Francisco.

More importantly than parkland is the amount of tree cover that our built environment has.[28] Tree cover is important because trees provide essential ecosystem services: they remove air pollution, retain storm water by keeping it from going down the drain and overflowing our sewage systems, and sequester carbon. Trees do all of this for free; the equivalent services provided by mechanical facilities would cost millions of dollars. A mature, large tree provides up to one thousand times more of these services than a mown lawn of the same area.

An urban ecosystem analysis performed in 2003 by the organization American Forests found that the tree cover in Buffalo was only 12% of the land area. That was before losing 100,000 trees in the 2006 October surprise storm. By comparison, the national average is 27.1%, and the most heavily forested city in the United States is Atlanta at 36.7%. Buffalo looks positively naked compared to Houston at 30%, Austin at 34%, Boston at 29%, Dallas at 28%, Syracuse at 26.6%, and New York City at 24%. American Forests recommends an average of 40% tree canopy for American cities.[29]

Toxic Waste and Brownfields

The Western New York Environmental Alliance's (WNYEA) waste and pollution working group produced, with the UB Design Group, the most comprehensive and scientific report on the state of the region's (including Cattaraugus County) environmental capital, "Mapping Waste: Setting The Stage To Clean Up the Niagara".[30]

Here are some highlights from its executive summary:

• Much of WNY's contamination is concentrated in our population centers first, because that was the location of early industry and hence, the legacy waste, and second, these areas continue as the center of "active" waste. This pattern increases the threats to the health of more people, especially our children. Further, many of these sites are located in low income areas, raising questions of environmental justice.

• Western New York has a substantial burden of both legacy and ongoing contamination in comparison to the rest of NYS. At least one of the three study counties was near the top of the list in total number of sites with each contamination issues study, leading us to suggest that WNY and its residents are unfairly burdened compared to the rest of NY.

• The presence of the U.S. Department of Energy Niagara Falls Storage site in the Niagara County Lake Ontario Ordinance Works (LOOW) site and the U.S. Department of Energy West Valley Demonstration Project in Cattaraugus County, show that Western New York bears a disproportionately high burden for storing high-level radioactive waste.

• Although burdened unfairly by contamination, Western New York residents have proven that community action can make a difference. The Love Canal tragedy catalyzed an environmental justice movement, championed by Lois Gibbs and other community members, that saw the creation of the federal and state Superfund programs for remediating similar sites.[31]

In terms of environmental Superfund sites, the average for a county in New York State is 21, yet Erie County has 87 and Niagara County has 67. For brownfield cleanup sites, the average for a county in New York State is four while Erie County has 31 and Niagara County has 11. In terms of solid waste landfills, the average for a county in New York State is 23 yet Erie County has 71 and Niagara County has 36.[32]

How is the generation and accumulation of waste trending? Sierra Club's Lynda Schneekloth, one of the contributors to the study mentioned above, says, "It's going up, it's going up. The state of New York talks about having a 80% reduction in the waste stream by 2030. That's a goal.... It's a stupid way to get rid of waste. We should just stop producing it. Niagara Falls is doing a lot of industrial waste burning.... it's not okay to have train after train after train of New York City's trash brought into Western New York for us to burn and breathe the mercury that's left over."[33]

Western New York has major toxic waste sites. In addition to the West Valley Demonstration Project and Lake Ontario Ordinance Works mentioned above, there is CWM in Lewiston, the only active toxic waste dump in the Northeast. Which is the worst? Schneekloth says, "West Valley because the kind of toxicity is there for millions of years and at this point it's built on unstable ground. If we had a flood like they just had in Colorado last year, we would have radioactivity leaking into the lakes. We are that close."[34]

Martin Doster, regional engineer for the New York State Department of Environmental Conservation's (DEC) environmental cleanup, has also managed the spill response comments on the DEC's mission is to improve and protect New York State's natural resources and environment and to prevent, control, and abate pollution. How well is DEC doing that?

Doster replies, "speaking from the perspective of remedial programs, which is typically land and groundwater, and brownfield remediation and recycling land, I have nothing but positive things to say. I think Western New York has done a very good job in targeting the worst cases of pollution and getting those remedied and, in some cases, flipping the properties to recycling the land, which is ultimately the home run in our business."[35] An example would be the old Republic steel facility on South Park Avenue, which operated from 1902 to 1980, left behind severely contaminated groundwater with toxic waste, benzene, lead, and petroleum. Using the state's resources, working with Erie County and the city of Buffalo, the team was able to get money out of bankruptcy court to address cleanup. Today, that property has been remediated to a commercial level. The city of Buffalo used Brownfield Opportunity Area planning grants (where the state of New York pays 90 cents on the dollar) to do planning: looking at brownfields, land-use plans, the site's history and projecting 50 years into the future. For past generations this land was very productive: a lot of paychecks, a lot of food on the table, a lot of jobs. Now there is a master buildout plan for this site, now the RiverBend clean energy corridor, which is bringing in two major companies. Doster says,"So that's a home run in my business. I wish I could say we have scores of these in Western New York, but I think we certainly have dozens of these, this model where we've been able to recycle these contaminated lands and at the same time protect the environment."[36]

DEC measures how many sites they've cleaned up and how many pounds of toxics they've taken out of the environment, but how does that make a difference in the bigger environmental arena? Many different entities: the U.S., the Canadians, the state, sometimes the locals and not for profits, measure this. Is it making a difference? Doster says, "My gut tells me that we're making a phenomenal difference in the environment. Is that because the Rust Belt has transitioned from dirty industry into something else? Is it a direct result of our remediation programs? Or is it simply nature cleaning itself up?"[37]

Regarding chemical and pollution control, how are we doing? Doster says, "Chemical control, pollution control is very good. The level of expectation has risen so high that today when you see an oil sheen in a creek or you see some dead fish or find a drum someplace, it's a big deal. You go back 20 years, that was a common occurrence, it was not a big deal." This generation doesn't know what it was like to have a dead Lake Erie or to have different colors going over Niagara Falls, or all the things we were dealing with back in the 80s. So the level of expectations is higher. One of the results is that, "Our lakes are cleaner than they've been really since the Postindustrial Era."[38]

How do we compare with the rest of New York state and the nation? Doster replied, "Between the cities of Niagara Falls and Buffalo, we have some of the largest acreage of brownfields anywhere except for maybe Detroit. Given that... we always have the largest percentage of land to be cleaned up, so obviously we have the largest percentage of cleanups done in the state. ... So we' re doing good."[39]

Doster continues, "I think we have a burden that's higher than North Carolina or Florida that haven't had that kind of 80-year jumpstart that we have, 80 years of industry. Other people hopefully are learning from that and when they site their new factories in North Carolina or Georgia they are learning from the mistakes of the past."[40]

Are brownfield sites forever stained? Can there ever be a full restoration to a point where the soil can be fertile and safe for growing food? Doster says it's the "How clean is clean debate. One must recognize, given all the other needs of our population, there is not enough money to clean up sites so that they all meet the standards where one could plant tomatoes or picnic on the ground and build a home there. The technologies are there, we certainly could do that."[41] It comes down to our decisions as a society as to how we're going to spend capital because there is only so much to spend. The brownfield program recognizes that not all land is going to be residential requiring the highest cleanup level and allows cleanups to go to different standards: industrial, commercial, or residential. Doster says, "Is that the solution to the debate on whether or not we should take all the chemistry out of the environment? No, but I think that's a pragmatic solution." Do we really need to take out all the benzene, toluene, xylenes, the petroleum contamination from a gas station? "Petroleum will naturally decay. A little sunlight, a little microorganisms, a little energy and very quickly petroleum oil, that kind of contamination, will quickly degrade down to the base elements. We need to recognize that and take into account that nature can do a lot about recovery as well. So we can focus our limited capital on the true environmental crime: polychlorinated biphenyls, PCBs, biocummulative contaminants, endocrine disruptors, things that are known carcinogens, those are the ones we should be focusing on."[42]

Wildlife

One important survey of wildlife is taken every year. Loren Smith describes it: "National Audubon runs the Christmas Bird Count. So Buffalo Audubon works closely with the Buffalo Ornithological Society and other individuals who participate in the Christmas Bird Count locally."[43] Buffalo Audubon also informally participates in Breeding Bird Atlas surveys and they do bird banding at Beaver Meadow and other places as well. What does this bird count tell us about the state of the environment? Is it akin to the canary in the coal mines analogy?

Smith explains that the Christmas Bird Count is the longest running, rigorous citizen science census of bird populations across the United States and beyond. The National Audubon Society analyzes avian population shifts and timing of presence and absence of birds and relates that to climate change. "So literally it can be seen as the canary in the coal mine. Also there have been papers that have been focusing locally on the arrival and departure times of birds that are showing statistically significant change over the last several decades in terms of Western New York populations."[44] What do those changes tell us?

Smith says, " It tells us that climate change is not just a global issue, that it does impact us right here in Western New York, in our own backyards, in ways we might not necessarily be able to predict.... all the birds all across the country, are definitely showing patterns in the biological response to climate change."[45]

Carbon footprint

When it comes to carbon emissions, the region's residents behave better than the nation as a whole. The Brookings Institute reports, "The average resident in metropolitan Buffalo emitted 1.995 metric tons of carbon from residential and transportation energy consumption in 2005. Emissions in the 100 largest metros averaged 2.235 metric ton per capita while the U.S. per capita carbon footprint equaled 2.602 metric tons. The metro area's total vehicle miles travelled (VMT) from passenger and freight vehicles amounted to 7,066 per capita in 2005. The 100 largest metros and the nation as a whole recorded 9,079 miles per capita and 10,083 miles per capita, respectively."[46]

Looking Forward

Jay Burney wrote, "From this writer's perspective the future is resurgent," meaning, "As we move further into this century, people are more and more aware of the obstacles to a sustainable future, people have become more engaged, and there are more projects looking at how we can conserve and protect and develop our resources. So the resurgence is there's more awareness, there is more engagement."[47] He doesn't know if we have or intend to do enough to protect our resources. "But people are trying." They should, he says, because this region is blessed with world-class natural assets that could provide economic benefits such as, "Some of the greatest avian and ornithological happenings on the globe happen right here in Western New York. Ecotourism and bird watching are two of the biggest growing industries in the world, and we have so much happening here. We can be equitable to the Galapagos Islands and Yellowstone in terms of the kinds of ecological things that are happening here."[48]

Buffalo Niagara Riverkeeper and partners recently achieved great success in cleaning up contaminated sediment from the bottom of the Buffalo River with the help of public agencies and a private corporation. Jill Jedlicka explains this unique partnership: "I would like to think that we were part of breaking the mold because ten years ago we started having unique partnerships with private corporations and having an environmental organization work with a government agency, whether it's the Corps (United States Army Corps of Engineers), or the DEC– that just didn't happen."[49] Those agencies would look to Buffalo to find out what was going on here. Sometimes government agencies have negative reputations but Jedlicka defends them, "Because the folks who are working here in the Buffalo district live, work and play here, they are vested in what happens here."[50] Erin Heaney and Jay Burney said pretty much the same thing about the people they work with, and Martin Doster is a perfect example of that: somebody whose heart and passion is with the community.

Typically, economic development agencies and their plans ignore environmental capital, but the 2013 REDC annual report refers to Buffalo Niagara Riverkeeper's work as balancing economic development with environmental preservation. Jedlicka sees the REDC as defining the future of Western New York's revitalization.[51] Riverkeeper noticed very early on that water was not part of their conversation other than the fact that it's often referenced for tourism because of Niagara Falls or the fact that it's an asset or a commodity that could be bought or sold or utilized. No part of the conversation was about enhancing, protecting, or restoring quality. Now, not only in Western New York, but in a lot of Great Lakes communities, there's recognition of issues such as climate change and the water shortages in the Southwest and the Southeast versus the fact that we have 20% of the world's surface freshwater in our front yard. Now the challenge becomes, from an economy standpoint, how do you leverage that asset to give this region the competitive advantage and to take that a step further, to enhance and restore it as well? Riverkeeper engaged with the REDC and "once we started talking about our philosophy and goals and what we're trying to do, they did see the synergy and the importance of it." Jedlicka says, "So our engagement with the economic development council is evolving, it's very positive, and it's a very open dialogue right now and we're really excited about where it's going."[52]

The Niagara River Greenway Commission resulted from the federal government's relicensing of the Robert Moses power project. Lynda Schneekloth assesses its impact on the region's human, social, and economic capital: "The first thing that seems important to me is that it exists at all because there has not been a good history of these kinds of relicensing as ending in something as substantial as the Greenway commission and $9 million a year." She went on to say, "I'm a firm believer in the nature deficit disorder. That we as a species, especially in our modern cultures, have lost contact with the natural world and so our not being able to actually access wildness."[53]

Schneekloth was one of the founders of the Western New York Environmental Alliance. "Every time I've talked about this in other places, people were astounded. It is truly a remarkable thing."[54] The Community Foundation brought people together, convened a series of meetings with environmental community leaders, and asked them what to do. The biggest issue that kept coming up was the fractured nature of the environmental community. These leaders thought that some kind of an organization or a coordinating function was needed. It actually became an alliance and has over 100 member organizations but probably "about thirty organizations are active which is a pretty good percentage,"[55] says Schneekloth.

On the REDC, Schneekloth, through the Sierra Club, tried to get energy and stopping the waste economy ("we're the armpit of whatever," she laments) as one of the REDC's high priorities. But those didn't even make it to the top three. She attributes Riverkeeper's success because they did a campaign on the blue economy and put the language "economy" in there.[56]

Erin Heaney's summary of how well our community leaders are taking care of our environmental and public health and well-being is, "they've got a lot of work to do. I think that they are only going to do as well as we encourage them to, force them to." She doesn't "see a lot of folks championing the environment as their top one or two issues." Citizens "have to organize and create a tremendous amount of public pressure or encouragement to see an elected official back the things that we're doing." One of the biggest challenges is the misconception that "we're in a rough economy and there's a perception, I don't think it's real, that you have to trade off jobs or economic growth for stronger environmental protection. That's not been our experience [but] there is a perception and that's very real and that molds the environment that [officials are] working in. So I think there's room for improvement."[57]

PART TWO:
....

FALSE NARRATIVES
AND REAL REASONS

During the hip, clever, cult television series *The X-Files*, there was a sinister villain called the Cigarette Smoking Man, described by one of the main characters as "…the most dangerous man alive." During episode seven of the fourth season, "Musings of a Cigarette-Smoking Man," in which this villain-instigator of every conspiracy of the latter half of the 20th century writes his memoirs under a nom-de-plume. This is what he has to say about us:

CSM: "What I don't want to see is the Bills winning a Super Bowl. As long as I'm alive that doesn't happen."

Aide: "Could be tough, sir. Buffalo wants it bad."[1]

At times, when bad news piles up, doesn't it seem as though we're cursed? Some people think so. In January 2008 paranormalist Mason C. Winfield III was the featured guest at a "Throw off the Curse" benefit for the Landmark Society. Winfield theorizes the curse hanging over this region began with the opening of the Erie Canal. Winfield chanted "God bless our Sabres and Bills" but a lot of good that did: The Bills went on to six more losing seasons and the Sabres were worst in the NHL last season.[2]

Speaking of curses, what's with Dallas?

Figure II-1: The faithful watch and cheer as the Buffalo Bills lead the Dallas Cowboys for 59 minutes, 59 seconds of a regulation game when the Dallas kicker puts one through the uprights with no time left: Dallas 25, Buffalo 24

Doesn't it seem that Dallas has supernormal powers over Buffalo teams? Consider the October 8, 2007, nationally-broadcast Monday night football game when the Bills snatched defeat from the jaws of victory (or Dallas snatched victory... oh, you get it). Or the back-to-back spankings Dallas handed the Bills in Super Bowls XXVII and XXVIII. And "No goal" is still an open wound.

What could have cursed us? Was it the assassination of a president? Dallas suffered one of those tragedies too.

Here's another thing: Dallas, and the whole Sunbelt which sucks people out of the Northeast, is made possible by the invention of air conditioning. The growth and continuing economic success of the region is only possible because air conditioning makes it tolerable to live, work, and play there.

Air conditioning was invented by one Willis Haviland Carrier. *Time* magazine named him one of the 100 Most Influential People of the Twentieth Century. Author Molly Ivins wrote, "…a kindly engineer from the Snowbelt made the Sunbelt boom."[3] Willis was born and grew up in Angola, New York. Angola is so close to Buffalo, it could be a suburb. Do you see the irony here? Willis Carrier was working at Buffalo Forge at the time of his invention, but when they closed their engineering department, he formed his own company and moved his operation. Today, the Carrier Corporation is global, with 43,000 employees, $12.5 billion in revenues, and it's headquartered in Farmington, Connecticut. The irony doesn't end there. Willis Carrier died in 1950 and is buried in Forest Lawn Cemetery…in Buffalo. Who says you can't go home again?

Lake Effect

It's not the Perfect Storm, the one Sebastian Junger wrote about—a.k.a. the 1991 Halloween Nor'easter—whose movie version starred, among others, Cheektowaga's William Fichtner—but it does require planetary-scale features and forces to create. Among other things: the alignment of global wind direction with the axis of one of the largest lakes on the surface of the earth plus a seasonal lag of water vs. air temperatures only happens in a few places on the North American continent over just a few square miles. And, wouldn't you know it, Buffalo is in the middle of one of those spots. Because of one bad lake effect storm in January 1977, we've had a bad weather reputation ever since.

Another false narrative has it that the flight to the suburbs was sparked by a single race riot on the [boat] Canadiana in the early 1950s. A major demographic shift from the city of Buffalo into the surrounding suburbs occurred from 1950 to 1960. The population of the city itself dropped 8.2%, but the population of the region increased by 20% and the population outside the central city increased by 52.1%.[4] This tremendous shift to the suburbs was prompted not by racism but rather by a bubble of new household formation. A perfect storm of economic prosperity in the 1950s, new family formation at the peak of the "baby boom", and the economic stimulus of the G.I. Bill created a movement of families that had been living in three-generation households, into a brand-new development pattern called the "suburbs." From 1947 to 1951, William Levitt built the prototype of postwar suburban development, Levittown, New York. "An important provision of the G.I. Bill was low interest, zero-down-payment home loans for servicemen. This enabled millions of American families to move out of urban homes and into suburban homes,"[5] and would help realize the American dream of owning their own brand-new home.

I know this phenomenon well because it happened to my father and my father-in-law. In the early part of the 1950s, they lived with their new brides and young babies in households owned by their mothers-in-law. When my dad moved to a new subdivision in Cheektowaga in 1954, initially the street had fifteen three-bedroom, one-story ranch houses. Of the fifteen, eleven were owned by WWII veterans, within a few years of age of each other, early in their marriages, with many children. Age range of their children was pretty much the same. And racism was the furthest thing from their minds.

By that decade, the city of Buffalo was pretty much built out to its boundaries. Many of those homes were doubles; the American dream created by Levitt was a single. Buffalo did not have the extra space for the construction of brand-new homes. Instead of expanding the boundaries, city fathers allowed people to move into the inner ring suburbs of Cheektowaga, West Seneca, and Tonawanda. It looked like the city was losing population but actually the region grew in population between 1950 and 1960, growth that would continue for at least another decade.

Figure II-2. Showing the growth of inner ring suburbs 1950 to 1960.

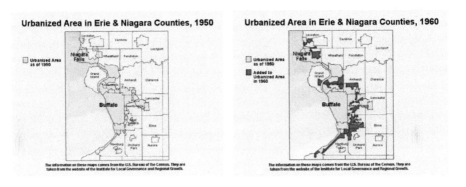

Source: University at Buffalo Regional Institute

The St. Lawrence Seaway myth

One of the great false narratives that many of the local population subscribe to is the St. Lawrence Seaway myth, that the beginning of the region's decline coincided with the opening of the St. Lawrence Seaway. Problem is, population loss began before the Seaway's opening April 1959 and there were larger phenomena that occurred before the opening of the Seaway which certainly had a far greater impact on the region. Diana Dillaway, author of the excellent book on the region's decline *Power Failure*, explains:

> Many Buffalonians attributed manufacturing's decline primarily to two events—the opening of the St. Lawrence Seaway (1959) and the loss of the steel industry (1971 – 1983). Time provides broader perspective, however, and I will argue that five factors contributed to Buffalo's economic decline. First, there were changes in the transportation routes for raw materials and goods. Second, the steel industry faced competition and technological change. Third, Buffalo lost home-owned industries and corporate headquarters. Fourth, the labor movement brought about militant labor demands and high wages. Fifth, Buffalo's political and economic organizations competed for power to the detriment of the city. These five factors set the stage for many, if not all, of the challenges facing Buffalo in -the second half of the twentieth century.[6]

When the country was not in war production, Buffalo's local economy took significant dives, as in 1946 when eighty thousand people became unemployed almost overnight. The biggest single loss was when Curtiss-Wright closed its operation and moved to Columbus, Ohio, shutting forty thousand people out of their jobs.[7]

The first of these larger phenomena with greater impact was the loss of the local aviation industry. During and shortly after World War II, there was a booming aircraft industry here in Western New York: Curtiss Wright, Bell Aircraft, and various supporting industries. As the war effort tapered off, jobs associated with this industry were either cut or moved to other parts of the country. The History of Buffalo website records, "By September 1945, the 40,000 people working at Curtiss-Wright has been reduced to 5,500 and the ripple is felt throughout the whole economy. By Christmas, 1946 there are over 80,000 people, close to fifteen percent of the area work force, without work."[8] This is a significantly larger number than those employed by the maritime industry displaced by the Seaway.

The decline of the port of Buffalo resulted largely from the major shift in transportation modes in the U.S. After completion of the Dwight D. Eisenhower Interstate Highway system, trucking took off and so did air freight. Freight carried on the Great Lakes waterways declined from 99.5 billions of tons miles in 1960 to 83.1 in 1988. This decline continues: Freight carried on Great Lakes waterways declined from 148.1 million tons in 1985 to 108.7 million tons in 2009.[9] The pictures below illustrate that shift in transportation modes: They're the same spot just about 50 years apart. On the left is an all-but-abandoned Erie Canal at the end of its life; on the right, a section of interstate highway I-190 that replaced it.

Figure II-3: The view looking south from Porter Avenue bridge in 1950 and 2005.

Many forces, both positive and negative, have led the region to this point. Many good writers have eloquently explained large historical forces that shaped the region, e.g. "The Power Trail" by Gawronski, Kasikova, Schneekloth, and Yots, and "Olmsted in Buffalo and Niagara" by Schneekloth, Shibley, and Yots. Part Two explores four major sets of dynamics that have been keeping our region from reaching its potential.

CHAPTER FIVE

SPRAWL AND SEGREGATION

Part One shows that the state of the region is a complex thing, not easily summarized by one number or statement. Likewise, the causes for our current state are numerous and complex. One of the most negative and damaging forces present that prevents us from realizing our potential is sprawl. Buffalo Niagara is a poster child for sprawl, because unlike other regions where sprawl is driven by population growth, here there is no good reason for it. This hinders the growth of all our capital. Buffalo Niagara is moving in the opposite direction from...

The Trend Toward Cities

The United Nations Population Fund reported in 2007:

> The world is undergoing the largest wave of urban growth in history. In 2008, for the first time in history, more than half of the world's population will be living in towns and cities.

> In principle, cities offer a more favorable setting for the resolution of social and environmental problems than rural areas. Cities generate jobs and income. With good governance, they can deliver education, health care and other services more efficiently than less densely settled areas simply because of their advantages of scale and proximity.

> Cities also present opportunities for social mobilization and women's empowerment. And the density of urban life can relieve pressure on natural

habitats and areas of biodiversity. The challenge for the next few decades is learning how to exploit the possibilities urbanization offers. The future of humanity depends on it.[1]

Scientific American's editors declare, "Many experts have come to realize that people are better off when they live in a city....Indeed, the city is come to look less like a source of problems that as an opportunity to fix them."[2]

Brookings Institution demographer William Frey says,"Americans' growing love affair with cities shows few signs of abating...Census data...show that in 2013 Americans kept moving to cities, favoring them over suburbs... the USA's urban growth shows no signs of ending. 'This looks like it could be the decade of the City,' he says."[3]

In a special themed issue on cities, National Geographic reports this example:

> More than half of Metropolitan Seoul's [South Korea] 24 million residents live in high-rises, deeming them safer, more energy-efficient, and a better investment than single-family dwellings.... Between 1960 and 2000, South Korea went from being one of the world's poorest countries, with a per capita GDP of less than $100, to being richer than some in Europe... Seoul today is one of the densest cities in the world. South Koreans have, a carbon footprint less than half the size of the New Yorker's. Their life expectancy has increased from 51 years to 79—a year longer than for Americans."[4]

Seoul is now the number ten most influential city in the world, using metrics of human, political, and economic capital, according to global management firm A. T. Kearney's Global Cities Index.[5] This is an example of why the trend toward cities is a positive one.

Why cities are good and sprawl is bad

In chemistry terms, think "dilution" and "concentration": The more concentrated something is, the stronger it is. Sprawl is the dilution of resources. In physics terms, think mass, density, and gravitational attraction. The greater the mass, the greater the attraction. Something that is spread out and dilute has little mass; something that is dense and concentrated has a great deal of mass. Similarly, sprawl is weak; dense concentration and mass attract greatly.

The economics principle of "economies of agglomeration" describes the benefits that derive from clustering together. This principle is related to the economies of scale and the benefits they afford. Physicists Luis M. A. Bettencourt and Geoffrey B. West explain:

> Why, then, do people throughout the world keep leaving the countryside for the town? Recent research that is forming a multidisciplinary science of cities is beginning to reveal the answer: cities concentrate, accelerate, and diversify social and economic activity.... People living in denser habitats typically have smaller energy footprints, require less infrastructure and consume less of the worlds resources per capita. Compared with suburban or rural areas, cities do more with less. The bigger [the] cities, the more productive and efficient they tend to become.[6]

Bettencourt and West say how a new science of cities has "unveiled several mathematical 'laws' that explain how concentrating people in one place affects economic activity, return on infrastructure investment, and social vitality." They go on to explain in more detail,

> When the size of the city doubles, it's material infrastructure—anything from the number of gas stations to the total length of its pipes, roads or electrical wires—does not. Instead these quantities rise more slowly than population size: the city of eight million typically needs 15% less the same infrastructure than do two cities of four million each....On average, the bigger the city, the more efficient its use of infrastructure, leading to important savings and materials, energy and emissions.[7]

Harvard economist Edward Glaeser has this point of view:

> There's no such thing as a poor urbanized country; there's no such thing as a rich rural country," he said.... Poor people flock to cities because that's where the money is, he said, and cities produce more because "the absence of space between people" reduces the cost of transporting goods people and

ideas....Successful cities "increase the returns to being smart" by enabling people to learn from one another. In cities with higher average education, even the uneducated earn higher wages; that's evidence of "human capital spillover." Spillover works best face-to-face. No technology yet invented – not the telephone, the Internet, or videoconferencing – delivers the fertile chance encounters that cities have delivered since the Roman Forum was new. Nor do they deliver nonverbal, contextual cues that help us convey complex ideas – to see from the glassy eyes of our listeners, for instance, that we're talking too fast.[8]

National Geographic argues why cities are the best cure for our planet's growing pains. Their reasons include:

• City roads, sewers, and power lines are shorter, their apartments take less energy to heat and cool;

• Dense cities tend to emit less CO_2 per person than the national average;

• Cities allow half of humanity to live on around 4 percent of the arable land, leaving more space for open country.[9]

They go on to write, "The fear of urbanization has not been good for cities, or for their countries, or for the planet."[10]

Edward Glaeser believes "In the 20th century American cities were redesigned around cars...Car-centered sprawl gobbles farmland, energy, and other resources. These days, planners in the U.S. want to repopulate downtowns and densify suburbs." He goes on to say, "It would be a lot better for the planet, [if people end up]in dense cities built around the elevator, rather than in sprawling areas built around the car..." concluding that urbanization may be "...the most sustainable solution to our planet's environmental challenges."[11]

Sprawl has a negative effect and urban concentration has a positive effect by their very physical configuration on human and social capital. Architect Michael Brill expressed it well: "Many people see social relationships as either private or public. They don't distinguish an important third form, community life....Public life is sociability with a diversity of strangers; community life is sociability with people you know somewhat. With our long-term and increasing emphasis on the private realm, we are losing both of these forms of broader social relationships, and many mourn that loss."[12] So as Buffalo Niagara residents move farther away from each other, their public life diminishes.

He goes on to explain that public and community life operate at very different scales and density, "each requires different physical environments in order to be robust."[13] To him, the desired behavior is about neighboring: relationships with shopkeepers that are more than economic; kids playing in a small local park; the chatting happening between those strolling pedestrian-scaled streets and on adjacent porches. The behaviors that Brill talks about are encouraged by city design—walkable streets and front porches— and discouraged by suburban and ex-urban design—streets without sidewalks and houses with backyard decks. These are the physical features that increase public life and, therefore, social capital.

Robert Putnam considers mobility and sprawl to be one of the major causes of the decline of social capital. He notes, "mobility undermines civic engagement and community-based social capital."[14]

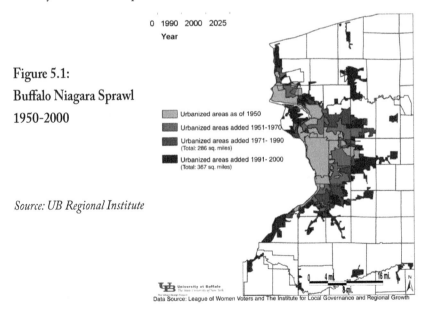

Figure 5.1:
Buffalo Niagara Sprawl
1950-2000

Source: UB Regional Institute

Why this region is different

Buffalo Niagara is moving in the opposite direction. Even as its population declines, it sprawls outward, spreads itself thin and reduces its density. We have fewer people but use more land. Buffalo sprawls at about four times the national rate. "Between 1980 and 2000, the Buffalo metro area consumed 4.03 acres of rural land—areas with less than one housing unit per 40 acres—for every new housing unit built, more than the 99-metro average of 0.90 rural acres per new housing unit."[15]

One result of this sprawl is the fact that Erie County maintains more miles of road than any county in the state, nearly 50% more miles than the number two county, Onondaga[16], another example of why sprawl is a negative force.

Smart Growth America does an annual study to examine the costs and benefits of sprawling development.[17] In Measuring Sprawl 2014, they researched and analyzed development patterns in 221 metropolitan areas and 994 counties in the U.S. Using four primary factors—residential and employment density; neighborhood mix of homes, jobs and services; strength of activity centers in downtown; and accessibility of the street network—they come up with a Sprawl Index score. They write:

> This report also examines how index scores relate to life in that community. The researchers found that several quality of life factors improve as Sprawl Index scores rise. Individuals in compact, connected metro areas have greater economic mobility. Individuals in these areas spend less on the combined cost of housing and transportation, and have greater options for the type of transportation to take. In addition, individuals in compact, connected metro areas tend to live longer, safer, healthier lives than their peers in metro areas with sprawl. Obesity is less prevalent in compact counties, and fatal car crashes are less common.[18]

In the 2014 report, Buffalo Niagara Metro ranks 97th with a score of 106.36.

Ironically, the Buffalo Niagara Falls metropolitan area is only one of sixteen in the United States that has an incorporated place with a density of over 10,000 people per square mile—the village of Kenmore.[19] The reason for this is that almost the total area of Kenmore is residential development, 82% vs. 57% for the City of Buffalo. Kenmore is considered to be a very livable neighborhood and an example of why density is not a bad concept.

The editors of *Scientific American* these conclusions about sprawl:

> In matters of housing, education, transportation, the environment and social services, existing rules and spending priorities give cities a raw deal. Cheap gas, highway subsidies, tax incentives for home ownership, complacency over urban education and the apportionment of legislators all give preferential treatment to suburbs and rural areas.
>
> The five least-populated states got twice as much (stimulus) money per capita as the rest. Anti-urban policies hurt denizens not just of downtown urban cores but also broader metropolitan regions—and, arguably, the nation as a whole. Cities contribute to economic growth out of proportion to their populations. When they are dragged down, everyone pays the price; when they do well, so do their hinterlands....
>
> Ultimately, the trouble is that the U.S. political system is rigged against densely populated areas....
>
> The basic issue is fairness. Why should government policy favor owning over renting, driving over mass transit, where kids in one school district over another? The current incentives encourage people to settle in the outskirts where they might otherwise prefer to live downtown – a bias that makes little sense even when you leave out its environmental costs....[20]

Bettancourt and West warn,

> Well-run modern cities have demonstrated the pervasive ills are not inescapable. The problems result primarily from nonexistent or poor planning and a lack of good governance. The development of these organizational traits may, in fact, be the most important long-lasting effect of urbanization because it paves the way for socioeconomic development at the national level.... Unbridled growth can nonetheless create crises that, in the extreme, could cause a city to collapse.[21]

UB professor Uriel Halbreich expressed it well in a *Buffalo News* article when he said, "We need the critical mass that is one of the main attributes of an upwardly striving city. That mass would evolve and should be geographically located in the core of the area, as an attractive 'Buffalo Niagara city center' to which all roads lead. We should reverse the centrifugal forces of suburban sprawl and the weakening of the inner-city that became the vacuum at the center of a 'bagel' metropolitan area, creating instead a strong magnet in the core."[22]

Segregation

Segregate: to separate or isolate from others or from a main body.

Inextricably linked to sprawl is the fact that region has sixty-four municipal governments—six cities, thirty-seven towns, twenty-one villages; two county governments; and two Indian reservations. Each of the municipal structures has been empowered by the state, under the municipal home rule law to act independently of their neighbors. The law does not provide language to restrict such powers with relation to any detriment that might result from such actions, other than what might be deemed unlawful or unconstitutional. In other words, they are entitled to operate independently of their neighbors, without consideration to the collective effect. The configuration of our region is de facto segregation.

One of the other definitions of segregation is the separation of races. One of the results of a fragmented region is the persistence of racial and ethnic disparities. Why does it matter? The Community Foundation for Greater Buffalo asserts that it matters to all of us because people of color constitute the only growing population in the region and they are also the youngest component of the population. The Buffalo Niagara region is the eighth most segregated between African-Americans and Caucasians in the United States. Reports of incidents of racial bias continue-and continue to increase. The Community Foundation's Cara Matteliano says, "We're a segregated community. That's the problem." The Community Foundation's vision statement calls for a vibrant region. Are we there yet? Matteliano replied, "No. I don't think we can be there yet but until we break down some of the racial barriers that divide our community. We have to resolve the racial difficulties in our community."[23]

Another telling sign of segregation is the racial composition of the region's suburbs.

Table 5.1: Majority racial composition by municipality

Municipality	% of population that is white
Erie County	80.0 %
City of Buffalo	50.2%
Town of Amherst	83.8%
Town of Cheektowaga	86.2%
Village of East Aurora	97.8%
Town of Orchard Park	96.7%
Town of West Seneca	97.3%
Village of Kenmore	92.8%
Niagara County	88.5%
City of Niagara Falls	72.0%
Town of Lockport	85.0%
Town of Lewiston	95.6%

Source: American Fact Finder, census.gov, Community Facts, table DP-1. Accessed 8/2/14.

Michael Brill writes about the sociopolitical effects of segregation: "What do we lose when we don't cultivate our public life, this important form of social relationships with a diversity of strangers? We lose an important factor in the growth of individuals, in a culture that values individualism. We lose a focus of opposition to the power of the state in the Corporation. We lose the marvel of the stranger."[24]

He goes on to say that community life is being threatened "by technologies and networks that spatially uncouple work and, increasingly, commerce, from metropolitan centers, enabling white-collar workers to work from their homes, close to home neighborhood satellite offices... without going downtown. With corporate downsizing there is also a substantial increase in outsourcing, with highly skilled, white-collar temporary employees often working from their homes."[25] This is another force separating us that we have to deal with.

The REDC addresses poverty and commits to tackling the underlying causes. They note how homogeneous the racial and ethnic composition of the Western New York workforce (85% white) is compared to New York State (56%) and the U.S. (64%). Their key metrics are useful: percent minorities in the labor force, graduation rate, number of degrees awarded, and the average annual wage. These percentages are not far off from the actual racial and ethnic composition of those geographic populations: The Buffalo Niagara metro area is 81.6% white and New York State is 65.7% white, but it does indicate that the metro area is less diverse than the state. REDC recognizes and graphically illustrates some of the major underlying causes of poverty and barriers to adequate employment: access to public transportation, safe and affordable childcare, and affordable quality housing options.

PPG's Sam Magavern has this take: "If you took that 14% poverty rate and you distributed it equally among all the school districts, all the school districts would be doing fine. If the Buffalo school district had a 14% poverty rate, it would be doing just fine.... It's very challenging because the balance is tipped so far where you've got three quarters of the region's population living outside the core cities, Buffalo and Niagara Falls. So the balance of power is so nonurban right now."[26] So when it comes to "a practical issue like education or something, people's self-interest is a little too strong to ask them to share burdens more equally. So it's tough."[27] This tells us that segregation is self-perpetuating in a negative way.

Kevin Gaughan compared the number of school districts in Erie County versus five other fast-growing regions in the United States. In his chart, Erie County had 29 school districts while Fairfax County, VA had only two school districts, Montgomery County, MD had only one school district, and Glenn Burke County, NC (home to Charlotte) had only one school district. Each of these counties had a population greater in 2010 than Erie County.[28] We can fairly conclude that large unified school districts are not only manageable but also would not hurt a region's growth.

Another expression of segregation can be found in agriculture. "A total of 37,297 Erie County residents live in the Census Tracts considered to be food deserts. Within them, 71% of people have "low access" to a supermarket or grocery store, including minor children (20.1%) and seniors (9.3%). This means that at least 33% of the Census Tract's population resides more than one mile from a supermarket or large grocery store in urban areas and more than ten miles in rural areas."[29] Separation of population from food sources is part of "food insecurity" creating, not solving, problems. Even the REDC recognizes this as a problem "with growing concerns over local food system sustainability and community health."[30]

In conclusion, the sprawling development of the region's residents and businesses is consuming more of our resources, weakening our community.

CHAPTER SIX

LEADERSHIP

The introduction to this book uses a 1901 quote that described a dynamic world-class city. At that time, the leadership of the region which created that world-class city was a small group of powerful and wealthy elite individuals lacking in racial, ethnic, and gender diversity. They worked privately without public input. William Dorscheimer brought Frederick Law Olmsted here; Darwin Martin brought Frank Lloyd Wright here; New York City banker Edward Dean Adams brought Nikola Tesla, George Westinghouse, and Thomas Edison here. That leadership worked well for our region. Could that model work now? Robert Shibley, dean of the University at Buffalo, School of Architecture and Planning thinks, "We live in a very different time than they did."[1] If they were here today, could they do the same thing? "My guess is if they were operating in the same mold that they were when they did what they did, the answer would be no. The context—political, social, and economic—is dramatically different."[2] Things changed, however, in the middle of the 20th century. From then to the present, our region's public and private sector leadership–elected officials and their appointees, as well as the wealthy, powerful, and well-connected business community—have not served the community very well.

"The story at this point sounds like that of most other cities. The difference lies in the details of the relations of power, attitudes of leadership, and the process of planning."[3] It's certainly true that leadership is an issue in all other communities, but it's a matter of degree. Judging by the how well this region does relative to other regions in the nation, this region is especially poorly served by its leadership.

There is no better book about the region than Buffalo native Diana Dillaway's *Power Failure*. Although confined to mostly the second half of the 20th century, the depth and breadth of this book is far greater than any written about this subject. Dillaway conducted interviews with the region's leaders from business, politics, and community, many of whom were present during pivotal decision-making events. The next four sections borrow extensively from her research and interviews.

Characteristics of Regional Leadership

Dillaway says, generally, "Powerful individuals or organizations... do not always provide leadership. In fact, people with the greatest power often do not lead at all."[4] They use their power in several ways: refusing to share power; selling it; or using it selfishly to benefit only themselves.

According to Dillaway, "Buffalo's leaders did what they could to protect the status quo."[5] Political parties protected their patronage and power, economic leaders protected elite positions of prestige and power, and labor's militant power blocked new and innovative approaches that might modernize production processes.

"Until the 1980s, Buffalo's economic elite was almost without exception white, Anglo-Saxon, and Protestant (WASP)."[6] These elites came from the banking industry, businesses tied to land-based development, real estate, insurance, and law. Consequently some considered "Buffalo's leadership to be radically conservative, perhaps even racist..."[7]

One of Dillaway's interviewees, a banker, said, "Buffalo's business elite has always been dominated by bankers and their lawyers." As far back as the 1930s, "the lawyers came as close as any group [to] constituting an aristocracy."[8] A local developer adds this observation on local business leadership, "Bankers are risk-averse and they have no imagination."[9]

A common theme from Dillaway's sources was, "Buffalo's entire leadership— political, economic, and community—remained obsessed with issues of power and control," and focused on "the protection of their political and ethnocentric ways of life."[10]

By the late 1990s, "One flaw remained. The structure of power had not changed." A *Buffalo News* study "found that bankers and lawyers alone constituted more half of local and regional boards and private sector." Even though "government was a dominant player throughout the region...it becomes clear that the private sector leadership dominated." Dillaway quotes a *Buffalo News* study which found that "boards of directors found certain people and certain professions—government, banking and law—dominating the Buffalo Niagara region's power structure." That article went on to say, "Board member redundancy concentrated power further, and the fact that greater breadth was not reached (for whatever reason) made for a 'shallow pool of talent.'"[11]

Characteristics of Regional Politics

Dillaway declares that, for decades, "Political leaders, for their part, continued to use the power of electoral politics as a kind of jobs program for" their respective ethnic communities. The office of Mayor, for instance, brought patronage and jobs and "as a result, reelection was foremost in each sitting mayor's mind, making him a follower by nature and subservient to elite interests."[12] Is it any different today? Do current leaders continue to reward supporters with jobs and favors?

By the mid-fifties, the Republican Party declined in the city of Buffalo, which "essentially went to one-party rule." Buffalo has elected only one Republican mayor since 1960. The Democratic Party bears a great deal of blame for what happened to Buffalo because, as Dillaway writes, "The Democratic Party controlled the city and placed great importance on positions at all levels of the structure."[13] The decline in the city since then occurred on their watch; while they were in charge.

In the '70s, a committee recommended revisions to the city charter which the Common Council turned down. The city council's actions outraged Buffalo's citizens to the point that, in the 1977 election, they voted eleven incumbent council members out of office. This sentiment also played a role in the mayoral election. Dillaway quotes a community organizer and public official saying, "1977 was almost a fateful moment in Buffalo history. Community coordinators and activists actually ran a slate of candidates for every single council seat, every single committeeman's seat, every single

Erie County legislative seat that was in the city of Buffalo.... We decided, basically, to challenge entire Democratic Party in Buffalo."[14] Yet, it did not change much as the following paragraphs explain.

This, plus economic decline, "set the stage for the election of Jimmy Griffin, an independent mayor, a former Democrat, who changed the rules of the city's planning and budgeting process—and thus the structure of power within the public sector. A great divide between the Office of the Mayor and Common Council transpired and ensued for the sixteen years of Griffin's tenure making inclusive urban planning for downtown, city neighborhoods, and the waterfront impossible."[15]

By Griffin's fourth term, Dillaway writes, "The institutions of city government were practically immobilized because of the standoff between the mayor and city council over the use of these funds."[16] One of Dillaway's interviewees said, "I... thought Joe Crangle [Chairman of the Democratic Party] was divisive, but I hadn't really seen divisiveness until Griffin."[17]

Relations between Griffin and the city council headed to an impasse. She writes, "Mayor Griffin had campaigned against the business elite but reversed himself once elected. Further, he created nonprofit economic development vehicles that enabled him to bypass the city council in legislating and budgeting for urban development. At the same time, he fulfilled his campaign promise to sideline the Democratic machine, replacing one system of patronage with another—his own."[18]

Characteristics of Regional Business

In the business community, Dillaway faults "The disappearance of locally-owned industries and Buffalo's subsequent reliance on multinational corporations [as contributing] to the city's economic decline." Multinational corporations with their concentrated capital had the "power to make decisions overriding local interests or even regional considerations."[19]

"Companies with out-of-town headquarters were twice as likely to close as locally-owned companies. Executives of absentee-managed firms tend to be less engaged in local politics," because "local executives are not part of corporate top management, they often are not part of the city's leadership elite." In this region the majority of businesses in the dominant industries "have absentee owners, resulting in an underrepresentation of key interests within the local leadership structure."[20]

She summarizes that,"[t]he business leadership did not watch what was happening. They did not argue and fight about the issues. For most of the 1970s, Buffalonians blamed problems on other things: the oil embargo of 1973; the cost of energy; then in 1979, the second oil shock; and beyond that Buffalo lost its automobile production and went out of the steel business."[21]

The Turning Point, the 1950s

Dillaway describes how, by mid-century, leadership had radically changed. "Leadership takes courage and willingness to risk change. The city of Buffalo did not have such a leader among those who were in positions of great power when it faced its greatest challenges in the 1960s and 1970s."[22]

During the 1950s, when the region's fortunes began to turn around and decline, Thomas DeSantis describes how "When the old industries were failing and closing and laying people off, we spent probably a decade or two trying to repair and revive something that was [a lost cause]. Entropy had taken over. It wasn't coming back. We were just prolonging the inevitable." He mentioned the electric utility Niagara Mohawk reports, back in the 50s, which saw the world changing, that all the industries had really peaked during the war effort. Niagara Mohawk knew it was unsustainable; it was just going to fall off and the rest of the world was going to move beyond us. "But," DeSantis says, "everyone tried to hang onto that just a little too long."[23]

Dillaway adds, "In fact, Buffalo's business, political, and community leaders—with some rare but interesting exceptions—were zealous in their defense of the status quo in the face of an economic slowdown and, later, spiraling decline."[24] Her book tells the story of how leadership failure brought the region to its current sad state.

"In the 1960s, the signals of Buffalo's economic decline became pronounced, quite clear to a few but by no means clear to all."[25] She concluded, "The city's leadership apparently rationalized the economic downturns and departures, denying any cause for concern."[26]

Dillaway claims during the 1950s and early 1960s, four men ran the city: the presidents of the city's three commercial banks... and the editor-in-chief (aligned with the owner-publisher) of the *Buffalo Evening News*."[27] These people and others in the city's leadership "let opportunities slip by. In fact, some of Buffalo's most powerful leaders fought them. No one doubts that Buffalo's elite, with their connections to the governor and to state legislators, could have forestalled Buffalo's decline,"[28] because, "Events unfolded in such a way that, had the opportunities been seized, Buffalo's leaders could have slowed or reversed the city's economic decline."[29] The opportunities included the urban renewal movement, Rockefeller's commitment to spend $100 million to develop a new State University campus at Buffalo, and federal and state funds for urban transit systems and regional transportation projects.

Buffalo's leadership preferred the suburbs. Dillaway again, "Selfish interests were at play.... the WASP elite needed to defend its culture, which, with its economic power, lay at the center of its identity. A downtown University... meant that thousands of students would bring their progressive politics and ideas into the heart of the city. It would also bring into the city a more progressive political constituency in electorate."[30]

Dillaway quotes a BUILD archives report: "Some very powerful people apparently want Buffalo to die. The University goes out to a floodplain. The medical school follows, breaking its promises. The Chamber of Commerce wants to run the stadium out of the city. And now the state and county want to strip a badly needed hospital from us. Apparently some men are willing to decimate Buffalo, and declare [suburban] Amherst the center of a new city."[31]

This crisis of leadership caused Buffalo's spiraling decline.

The Major Failures

"In 1962 Governor Nelson Rockefeller announced that the State University of New York (SUNY) planned to acquire the University of Buffalo, a private university and intended to build a second, much larger campus. Two options were considered: a suburban, Amherst campus and a campus in downtown Buffalo. Several individuals from the business elite opposed the downtown campus. The outgoing university president favored a suburban campus."[32]

Dillaway describes incidents during the debate, "A banker, who also chaired the Albright Knox Art Gallery board, blocked the display of the model of the proposed downtown university at the gallery.... Another banker made his feelings known informally to anyone who would listen, most especially among the social networks of the establishment: 'We don't want all those [New York radicals and people of color] running around downtown.' As fate would have it, both leaders sat on the University's Board of Trustees—one headed the board and the other chaired the Construction Fund."[33]

The University Council preferred the suburban location; you know the result.

In 1964 Buffalo there was talk of replacing War Memorial Stadium as a stadium for the Buffalo Bills, whether to renovate the old stadium or build a new stadium someplace else. An Arthur D. Little report agreed with Buffalo's Planning Department and most others that a location close to the central business district would be optimal in order to get "maximum utility from Stadium associated enterprises."[34]

But, Dillaway adds, "The Buffalo area Chamber of Commerce refuted this conclusion. ...in favor of a two-stadium complex outside the city in the Town of Amherst." Their board of directors had ignored professional advice and chosen a suburb over downtown unanimously. Their implementation committee "consisted of four attorneys, two bankers, two builders, three industrial executives, education administrators, sports team owners, and others." The *Buffalo Evening News* opposed the downtown location because the stadium would be built around its new office building.[35] The New York State Urban Development Corporation chose Orchard Park.

It got worse. In 1969, Erie County made an agreement with the private group headed by businessman Edward Cottrell to build a domed stadium in Lancaster. When construction bids came in over their estimates, the county reneged on the agreement, which led Cottrell to file a suit in 1971 which was settled in 1984 for $53 million.

Even more mistakes were made, such as replacing Olmsted's Humboldt Parkway with the Kensington Expressway and putting the rapid transit system on the surface of Main Street in the central business district.

Are Things Changing?

Attorney and activist Paul Wolf whose website, the Center For Reinventing Government, is extremely useful for citizens, has decades of experience in public service, including four years as chief of staff to the Buffalo Common Council. Calling to mind the cliché "you can't manage what you can't measure," how do we measure today's leadership?36 Wolf answers, "I think each government has to make their own metrics and make their own determinations as far as what they want to measure and how they want to measure it," and encourages government to do that. His website disseminates information for people to read and think about trying to do some of these things.

One of those things is performance-based budgeting. He recently met with Williamsville officials who were implementing that system. "The Erie County charter says that they're supposed to do performance-based budgeting but they really don't," he said.

When you start measuring things, accountability follows. Wolf says, "A lot of people are a little uncomfortable about that because now those numbers can be used to say you're doing a poor job. And people resist accountability in government in a lot of ways." He's shocked at how few city councils and town boards actually set goals and objectives, which results in their "trying to do hundreds of things at the same time which you really don't accomplish well."

Wolf places some of the blame on the electorate. "I think a lot of that comes from citizens themselves pushing. I fault the public more so than I do the elected officials in a lot of ways. I think you get the government you demand, and we're not very demanding, quite honestly." During his public service he saw that, for instance, elected officials rarely hear from people that government should be more open. He explains this way: "Most people, when an elected official comes to the door, they're concerned about their sidewalk, their street, the tree that is falling down; they probably don't talk about open government, so I think in a lot of ways that's the public's fault." It comes down to electing people because they respond to our neighborhood concerns and that's important. "The reality is, when you go door-to-door, nobody's going to ask you what policies did you support? They're going to say, 'when I called you about my sidewalk you did or didn't do something.' So nobody cares about policy, big picture, long-term thinking." The bottom line for him is that, "I think citizens drive a lot of this and politicians respond. Politicians respond to pressure. They don't get that pressure." This is why reactive politicians behave the way they do; leaders don't need that kind of pressure.

Wolf calls for more information online. For instance, you should be able to go online and find out what building permits have been issued, see the crime reports for your neighborhood, the health department inspections for restaurants, etc. Usually they're not online; if you want it, you have to file a request and it takes weeks. Wolf encourages people to take a more proactive approach.

How? He describes a problem: "Usually public input in government is a public hearing. If your public hearing is at 2 o'clock and you work, maybe you are interested but you're not able to attend. So we're all shocked that one or two people show up for a public hearing or sometimes it's held in the evening which is great, but how are these things usually publicized? There's usually a legal notice that goes in the paper that nobody reads that's full of legal gibberish."

One step Wolf suggests to encourage public participation is using things called wikis or wikispaces—a type of website that allows users to create content—where legislators can propose legislation and people make changes to it, debate and discuss what should be in a piece of legislation. Wolf says no local elected official here is doing that, but the Partnership for Public Good has created some wikis to contribute to discussions about issues.

Citizen apathy is a part of the problem. Wolf says, "I understand people are frustrated with elected officials … 'They're all bums, they're all no good' isn't a good answer" and does not justify sitting in home and not participating. When Wolf ran for office in Tonawanda, the primary had a 10% turnout.

Government needs to strive for continuous improvement, but how do you measure that? Wolf suggests Lean Six Sigma as a technique involved in tracking and measuring. Some offices and nonprofits use it; Erie County was doing it for a while under Chris

Collins. Wolf supported it and thought it went well. "Some people don't like being measured, being held accountable. So when Mark Poloncarz came in, one of the first things he did was kill that program."

One of the goals of the county executive's office is to respond to citizens faster regarding concerns that reach them by letter or phone call. Are they measuring how long it was taking before they respond to a citizen? Are they getting better at it or worse at it? "That's not being done" right now in Erie County. Are we continually improving? Wolf says, "There are plenty of communities where this conversation isn't taking place at all."

Wolf promoted term limits in Amherst as a way of reducing political power and people being in office forever, and the Amherst town board now has term limits. But, says Wolf, "A couple board members didn't like it because they were going to have to leave. People don't want to leave when they get into elected office." He has mixed feelings about term limits, however, "because ultimately the voters should decide if you like the job somebody's doing. But there are so many advantages to being an incumbent you have to have term limits because challengers just can't win. The deck is too stacked against them." So he does support consolidation, downsizing, and term limits.

To Wolf one of the biggest problems we have with government is who our elected officials are. "Most people who run for office haven't had a lot of community involvement experience, they have been political people," such as committee members who have a patronage job and who came up through the political system, that people with power get behind and support.

Since incumbents have something like a 90% reelection rate, one of the ways to level the field is public financing of elections. Wolf thinks we need more people running for office who aren't wedded to special interest money. "More than anything we have to change how people are elected." He favors nonpartisan elections. "At the local level I don't know if there's a Democratic or Republican way to pick up garbage or do police protection, quite honestly." When Wolf ran for Town Clerk in Tonawanda, people would ask him if he was a Democrat or a Republican. "Does it really matter for town clerk? The Town Clerk's office processes paperwork." Open primaries would allow all registered voters to vote, whether they are blank, Democrat, or Republican.

Wolf also favors a professional city manager to run government. "We need to take out the politics and the patronage." A city can still have a mayor who would act like a spokesperson, the cheerleader for the city, but the city manager hires the department heads and runs day-to-day government. The mayor and city council could set priorities but leave it to professional management to implement. "All the city manager cares about is qualifications," because the manager has a contract and the only way that gets renewed is if he gets the job done. City managers ethically can't go to fundraisers. All they care about is hiring the right people and getting the job done." Wolf adds that the current civil service system can be manipulated "so we can hire people because they're friends, they're supporters, not because of their skills and qualifications." If the organization isn't hiring because of talent, it affects morale.

One of Wolf's biggest complaints is how elected officials spend their time and what they do. He did analyses the past couple years looking at every resolution that councilmembers filed. Most were permit fees for a community group that wants a festival or an event. Why can't we just have it so that nonprofits don't pay? Wolf says politicians "want you to come to [them] and ask [them], 'can you file this for me so we don't have to pay the permit?' So a lot of what they do is waiving permit fees, and approving the hanging of a banner across the street." The city of Buffalo 311 call center tried to take this away from councilmembers. It was set up that if you have a problem, you call this number and the department deals with it. "You don't need nine mini-mayors dealing with all these." Wolf suggests these permits should be administrative —an individual in the permits department asks if you have insurance and use the proper equipment and supplies to hang it. Instead it goes to the Common Council. Why? Wolf answers from the perspective of the councilmember, "I want to you come to me and I want you to ask and I want you to remember." He adds, "They don't do that in Rochester, which has part-time council and all this stuff is dealt with by department heads." When Wolf breaks it all down, how many resolutions are anything of substance, he concludes, "When I get down to it, there's like 20% [that] is anything of substance."

He also studied the County Legislature and says they're even worse. "Ninety percent of what the county legislature does is mandated by the state. It's a pass-through. Do we need eleven people to debate and discuss? All their resolutions are honoring so-and-so for becoming an eagle scout, honoring so-and-so for her 90th birthday, honoring a lot of people who have died." Why is this so? He replies, "It's trolling for votes." Legislators make proclamations honoring relatives of constituents. Wolf says, "If you look at their meeting agenda, almost all the votes are honoring people. All symbolic resolutions again calling upon the federal government to do this, do that, they pass two or three laws a year. And the rest of it is just busy work."

Phil Haberstro has been dealing with public leadership for more than two decades now. One thing he finds lacking is "understanding how we develop leadership in our community and, 'restocking the pond'. Understanding you have to have a way of progression." The types of leadership we don't need include the "'I'm the big cheese' and 'my way or the highway' type of mentality. If the building is on fire, we don't need a committee meeting."[37]

Another shortcoming Haberstro finds, "I can't see us being successful if we don't shed some of the old boy network mentalities. If you leave the women out of the picture, you're forsaking a significant amount of talent and brainpower." He stresses we are competing globally with people in China and India. He heard that "there are more students in the Chinese high school honors program then there are in the United States high schools period. Everything we can do as a society, in a community to strengthen the capacity of our team members and build their abilities to do this. If we talk to elected officials, do they understand not politics, but social capital?"[38] As shown in Part One and Chapter 2, most of the time they do not talk about social capital, which leads one to suspect they do not even think in those terms.

Marlies Wesolowski has a great deal of experience with local leadership and thinks policies that have been adopted by the federal, state, or local governments have undermined communities' abilities to be healthy and well. She says it's not one thing, it's a combination of things. For instance, "Different mayors treated parts of the community differently than what they would others. You can tell that by the disinvestment." Some neighborhoods see a lot of investment; others see very little. "It's almost as if the city fathers and others wrote off parts of the city and treated [them] as if they were disposable."[39] The Matt Urban Center, which she runs, operates many programs for the East side because she sees a great need. She wouldn't mind doing less if she saw some other entity coming in, rolling up their sleeves, and pitching in, but she doesn't "see anyone doing that, though."[40] To fill that void, her organization and people are doing just that, rolling up their sleeves and pitching in and doing the best they can.

Is there hope for the future? Robert Shibley talks about the new leaders in our community in chapter 10.

CHAPTER SEVEN

JOBS AND THE ECONOMY

What's the problem?

In chapter 3, data show that the regional economy is subpar. Our economic capital does not reflect our potential, and it is hardly growing, at a rate below that of the rest of the state and the nation. How would the economic capital of New York State look if you subtracted New York City, the world's leading city and financial capital, and Albany, the state capital?

It's not just us: it's a Great Lakes problem

As noted in chapter 1, the Great Lakes regions, including the metro areas of Detroit, Pittsburgh, Cleveland, and Toledo, suffer population loss. As noted in chapter 3, the New York Fed's economist Richard Deitz reported that flat economic growth is also a Great Lakes/Northeast problem. Urbanist Edward Glaeser explains why:

> When so many cities are booming, why are some in decline? Cities naturally

rise and fall as technologies change. Detroit and the other cities of the Great Lakes established themselves as agricultural transport hubs before the Civil War. Afterward, they enjoyed a second growth spurt as American industry settled along waterways for easy access to raw material such as iron ore. But their geographical advantages eroded over the course of the 20th century as the real cost of moving a ton a mile by rail dropped by more than 90%. Manufacturers relocated to lower wage areas such as the South. Social fractures often came to dominate politics as well.[1]

Richard Deitz has this analysis:

> If you think about when the Great Lakes [region] was in its heyday, we had these great locational advantages and productivity advantages, being a hub for manufacturing, distribution of goods from the East to the West, the steel industry in Buffalo, these were all what made a lot of the Great Lakes areas great. These things don't matter anymore.

> There are things that matter in the economy of the 21st century; they are not the same things that mattered in the 20th century. Some of the more important things that matter in the 21st century are being in large cities, amenities, and climate. These are things that we really don't have in abundance; at least we don't top the list, is probably a better way to put it.[2]

Are New York State and its taxes the problem?

A Cornell University expert says state policies make it hard for upstate New York's cities to regain their past economic vitality. In an interview with reporter Ryan Delaney, Mildred Warner said, "Basically, that means more people would move back into cities if roads and parks and such were in better condition. But these need to be invested in; they need to be maintained,"[3] adding that is often the function of local government and requires money.

Delaney writes, "The professor is critical of policies coming from Albany: curbing property tax rates and investing in glitzy economic projects rather than concentrating on basic infrastructure. 'Actually,' she adds, 'state policy is starving the cities. And it's making it impossible to make the kinds of investments in quality of life that they need in order to attract and retain their residents.'"4

Warner also blames mandates like rising pension and health care bills. To reinforce Mildred Warner's statements, Paul Wolf says, "You hear a lot of people complaining about state mandates," and explains that the big issue is when the state asks the locals to do this but haven't given them any money. Mandates cost staff, time, and resources, so that's the biggest complaining Wolf hears: "We've got all these rules and regulations but no money comes with that."5 He offers this example: In the city of Buffalo when you demolish a home, you have to determine whether asbestos is present because there are rules and regulations about releasing it. One of the fees that has to be paid to the state is called the asbestos notification fee. It's a form that just says there is asbestos in this building and you have to pay the fee to the state, which just increases the cost to the city. Wolf says, "There's no benefit to us for this in any way; it's just a reporting item and a way for the state to collect money."6

Delaney summarizes, "Across upstate New York, the cities have higher concentrations of poverty than the suburbs. [Quoting Warner] 'So the cities are almost the like the hole in the doughnut. And the doughnut of wealth is around the city. And we've got to have more regional strategies.'"7

Another way to look at it includes the independent studies of the cost of doing business. A CNBC study on the top states for doing business ranks New York tied for 40th, last in the cost of business and cost of living; first in education, fourth in access to capital, and third in tech and innovation.8 Forbes ranks the Buffalo metro area 75th out of 100 for "Best Places for Business and Careers" due in large part to its cost of business rank of 111th.9

The Tax Foundation declares that New York State has the highest state and local tax burden of all the states of the union and has held that dubious title since at least 1977. The tax climate includes corporate, individual income, sales, unemployment insurance, and property taxes. In 2013, they said New York State also had the worst business tax climate in the nation.10

A dissenting opinion can be found in a study done by the Center for Budget and

Policy Priorities,[11] researcher Michael Mazerov found that state taxes have a negligible impact on Americans' interstate moves. This study argues that state and local income taxes are not a factor in relocation and found that large numbers of people have been moving, for decades, away from the Northeast to the South and Southwest for employment opportunities, less expensive housing, and, especially for retirees, a warmer climate. One of the study's major conclusions is that jobs and family are top reasons.

Deep tax cuts that result in deterioration of services and infrastructure would make these places less desirable to live. Report highlights include:

• Only a small percentage (1.522%) of people relocate interstate and "the vast majority cite new, transferred, or lost jobs or family-related reasons." The rate of interstate migration is small and has been declining since 1990.

• People are just as likely to move to high-tech states. New York, however is an exception: "New York experienced the highest net out-migration of any state for the 1993-2011 period for which the IRS has data, but even there, households moving in from other states replaced two-thirds of those that moved out (and the rest were replaced by international in-migration and new births, with the result that New York's population is still growing at a moderate rate)."

• "Climate is a major driver of interstate migration; people—especially retirees—continue to move from cold, snowy states to Sunbelt states regardless of the tax levels in either the origin or destination state."

• "Reductions in housing costs, not taxes, are what save families the most money when they move from states like New York and California to states like Texas and Florida."[12]

Exceptions to these points apply to Buffalo metro:

• The region's low housing costs are not a reason to move away from or not to relocate here.

• Cold weather regions can thrive—take, for instance, Minnesota's Twin Cities region and Toronto. Both Minneapolis and St. Paul are growing in population and economy.

• Income taxes are a factor for high income individuals such as corporate CEOs who may make relocation decisions for their companies.

The Tax Foundation did a five-part series responding to Mazerov's study, called "The Facts on Interstate Migration".[13] In part two of their report, they show New York State as having the highest percentage, of the 50 states, of population born in-state and the lowest percentage of population born in a different state. While acknowledging Mazerov's claim that the U.S. interstate migration rate is "only" 1.5%, this report notes that is about 5.5 million people, hardly insignificant. Also, the U.S. interstate migration rate is about ten times that of the European Union. Comparisons with Canada and Mexico as well show that the U.S. is one of the most mobile nations.

The report's author, Lyman Stone, counters Mazerov's argument that taxes don't matter much directly, but they do indirectly affect jobs. The big picture is that lower taxes encourage economic growth which, in turn, creates jobs. Lower taxes offer a competitive edge to states competing with other states for skilled workers or workers in demand. Lower taxes mean higher after-tax income, a key recruitment factor. Stone also argues against climate as an important factor, asking why California has the second lowest share of replacement population despite its good climate.[14]

Considering the Tax Foundation's ranking of New York as the highest tax burden of the 50 states, Stone concludes that "high inward migration states tend to have lower tax burdens" and "all of these exceptional out-migration states have generally had higher than average tax burdens."[15] This strongly reinforces the point that tax burdens have negative effects.

Many factors affect the relocation of businesses and individuals, and the priorities for each one of these factors vary by the individual case. Regardless of how important state tax burden is, being the worst in the nation does impede economic growth. It may not affect the capital region around Albany, where tax policy is made, or the New York City metro area, which is a special case, world-class economy all by itself and where the majority of the state population resides. But this tax climate hurts the rest of the state, especially Buffalo Niagara.

Sam Magavern addresses the migration issue, "It's just a national trend that when people grow up, they go off to school and look for work, they end up moving other places."[16] He acknowledges the climate issues, obviously, and slow job growth compared to other regions and concludes, "The research is pretty unclear. It's very hard to say to what extent people follow jobs and to what extent jobs follow people."[17] He finds it interesting to look at "who has and hasn't moved to Buffalo? The most striking thing is that foreign-born population is very small here compared to other major metros. Latin Americans and Asian-Americans aren't settling in Buffalo. The only exception is the refugee population, which is booming, but it's a pretty small sliver when compared to a city that has a big Mexican-American population. So that's quite different from how people are thinking about why everyone's fleeing."[18] The placement of refugees is determined in large part by the Federal government based on cost of living expenses where they want their budgets to provide the most benefit. This is the principle reason why so many refugees are placed here. Would southeast Asians or Africans from the Sahel choose Buffalo's climate?

Richard Deitz observed that our highly educated workforce has a downside. "It's a mobile population so in some sense, if you've got good jobs to offer, these days people will find you. So it's not necessary to be right next to where people are getting their degrees or where they live."

Deitz co-wrote an article on the brain gain/drain which concludes,

> Research suggests that job opportunities and local amenities influence choice of location. While regional amenities such as favorable climate, cultural offerings, and family and social networks are attractive forces, they may not be enough to attract college-educated workers if good job opportunities do not exist. Similarly, job prospects may not be sufficient to sway a relocation decision if a region is not perceived to be a desirable place to live. Both factors are important policy considerations.[19]

Those high taxes translate into many benefits and services for residents. The Matt Urban Center offers many services to residents of the East Side: housing, senior services, weatherization, homeless outreach, work skills training, crime victims assistance, food pantries, and so on. Marlies Wesolowski works with government and relies in part on government funding to provide these services. Regarding government, however, she says, "Whenever government is involved it usually costs twice as much as what it would if it were private or an NGO. It's just a matter of fact," explaining that it's due to more strings being attached than what really needs to be there. She believes, "It's a whole lot cheaper having a not-for-profit provide the services than it is for a government entity."[20] The government bureaucracy tends to be a roadblock or logjam that gets in the way of what needs to happen.

How Industrial Development Agencies (IDAs) handle economic development

Private and public sector leaders do collaborate on strategies and programs to stimulate economic development, and one of their key tools is the IDA. These agencies—and there are nine in the region—package incentives on a case-by-case basis to stimulate expansion, relocation, and/or new construction, by mitigating or offsetting the high costs of doing business that are common across the region and state.

In her book, Diana Dillaway states these agencies can be a hindrance:

> Similarly, strategic planning in the eight-county Western New York region proved difficult (emphasis mine) where roughly seventy-five to eighty public and quasi-public organizations worked on economic development from 1970 to 1985. These included different chambers of commerce, county and subcounty industrial development agencies (IDAs), job-training programs, and other nonprofit corporations with the task of supporting or energizing business.[21]

A 2007 study funded by the Ford Foundation summarized another negative effect on the region. They examined the geographic distribution of the property tax exemptions given by the nine IDAs and they discovered those IDAs

> ...have subsidized job creation outside of the region's oldest, most densely populated and most transit-accessible areas, despite the fact those areas are most in need of jobs and reinvestment. The exemptions' sprawling, pro-suburban bias is especially evident in Erie County and far less problematic in Niagara.

The findings suggest that economic development tax breaks are worsening what is often called a "spatial mismatch" in many U.S. urban areas, with poverty and unemployment concentrated the core and new job creation occurring mostly in suburban areas. By any common measure, the central cities of Buffalo and Niagara Falls need the most economic help.

Yet the disproportionately high share of IDA-granted tax exemptions in wealthy suburbs such as Amherst shows that these state-regulated incentives are being used to attract investment outside of the region's neediest areas. Like many other upstate New York regions, the Buffalo/Niagara metro area (composed of Erie and Niagara counties) has been sprawling, with land consumption marching on despite the fact that population has been decreasing since the 1970s. The result, as noted in the newly released Framework for Regional Growth for the two counties, is that sprawling development has "reduced the livability of older neighborhoods, eroded the competitive position of traditional centers of commerce and industry; increased fiscal stress; isolated low income, minority and elderly residents; and threatened the resources that make the region an attractive place to live.[22]

Architecture critic Jane Jacobs once wrote, "heavy and unremitting subsidies are transactions of decline, and once adopted, the need for them grows greater with time, and the wherewithal for supplying them grows less."[23] In other words, they hurt more than they help.

In her research and interviews, Dillaway found,

In the 1980s a new economic and political leadership, seeking to jumpstart the local economy, parlayed government funds into subsidies for private development and business retention schemes.... A range of projects, including new hotels and entertainment venues on Chippewa Street, generated excitement but had little lasting effect, fulfilling Jane Jacobs's assertion that subsidies are transactions of decline.[24]

Dillaway goes further in her criticism. "Local development agencies and officials under the present structure, respond only to the needs of the individual entrepreneur and not to the broader needs of the jurisdiction or region."[25]

Lately, IDAs have come under fire. A New York State Authorities Budget Office report showed that the local IDAs have poor results for their investment: For projects approved in 2008, the deficits between jobs created and jobs promised in Amherst was 138 and for the Erie County IDA, 276. Job creation comes expensive: The Buffalo and Erie County Industrial Land Development Corporation loaned $207,216 for every job created.[26] But reporting is not always accurate, and the two IDAs faulted by the report say the numbers were wrong.[27] This controversy illustrates an important point: There is no definitive way to know whether or not an IDA or a Chamber of Commerce is solely responsible for the job creation they claim.

An excellent example of the IDA process gone bad can be found in a report by the independent journalist blog Investigative Post on a 2014 real estate development.[28] One of the region' s richest privately held companies, owned by Buffalo's wealthiest family and one of its wealthiest individuals, has been receiving taxpayer subsidies since 2000. In cooperation with a prominent regional developer, they applied for and received from the Erie County Industrial Development Agency another ten-year round of assistance that will help it build a brand-new office tower in a market that already has two million square feet surplus of office space. The developer claims, "taxpayer assistance is required because the project is not otherwise economically feasible." Regarding this project, New York State Assemblyman Sean Ryan said, "The system is out of whack. How we do our IDA inducements in New York State, it's a broken system."[29]

Paul Wolf says, "I don't think government should be in the economic development business, quite honestly. I don't think they do it well. I would rather have government focus on the basics: police, fire, things of that nature," and let other people do the rest but, "getting people to agree to give up their power and authority is the hard part."[30]

Sam Magavern thinks we should "stop thinking of economic development giving money to companies to persuade them to come here or to stay here or just because. Which is how most of our industrial development works."[31] He prefers this money be invested in places and people: Schools, parks, roads, bridges, public transit. Instead, he says it's more common for businesses like "Philips Lytle moving from this tower

[HSBC] to that [Donovan building]. Delaware North moving down Delaware. That's what almost everything we do is."[32] This can create problems. Jonathan Epstein of the Buffalo News analyzed the effect of all the new construction downtown and concluded "new office demand creates vacancy woes."[33]

But there is a possible alternative to the role of the IDA. A new player in town since 2011, the Western New York Regional Economic Development Council (REDC)'s program has a more regional approach. The REDC has several strategies for business and job formation, including the Buffalo Business Plan Competition and the State Agency Resource Team. But by their own indicator, the percentage increase in the total number of new firms locally since their programs began is only half of the state's increase, which would indicate limited success.

Magavern's opinion of the Western New York Regional Economic Development Council is, "I'm glad there is one. I think highly of the leadership of it."[34] While it has an ability to come up with a fairly coherent vision and strategy, he's concerned that "it's a creation of this governor, wasn't created by an act of legislature, so it has a little bit of a provisional feel to it." He likes the work they've done so far overall, citing the RiverBend project which is, "within city limits, not contributing to sprawl, reusing brownfields."[35] It is important to remember, however, that the Buffalo Urban Development Corporation, the Office Of Strategic Planning, and DEC laid the groundwork for this project, creating some progress before the REDC arrived on the scene.

Eds and Meds: The Business

If you were to lump together education and health care services, they would form the largest sector of our regional economy. The sector is also the source of the most growth, offsetting losses in others such as manufacturing. But the future of this sector and its potential for growth is under a bit of a cloud.

Education is no longer a growth sector of our economy. In a *Buffalo News* article, reporter Denise Jewell Gee writes, "Private colleges across the region are facing a new reality. After fifty years of campus growth that buoyed enrollment numbers and led to new construction, the number of potential students coming out of high school is on the decline."[36] Gee quotes St. Bonaventure University president Sister Mary Carney as saying, "We're trying to get the same number of students to come here from our Western New York bases in spite of the fact that there are fewer of them. So each of us is sort of chasing a declining base."[37] The article goes on to say that colleges across the region "look toward a future in which there are fewer students applying to colleges."[38] Bottom line: In the future, declining demand and increased competition for local college openings is not a forecast for growth.

It's not just a regional problem. College enrollment at private, four-year nonprofit institutions across the nation has slowed down recently. The article goes on to say, "couple that with regional population declines, and the pressures facing local institutions is acute."[39]

In a special supplement before the school budget votes of May 2014, the *Buffalo News* published a graph which shows 28 school districts in Erie County with enrollment declining in 26 of the districts between 2009 and 2015. "While enrollment goes down in most districts, amount spent per student goes up."[40] This also means fewer students upstream of the colleges and universities.

The trend for college graduates to be unemployed or underemployed is growing. A 2013 New York Federal Reserve Board report states that 52% of recent (2008-2012) college graduates are underemployed or unemployed. In upstate New York it is 54%.[41] This, coupled with the increasing burden of student loan indebtedness, might also slow the increase in student enrollment in higher education.

On the meds side, one of the most exciting developments in the region in the last few decades is the explosion of new construction on the Buffalo Niagara Medical Campus. A series of recent *Buffalo News* articles report that the campus activity is also stimulating residential and commercial development in the blocks surrounding the campus. The campus is an innovation district, a place where economic, physical, and networking assets come together to create a critical mass for generating ideas and the commercial action that follows. As for attracting businesses, Richard Deitz says, "probably one of the biggest things is, again it depends on the type of company, being near other businesses that feed into what they're doing and what they can benefit from.

It's this clusters idea,–for a lot of businesses, there are advantages to being in a cluster."[42] Thomas DeSantis sees this activity as spurring further growth, "Like the first buildings that got built in the Buffalo Medical Campus. Somebody would have said, 'Okay, what's next?' And you wouldn't have been able to predict all the 'what's nexts' but you knew that things were coming. I think we're in that the same kind of position."[43]

The REDC's Progress Report 2013 states that the campus currently employs 12,000 people and they forecast growth to increase to 17,000 by 2017. How much of that is new job growth and how much results from the relocation of existing jobs—say from Children's Hospital on Bryant and the UB medical school on UB South campus— they don't say. So the growth forecast is not a net figure.

Buffalo Business First reports:

> The Buffalo Niagara Medical Campus has been the site of more than $1 billion in investment over the past decade, generating considerable political support and hope that it will change Western New York's economic fortunes. But until now, the major moves have amounted to a regional reshuffling of educational and health-care facilities, paid for by the institutions, taxpayers and philanthropists. The difficult part is yet to come. 'We haven't done anything yet,' said Patrick Whalen, COO of Buffalo Niagara Medical Campus Inc., which acts as a broad administrator for the direction of the campus. "Moving assets around is not economic development."[44]

The Community Foundation's Cara Matteliano expresses similar concerns:

> Because the medical campus has this big footprint, there are cranes and everything, they have to create good paying jobs. They can't just aggregate stuff. Currently I've seen some of the data that would suggests that they're just aggregating things. And they haven't gotten to the point where they've actually begun to generate a lot of additional jobs. That's sort of part one and part two, is you have to pay attention to somehow getting people in the Fruit Belt and the other neighborhoods around the medical campus to be taking good paying positions within the corridor. That's another one of

those entrepreneurship issues, too, because you still have community benefits agreements there that need to be fulfilled. There's a lot of missed stuff in the medical campus.[45]

Recently academics and reporters have been questioning the ability of eds and meds industries to drive local economies, especially in the Rust Belt. Writer Aaron Renn reports that these industries are at the end of their growth cycle and he analyzes the economics: Spending on these industries has grown over the last few years at a rate twice that of inflation, and he says, "Clearly, such a trend cannot go on indefinitely."[46] Duke economist Aaron Chatterji wrote:

> 'Ed and meds' have already accounted for a significant share of employment growth over the past several years. More important, these jobs are the only thing keeping many small and midsize American cities from sliding into deeper decline. Several regions are consciously building around these services under the logic that they cannot be outsourced, and local demand will continue to grow. Unfortunately, both assumptions are wrong, and that could mean bad news for many local job markets around the country.

> However, while the total number of jobs in these sectors could grow, it is not likely that all regions would benefit equally. For example, one might take for granted that there will be growing demand for orthopedic surgeons in Toledo, Ohio, and educational administrators in Iowa City. But the same forces that led other industries to cluster in specific regions (think technology in Silicon Valley or banking in New York) are now sweeping through education and health care.[47]

Urbanist Richard Florida calls out Buffalo and Rochester as metros having a large percentage of the economy in eds and meds but notes that we are not one of the metros with world-class clusters of medical and higher-ed institutions and therefore would not be among "the places most likely to benefit from greater competition and clustering of these industries."[48] Buffalo lags behind Rust Belt cities Pittsburgh, Cleveland, and Cincinnati, which all have had their medical campuses up and running for years now.

The most important point is growth in the healthcare sector really only comes from an increase in the illness of the population. Should healthcare succeed in increasing wellness, that would reduce demand for healthcare services, resulting in contraction in that sector. Our ultimate goal should be to reduce the size of this sector, secondarily to reducing the need for healthcare, shouldn't it?

Dr. Trevor Hancock, cofounder of the healthy communities movement, agrees: "Don't partner with those who make money from selling ill health, the tobacco industry and others; lose or don't make money if the health of the population improves—the 'medical-industrial complex'—or profit in ways that harm health."[49]

The points above seem to suggest limits to both the education and healthcare industries' ability to grow the region's economy.

CHAPTER EIGHT
....

PAROCHIAL THINKING

Parochial—narrowly restricted in scope or outlook.

A. T. Kearney, the global management consulting firm, produces the Global Cities Index. "Globally integrated cities are intimately linked to economic and human development. By creating an environment that spawns, attracts, and retains top talent, businesses, ideas, and capital, a global city can generate benefits that extend far beyond municipal boundaries."[1] They measure twenty-six metrics in five dimen¬sions: business activity, human capital, information exchange, cultural experience, and political engagement. The Buffalo of 1900 could very well have made that list, but don't look for the Buffalo of 2014 on it. Ironically, when Buffalo was at its population peak sometime in the 1950s, Toronto was a lesser city. In 2014, Toronto is listed as the number fourteen most globally significant city.

The people of this region, collectively speaking, could be fairly accused of not thinking globally, but parochially. It's not just about a matter of size; it has to do with depth and breadth of thinking, in dimensions of time and space. The existence of sixty-four governments in one region is sufficient proof this population cannot think regionally, much less globally. Examples below illustrate how the region has thought and acted in a parochial way, limiting the region's growth.

Have we learned from the past?

One thing we cannot change is our industrial legacy, and it's a dark cloud hanging over our heads. The DEC's Martin Doster, talking about former industrial sites called brownfields, says, "My activity in Western New York is large because of all our problems and we still have problems. ...What we can do with those properties that are bankrupt or falling in, decaying; how do we address that?"[2]

The Sierra Club's Schneekloth says, "It has to do with the history of the region. Go back to the power plants. We had power first, we brought in aluminum companies, chemical companies, long before there were any environmental laws," which weren't in place until the 1970s. "It's like Love Canal: people get so upset about Love Canal, they didn't do anything illegal by dumping there. [Back then] nothing differentiated hazardous waste from other kinds of waste. They knew better, but the reason we have so much historic legacy waste is for that reason,"[3] that the differentiation was stipulated by law.

We are still paying for it. Doster explains that [the EPA's] Superfund intended to put the burden of cost on the responsible party, and the only time taxpayer money is used is when there is no responsible party, such as when they refuse to do it or, more likely than not, they've gone bankrupt or no longer exist. By his estimate, in Western New York, 88% of all the money spent was borne by the responsible parties. He says, "In other words, the polluter pays and that's a big deal."[4] Still, the taxpayers have to pay some of it. Some money comes from the feds and some from the state but, in the end, it's taxpayer money. In the brownfield cleanup program, it's not the polluter that pays, necessarily, but the people who volunteer to clean up brownfield sites. The brownfield program, however, offers tax credits, which is taxpayer money going in, "sometimes lucrative tax credits, 25, 30% for both the cleanup and also economic development,"[5] Doster says. But it's working. "If you go downtown today, HarborCenter, Donovan building, medical campus, Buffalo Color, Health Now building, the new Delaware North headquarters at Delaware and Chippewa, every one of those are brownfields."[6]

Riverkeeper's Jedlicka says:

> We have a stigma attached to us, we have the aesthetics of the rotting infrastructure, we built a boom-and-bust economy that went bust and we're

left with liabilities. So when you hear rust, that's what you think about. ... It's not to say that didn't help to define who we are, because the steel industry, the chemical companies, all those things helped us become the country we are today. A lot of people forget Western New York played a pivotal role in the world wars, and the renaissance of the buildout of our country. What happened, when all that success happened, they left that environmental liability for us to deal with. We didn't necessarily feel the fruits of that labor. We did not get as much benefit as others did based on the backs of our workers, of our economy, and our home.[7]

But the rust continues. Erin Heaney of the Clean Air Coalition compares the current state of the region, with its greatly diminished industrial activity, to the past, when we were at the height of industrial activity. She said, "Things have gotten a lot better. Industry has declined and that's made our air quality better for sure, but the narrative about Buffalo, that there's no industry here, is totally false. Tonawanda has a pretty thriving manufacturing sector, fifty-three plants in a two-mile radius."[8] As shown in chapter three, employment data on the percentage of our overall economy contributed by manufacturing back up Heaney's contention.

On top of that, Schneekloth alerts us to the fact that, "We have very high levels of waste continuing to come into our region."[9] West Valley reprocesses nuclear waste and, Schneekloth says, Niagara Falls' "Covanta [is] going to bring in tons of waste from New York City, a twenty-year thing. So that's the part I can't see. Why are you continuing the waste economy? Why aren't you shifting that to a clean economy or tourism, I don't care what that is, why are you allowing this to continue? And I hear jobs, jobs, jobs. But I don't find that a good excuse. I think it's a sin, frankly."[10]

Cleanup has an upside. Riverkeeper's Jedlicka explains that the multiplier effect leverages dollars spent on cleanup into a positive economic impact. She says, "Brookings Institution has looked at a 1 to 2 ratio [dollars invested resulting in dollars impact] for Great Lakes investment. Because there's been so much investment just in the last two years alone (locally), fifty million going towards the river remediation and the ninety-two million for green sewer infrastructure committed by the Sewer Authority. All of that is going to have an economic impact."[11] But is creating a problem and then generating economic activity to fix it progress?

State and Federal Government

The state and federal government collect money from the region's residents and give some of it back. In fact, New York State gets more federal dollars per capita than the average state of the union. Not all federal money is equal, however: The majority of those federal dollars that the state receives is in transfer payments—Social Security, Medicare, Medicaid, etc. When the federal government invests their (non-transfer) dollars in Houston for NASA, it creates STEM jobs. Transfer payments create jobs as well when recipients purchase goods and services. But STEM jobs buy a lot more restaurant meals and groceries than SNAP benefits.

In his book *The Future*, Al Gore describes a global force: "Unfortunately, however, the U.S. no longer has a well-functioning self-government… American democracy has been hacked. The United States Congress… is now incapable of passing laws without permission from the corporate lobbies and other special interests that control their campaign finances." He describes a Congress serving the special interests that are providing most of the campaign money with which candidates purchase television commercials. He says Congress "no longer responds to any but the most emotional concerns of the American people. Its members are still 'representatives,' but the vast majority of them now represent the people and corporations who donate money, not the people who actually vote in their congressional districts."[12]

Gore also says, "With the future of human civilization hanging in the balance, both democracy and capitalism are badly failing to serve the deepest interest of humankind." Both are in need of repair. "Yet this difficult policy transition will require leadership and political courage that is presently in short supply, particularly in the United States."[13]

Democracy and capitalism are failing, resulting in "the ever-increasing inequalities of income and growing concentrations of wealth, and the paralysis of any efforts at reform." The public's ability to respond constructively "is dampened by the structure of our dominant means of mass communication, television, which serves mainly to promote consumption of products and entertain the public, while offering no means for interactive dialogue and collaborative decision-making."[14] It's no different in Buffalo Niagara.

In another book, Pulitzer Prize winner Thomas Friedman and economist Michael Mandelbaum described it thus, "That used to be us: how America fell behind in the world it invented." They talk about America's challenges requiring sacrifice "which makes generating collective action much more difficult."[15] What this means is it is now harder for a region's population to act together for the collective good.

These statements sometimes apply to local governments as well. While it may seem that the forces of federal and state government are beyond our control, the regional population can effect change. Gore believes, "Many supporters of democratic self-governance are placing their hopes on the revival of robust democratic discourse in the age of the Internet."[16] This would mean that change can begin at the grassroots level.

Why can't this region be a laboratory for innovation in social, economic, and environmental capital? Doster and his DEC have world-class experience in brownfield remediation. The city of Buffalo's Office of Strategic Planning has proposed a research and development incubator at RiverBend to utilize that expertise on reclamation of brownfields, developing new methods for remediating old industrial sites, drawing visitors from around the world to come here for advice. Several nonprofits are creating a new experiment in social capital called Open Buffalo.

Global change and innovation can once again start here.

Climate and the environment

Up until now, our climate has been a disadvantage, as mentioned by several experts in chapter 7, but that may be changing, as Chapter 12 will explore. In the meantime it remains a debit because of how we think about it.

When you talk to a call center outside this region and are asked by the representative where you're located, and you reply "Buffalo", they will often say, "Is it snowing there yet?" For people outside this region who have never visited here nor have relations here, our reputation is defined by snow, a great deal of it defined by one storm in January 1977. This negative image derives from a negative mindset by the media and some of the people that live here. For example, in a recent book about this region, a writer related his experience nine days after the blizzard first hit, "I, like the rest of the people of Buffalo, ventured out..." The rest of Buffalo wasn't like him. Back then, I worked at Roswell Park, which continued to operate without a glitch, and hours after the blizzard started, at the end of my shift, I took the bus home. That weekend, my wife and I and another couple walked to a restaurant which was open for business. On Monday morning, I went into work on time. Many, many people in this region went to work and did their jobs.

Media tend to focus on the bad part of our weather and ignore the many people and parts of our community—police and fire, ambulance, public transportation, utilities (especially the repair workers who are outside restoring service), some retail services, truckers who deliver food to stores, even media representatives themselves who go into work to make sure television is uninterrupted and the newspaper gets out. For many people, weather is just a minor annoyance and we get better at handling it. In January 2014 Erie County was hit by its first official blizzard since 1993. Emergency services coordinated by the Emergency Operation Center handled the emergency with no loss of life and returned the community to normal operations in just a couple of days. The CDC rates communities for emergency preparedness and Erie County's score increased from a 65% "F" in 2011 to 95% "A+" in 2013. But the media tells the world not how well we cope but how bad things are here, and we all suffer for it.

Climate is changing. Environmentalist Jay Burney writes "Climate changes aren't only in the future. It's today, it's last week, it's last year. People are starving, people are at war, and there are great climate catastrophes that are happening around the planet. We live in a consumer-driven comfort zone world that is exaggerated by the media.[18]"Climate change is happening, of that there is no question. The only question is how fast and how bad. "We're not prepared and we have no desire to be prepared or even know about it." Climate change is global. It is happening in Buffalo Niagara just the same as everywhere else on the planet.

Al Gore writes:

In 2011, the U.S. had eight climate-related disasters, each costing over $1 billion. Tropical storm Irene... nevertheless caused more than $15 billion in damage. Texas experienced the worst drought and highest temperatures in its history, and wildfires in 240 of its 242 counties. Thousands of daily all-time-high temperature records were broken or tied. Tornadoes, which climate researchers are still unwilling to link to global warming (partly because of the records of past tornadoes are incomplete and imprecise), ravaged text Tuscaloosa, Alabama, Joplin, Missouri, and many other communities; seven of them cause more than $1 billion in damage. In 2012, more than half of the counties in the US suffered from drought. Hurricane Sandy cost at least $71 billion.[20]

Environmental damage results, in part, from a failure to think globally in temporal terms. The community of people that lived in this place centuries ago, the Iroquois Nation, had this wisdom. The Great Law of Iroquois Confederacy said, "in every deliberation, we must consider the impact on the seventh generation.... Look and listen for the welfare of the whole people and have always in view not only the present but also the coming generations."[21] Sierra Club's Schneekloth related this incident, "I gave a talk one time and some guy stood up and said, 'I don't care about future generations.' I was dumbfounded."[22] One of the great challenges to improving our situation involves the individuals who do not care about future generations, who only care about themselves in the here and now, a classic example of parochial thinking.

Many environmentalists argue that ecosystem services and natural resources and the environment as a whole are treated as externalities by the economy. Resources that were in the Commons* are used, spoiled, depleted, exhausted by industries who escape the consequences, which are then borne by society at large.

Often you see the argument that economy trumps environment. How does the CAC's Erin Heaney address that? "I hear very similar stories from talking to the guys working at Tonawanda Coke and also the DuPont plant. They'll say this bluntly: they are trading years of their lives to have a good paying job now to be able to provide for their family. Can you blame them? They didn't believe that there is another option for them and there may not be."[23] One solution is to improve strong environmental and worker safety protections to minimize worker exposure. She says the bigger question is to transform our economy so nobody has to take a job where they have to make those choices. "I also think that the narrative sometimes gets used by people who have a lot of money to make by pitting workers and environmentals against each other when in reality we have a lot in common and could be fighting for protections for everybody."[24] Sometimes it's a real conflict but mostly, she says, "It could be used as a wedge by people who have a lot to gain from us not talking to each other."

In an economy of limited resources, how do you convince the electeds and the electorate to spend more on the environment at the expense of something else? Schneekloth says, "I think that the only way that we get people to pay attention is through the public health discourse. If I say, you're gonna get cancer in your lifetime because you live in this community, or I can show you four people on your block who are sick from environmentally related diseases and why do you think you're not susceptible? Then people pay more attention, elected officials pay more attention."[25] To the dilemma of jobs versus health she has observed, "Even here the union still would be willing to continue to pollute everybody in order to preserve seventy jobs."

She elaborates, "That's the story that Western capitalism, industrial culture, tells people that either you have a job or those environmentalists are trying to take a job away from you and therefore you can't provide for your family. We have to get a more powerful story that says you can have both of these and here's how."[26] Both the Sierra Club and the Clean Air Coalition are working on plans for replacement employment in the eventuality of Tonawanda's Huntley power plant closing.

DEC's Doster encounters many different circles of people in his work and "there's a group of people out there who don't give a rat's rear end about the environment. But they do care a lot about being able to turn the electricity on or getting in their car or about getting a job or about getting educated, and that's a big deal."[27] When working with people of like minds on the environmental side, it's an easy sell. But different groups of people have different perspectives. Regarding the East Side of Buffalo, where people are living in poverty, he says, "There's a lot of suffering going on there." So allocation of limited public resources becomes a debate among groups with differing priorities. Doster might want to spend $250,000 on a fish habitat, but the social services commissioner "would be seeing a whole different reading of this."

"It's a challenge," he says, " Being the third poorest city in the country, there are other pressing needs....So I'm not throwing darts at anybody because these are just societal issues that are some of the many things we wrestle with."[28]

Judging by the wellness indicators of our region, we could be doing a much better job of this.

The way we think about things

Geographically, Buffalo Niagara is a significant place on the globe like the Great Barrier Reef. So what does it do for the people of this region? Jay Burney suggests, "If we decide to use those things as a major focus of our economy, it could provide both jobs and industries."[29] Here, too, our thinking is an obstacle because our traditional economic investors still think of the environment as an externality that is a factor beyond their scope or outlook. "I don't know how we can shake the bonds of that kind of strategic thinking. That's a conversation we have to have and we are not really having it very effectively and there are a lot of reasons for that. How we think, what we think, is driven by a lot of forces [which] pay for our media, our conversations, and our politics. The money that drives that stuff is not necessarily the money that promotes social well-being."[30]

Local state of the environment reports do not include much in the way of reference points, because, as Burney explains, it is a problem of metrics. "When we talk about land-use it's in very traditional ways: industrial, residential, open-space and that kind of hard and fast measurements"[31] which ignores ecological services. Burney explains the concept of ecological services is a new idea to the people who use traditional land-use development, which is a shame because "the economic importance of ecological services is incredibly valuable, probably a thousand times more valuable than surface parking lots. The impact of a marsh in terms of what it provides—clean water, clean air—is a thousand times more valuable than the economic impact of a parking lot. We don't measure it that way because clean water and clean air are considered externalities."[32]

Ecological economics is a brand-new scientific discipline that is being developed across the country. Does anyone in town use this sort of science? Burney says, "There are some people, including myself, starting these kinds of discussions new to the area, but it's being met with a lot of resistance because they trump traditional values and we don't have the kinds of resources to push them out there as much as other folks, including the economic development gurus of WNY like Governor Cuomo's local government strategy or Wall Street strategy."[33]

One important example of how this thinking currently hurts our region's improvement is the issue of overflow from the region's combined sewer systems. About four billion gallons of sewage overflows from our community into the Great Lakes system and continues to be a threat not only to the water but also to the people who reside here and downstream. Correcting this problem might cost as much as $500 million. But it is not as sexy an investment as, say, HarborCenter. Burney thinks, "The people who invest money don't really think of that as where they want to invest their money because it doesn't show immediate returns, immediate impact," despite the fact that, long-term, it would improve the health of the region's population and the health of the Great Lakes. There are other threats to the lakes as well: a dead zone, toxic algal bloom created by agricultural runoff, and micro plastic particles that get into wildlife and people. "What does it cost to clean it up? It's almost an unspeakable question because the first question is how can we exploit that resource to make money? Again it goes back to profit."[34] Most people put our region's water at the top of the list of assets. How are we conserving these resources?

Not well, according to Burney, because of how we think about it. "The primary lens is the economic aspect of this resource. That's what our society does. How can we continue to grow our GDP through these kinds of resources? The environment becomes an externality. Is there an economic motive to restore the Great Lakes? Yes, we do believe in blue economy concepts, we do know that we need clean water in order to survive, but it's not the prime motive and it may be totally incapacitated by the motive to profit from natural resources."[35] Burney is pessimistic about change, "Long-term, I don't have a lot of positive thoughts about restoring and conserving the Great Lakes." One big project to improve things would be to eliminate sewer overflows, but that might be tough. As he puts it, "Would you rather spend $500 million on a stadium on the waterfront or $500 million on sewer systems for Buffalo?" In a very practical way we're developing the waterfront, spending a lot of public money on creating infrastructure to produce industry and mixed-use, but we're not spending that money on protecting the water. "The ECHDC, the Empire State Development Corporation, give it a lot of lip service, but aren't investing in it." Burney does credit the Buffalo Sewer Authority, who know what they need to do and are seeking funding for it, as well as organizations like Riverkeeper and its leaders, Julie Barrett O'Neill and Jill Jedlicka, who come to the table with ideas and legitimate programs and changes.

Would it help if state of the environment reports were to be used as tools in public policy and everyday life? Burney says, "Probably 99.9% of the people in Western New York don't know about [them]. The report is put together by a small staff of volunteers. It's issued to the County Legislature; whether or not they read it, it's hard to say. Are policies based on it? Very little is being done at the policy level. So, I don't think it's used very well.... I think we have to do other outreach about the state of the environment."[36]

Followers or leaders?

The Buffalo of 1900 was filled with leaders: William Dorsheimer, who convinced Frederick Law Olmsted to come here and do his best work; Edward Dean Adams, who brought together the world's top scientific talent of Edison, Kelvin, Tesla, Westinghouse, for a historic experiment in Niagara Falls; Darwin Martin, who convinced an up-and-coming young architect Frank Lloyd Wright to do some work in Buffalo; a young engineer for Buffalo Forge who changed the world with his invention of air conditioning. An innovative social movement began here with the Niagara Convention in 1905, and the world's first binational environmental treaty was signed here in 1909. What have we now? Our "new" medical campus is just now ramping up to emulate what's already been in operation in Rust Belt cities like Pittsburgh, Cleveland, and Cincinnati. Our waterfront, where good things are happening now, is still behind the development and excitement of the waterfronts of Toronto, Chicago, and Baltimore or even cities with lesser waterfronts such as San Antonio and Indianapolis. No social or political innovation has come from this region for decades.

Buffalo Audubon's Loren Smith, when talking about climate change, refers to a process of adaptation in macro evolutionary biology called the Red Queen hypothesis: You just have to run faster and faster just to keep up. If we want to become a leader again, we will have to run faster still.[37]

One example of that comes from Federal Reserve's Richard Deitz. Reflecting on education, he wondered, "Can you imagine if we were at the head of the pack in developing programs to help kids develop quantitative skills in high school and college? That's the kind of push that you really need if we want to get ahead."[38]

That's the kind of thinking the region needs. That begs the question, are we happy where we are or do we want to get ahead? That is what part three will explore.

The best explanation of the concept of the Commons—the resources accessible to all members of a community—can be found in the writing of Garrett Hardin.

PART THREE

RECONSTRUCTING BUFFALO NIAGARA: PRESCRIPTIONS

Thomas DeSantis' interview began with my saying, "Buffalo Niagara is a very special place. If we were to fully realize our potential we could be..." And he finished the sentence "... we'd even be more special. I agree."[1]

Cara Matteliano moved here from Maine in 1989 and noticed how the civic narrative went something like this, "Once we were a great city and then we lost all our jobs, and now we're terrible. And we're never going to be good again. We're all about the [Pan American Exposition] and these other things, but really we fell off the deep end." Matteliano has seen that change and now hears people saying, "We once were a really great city and we went through some hard times and we're going to be a really great city again. Just not the city we used to be." She thinks people realize "we're not going back, we're going somewhere different and that's a good place."[2]

Not everyone would agree that we need change. There certainly are people in Buffalo Niagara who feel things are fine just the way they are. These include people who aren't concerned with the status of the community beyond their personal space. There are many who feel we are already on the right track, no change in direction needed. But there are others who believe much more needs to be done.

Before we look at solutions, let's look at some things that will not solve the region's problems.

False Hopes and Silver Bullets

When used in mainstream media, the phrase "silver bullet" refers to a simple remedy for a complex problem. It's understandable to wish that the solutions to our region's woes would be so simple, but that's not the case. Here are a couple of the more prominent examples:

In 2014, one of the biggest local stories was the sale of the Buffalo Bills NFL franchise. Original owner Ralph C. Wilson passed away early in 2014 and the trust he set up solicited bids to sell the franchise to new owners. Over a period of several months, the *Buffalo News* published a series of stories speculating about the future of the Bills and reflecting the anxiety and angst of the community, especially with regard to the possibility that the team might leave. But does a football franchise do very much for the region?

Economists have been piling up research suggesting that pro sports franchises do not contribute much to the local economy and, depending on how much public funding they receive for stadia, they may, in fact, be a burden on the local economy. The counterargument from the sports industries and their supporters is that these franchises provide intangibles to the community: publicity, identity, pride. Do the Bills do this? Consider the fact that their lifetime record is .459. Often writers outside this area put "small-market" in front of "Buffalo". So how do the Bills contribute to our image; how do other people outside the region see us?

- *Business First Journals* did a study in 2011 of 85 metros in the U.S. and Canada and found that Buffalo was the #11 most overextended sports market, with a $30.9 billion dollar deficit in available personal income to support the two professional franchises.[3]

- *Sporting News* used to rank the Best Sports Cities in the U.S. Their last list in 2011 ranked Buffalo 41st [4] out of only 50 U.S. and Canadian cities that have at least one franchise and of the 31 with two or more franchises in the four major leagues —MLB, NFL, NBA, and NHL. Since then, the Bills have extended their streak of not making the playoffs.

- *Forbes* ranked Buffalo the fourth-most miserable sports city in America in 2013, where they let the fans down the boldest,[5] and that was before the Sabres finished dead last in the NHL 2013-2014 season.

• The *Buffalo News* reported that viewed by some in the NFL, when it comes to revenue, "Ralph Wilson Stadium in Orchard Park is a loser."[6]

• Weather.com named Buffalo the worst weather NFL city.[7]

Another silver bullet solution is "build the bridge." When traffic congestion on our international border crossing at the Peace Bridge between Buffalo and Fort Erie got to the point where the community decided that something had to be done about it, an early solution was a twin span. Some people in the community promoted the idea that this additional bridge should be something architecturally special, a "signature span." A design competition was held and, with some public input, one entry was chosen, a cable-stayed bridge by world-famous bridge architect Christopher Menn. Was it something special? It would not have any feature that would place it on the list of notable cable-stayed bridges.[8]

It still isn't built in part because the congestion problem is caused largely by the volume and speed of throughput at customs, not by the space to hold cars and trucks in line. Now the focus is not on a companion span but on expansion of customs processing facilities, which is a problem on the U.S side—the site is constrained by Olmsted Park and a residential neighborhood. Moving all customs processing to Fort Erie, where they have ample room, was blocked by national pride.

Regarding silver bullets, PPG's Sam Magavern tends to agree,

I think calling attention to the less noticeable victories is an important part of what we do because there's a tendency in the media and watercooler conversations to look at big projects and measure success by, have we built a new Peace Bridge? Are there new big buildings going up or that sort of thing? That's such a small part of progress and sometimes it's not progress. Building a new casino is not progress. Building Bass Pro would not have been progress. It's not clear that building a new Peace Bridge is progress.[9]

What will work: Framework for Regional Growth and One Region Forward

We need to think big and regionally. In 2006, a remarkable document was finalized: Framework for Regional Growth: Erie + Niagara Counties, New York (FfRG). This document was designed to fill a void—the absence of a regional vision. There is follow up: One Region Forward (ORF), "a broad-based, collaborative effort to promote more sustainable forms of development in Erie and Niagara counties—the Buffalo Niagara Region—in land use, transportation, housing, energy and climate, access to food, and more. It will combine research and public engagement with planning and action to help us meet the combined economic, environmental, and social challenges of the 21st century." ORF intends to do a plan of its own, the Regional Plan for Sustainable Development which "...will serve as a practical roadmap for improving mobility, promoting more efficient land use patterns, strengthening our basic infrastructure, growing a 21st century economy, ensuring broad access to healthy food, protecting housing and neighborhoods, and mounting our region's response to the challenge of global climate change." [ORF] will produce a federally recognized document that will give our region priority status for funding opportunities today and into the future.[10]

These excellent efforts come from a broad range of citizens working collaboratively on region-wide issues. One step an individual citizen can take to improve the region is to get involved with the One Region Forward project. This should be the focus of our energy in terms of regional planning.

In presenting "A New Capitalism for the 21st Century" Healthy Communities founder Trevor Hancock said, "The new capitalism must simultaneously increase ecological capital, social capital, economic capital, and human capital."[11] This is a call for more than the typical, narrowly-focused economic plans.

Magavern says, "There is no one strategy, no one place to focus our efforts. We can't just focus on job creation we must also be working simultaneously on improvement of the environment, the health of our citizens, and the relationships between them." He emphasizes one important part of it is that "public investment needs to go to public goods, and public goods draw people to want to live in a place." As an example, when you're thinking about young professionals, is arts and culture. "That's what gives the city of reputation as cool or not cool, which people very much respond to, so investing in arts and culture and history, historic neighborhoods, walkable neighborhoods, that's where many young professionals want to live is that kind of situation. That's the kind of big picture strategy."[12]

The last four chapters will offer original solutions and solutions from others which deal with all four aspects of our communities. These solutions may seem to the reader at times to be like silver bullets, but there is an important qualitative difference: Each one of the solutions integrates well with all the other types of capital and, to echo Magavern, there is no one thing that can be done without the others in order to make a difference.

One last thought from the Wellness Institute's Haberstro, "It's back again to the idea of creating your own future rather than letting it happen to you."[13]

CHAPTER NINE

HUMAN CAPITAL

John F. Kennedy's January 1961 inaugural address is perhaps most commonly remembered for his command to the American people, "Ask not what your country can do for you, ask what you can do for your country." This was a remarkable declaration coming from a politician. Instead of promising his constituents what he would do for them, he commanded them to commit themselves to improving our society. This was and is extremely rare. Watch and observe politicians as they run for office. Most of their speeches focus on what their office will be doing for their constituents. How often do you hear an elected politician exhort their constituents to action?

In July 1905, the "Negro-American" members of the conference known as the Niagara Movement assembled in Buffalo. This conference produced a document called the Niagara's Declaration of Principles, 1905. In it, a section called "Duties" states:

While we are demanding, and ought to demand, and will continue to demand the rights enumerated above, God forbid that we should ever forget to urge corresponding duties upon our people:

The duty to vote.

The duty to respect the rights of others.

The duty to work.

The duty to obey the laws.

The duty to be clean and orderly.

The duty to send our children to school.

The duty to respect ourselves, even as we respect others.[1]

In like spirit, our community leaders, whether they be elected, corporate executives, or the heads of nonprofits, should call citizens to duty to face the challenges of our region and commit themselves to improve the quality of life. Our leaders, public or private, should lead, demand, and expect. As an example, a story about the leadership of Dwight D. Eisenhower goes something like this: In a planning meeting before D-Day, Eisenhower called Allied generals and assembled them around a table on which he had a piece of string. When he pushed it, he showed them that he had a hard time getting the string to go where he wanted it to. But if he pulled it, it followed his fingers wherever he wanted. So he commanded his generals to use the battle cry "follow me" in action and to be at the front of their troops, leading them. Our region's leaders should lead by example and expect the region's residents to become more active in civic life.

Activist filmmaker Annie Leonard explains how we can do it. "I realized that each of us has two parts. We have a consumer part and a citizen part, a consumer muscle and a citizen muscle." The consumer muscle is exercised every day motivated by relentless advertisements. "So our consumer muscles are really well developed."[2]

But our citizen muscle has not been used as much as our consumer muscle. "That citizen muscle has atrophied and what worries me about that is that when we're faced with problems as enormous as the disruption of the global climate, or babies being born pre-polluted with the 160 industrial chemicals already in their blood at the moment of birth, these are really big systemic problems—and the best we can think of is carrying our own bag to the grocery store?"[3]

She insists we must continue to "do those responsible consumer things, but those are a good first step, a good place to start, not a good place to stop." But what we really need to do is engage our citizen muscles, think about people beyond your household, think about making change in your broader community and in your country. "It involves things like working together to change the rules of the games, rather than trying to perfect your day-to-day behavior within a fundamentally unsustainable context, let's change that context so that the more sustainable choice becomes the new default."[4]

It begins with the individual. It begins with a commitment to maintain ourselves in the best possible health so that we are not a burden to others. Think about it in terms of preflight airplane instructions, the part where we put on our air masks: We have to take care of ourselves before we can take care of others. This is our duty, not the duty of government, the healthcare industry, or others. Most of us were born well, in good health. It is our responsibility to maintain that good health.   Larry & Sharp have

This also applies to whatever talents we were born with. It is up to us, not the education system, to maximize our talents and to go through life practicing continuous self-improvement. In many of the reports referenced in previous chapters, when it gets to the section on recommendations, these reports almost always recommend actions by agencies or governments. In Erie County Department of Health's Community Health Assessment they list "available resources" and "screening and treatment providers" and "primary and preventive health care services", and "needed services" for some select health issues. In prescribing what needs to be done, in several places they list "increased staffing" but do not mention "increased priority". Why not spend more time in the curriculum in schools, and all grade levels, on health issues at the expense of some other topic? Nor do they say "demand people change." It's time the language got stronger.

One of the first steps for improving human capital in the region would be for all elected leaders and agencies to include indicators on human capital in their annual reports, mentioning the latest health measurements and the trend from the previous year. They should not be proud of how many taxpayer dollars were spent on building a new hospital or clinic because it's not effort that counts, it's results that count. Effort is measured in dollars spent; results are measured in health indicators. Their address should have an agenda of steps that individuals can take toward a sustainable lifestyle that would improve the quality of the region for all. One good example comes from the Western New York Environmental Alliance which has a shared agenda for action that begins with "We, the people of Western New York, are resolved to work collaboratively to improve our environment and our regional, international community."[5] How seldom do local executives begin their addresses with "we" and then ask their constituents to work toward a goal?

Marlies Wesolowski has a great deal of experience and expertise on the topic of human capital. She has seen it from both sides, "I came from a family that really struggled," and she, her mom, and her family "could have been very eligible for a lot of the services I provide. In some cases, we did, we lived in public housing, we used to go to soup kitchens and food pantries and get food, and Mom used to volunteer in order to pay back the food that we used to get from the food pantry."[6] What would she most like to see change?

Wesolowski said when Clinton and Gingrich struck an agreement on welfare reform, they "required people to perform some kind of community service. That was a good thing. I think that the move right now to take that piece out of the legislation where you don't have to do work, it's not required—I think that hurts. People really need to know that they have to contribute in some way, shape, or form." The Obama administration has "been pushing for a relaxation of the welfare-to-work. I think removing that will have a negative effect because it doesn't encourage people to strive to better themselves. It contributes to people wanting to live off the system."[7] She is not suggesting a return to the days of Ozzie and Harriet households because things have changed, "but we need to reinstill some of those old-fashioned family values because they're not here today."

Self-sufficient, independent people will make this region strong. To increase the value of our human capital, the quality of our human capital, let us call each individual to duty to realize this mission.

Growing our population

One Region Forward has projected that, if we stay on our current path, our region will lose about 100,000 people by 2050. How can we expect our population to grow?

In terms of migration, we lose more people than we gain. Our population is still healthy enough that births outnumber deaths every year. Sources disagree: the Federal Reserve Board thinks that our out-migration rates match the nation's average but that in-migration is the problem, "If upstate New York were a state, it would have the nation's lowest in-migration rate." But analysts in a *USA Today* article, as well as at the Center on Budget and Policy Priorities, suggest that the out-migration rate from New York State is clearly higher than the national average (see chapter 1).

It does seem, though, that we lose a lot of the best and brightest of our children. Anecdotal data from some of the region's top schools—City Honors, Nichols, the

Buffalo Seminary—back this up but we have no hard data from these schools or from metros across the nation to compare it to. Regardless, one thing we could do to grow our population is to retain more of our children. One particular message that schools could stress is the idea of "bloom where you're planted;" that is to say, where you're born is where you should live your life and realize your potential, regardless of whether you think the grass is greener elsewhere.

A potential future development could boost our in-migration rates. A *Scientific American* article states, "Experts predict that the sea level along the USA's east coast—affecting cities such as New York, New Orleans, Virginia Beach/Norfolk, and Miami—will rise by at least one meter by 2080. This will result in storms like Superstorm Sandy at least once every two years. One of the solutions is to recommend that people move out of the most vulnerable areas."[8] Where will these people move to? Someplace with a temperate climate, ample water, and an elevation high above sea level?

Jay Burney thinks that our population will grow with climate refugees. "I think it's entirely probable. We live in a region [which] will have fairly moderate weather patterns in the future. We won't be exposed to drought in dramatic episodes. We're not on the coast so we won't have sea rise issues. So our location is going to promote a quality of life we may not see in many other places on the planet. In addition, we do have this incredible resource," twenty percent of the Earth's surface freshwater which will turn out to be one of the most valuable assets on the planet. So Burney says, "We can and should expect climate refugees, war refugees, political and economic refugees. They will want to come to our area."[9] This may well happen well before the Scientific American's forecast of 2080. Steps could be taken now to plan for it.

Other ways of attracting newcomers to our region will be explored in chapter 11.

Health

The excellent Community Health Assessment (CHA) by Erie County's Department of Health cites many factors for poor health in the region, but it is especially important to reiterate a point made earlier in the Community Health Assessment: The major cause of diseases are lifestyle choices: diet, smoking, lack of exercise, etc. "With poor diet and physical inactivity fast becoming two of the leading preventable causes of death in America, the evidence we are seeing of these behaviors in the rates of obesity across the country and locally are astounding and escalating daily."[10]

The Buffalo Niagara Medical Campus is largely an investment in the treatment of people who are not well. Imagine what the results would be if all that money were invested instead in prevention of disease? Maybe not the same ratio as the proverbial ounce of prevention and pound of cure, but it certainly does cost less to maintain health than cure disease. For example, the CHA says, "Reduction in teen pregnancy is critical as for every dollar spent in family planning, four dollars are saved."[11]

Lifestyle choices are not entirely a matter of personal freedom as they have consequences for others beyond the individual who makes the choice. The CHA agrees: "Teen pregnancy can have serious consequences for the teen mother, the child, and to society in general."[12] Smoking tobacco is another example with serious consequences for society as a whole, "causing more than 440,000 deaths each year and resulting in an annual cost of more than $75 billion in direct medical costs. Nationally, smoking results in more than 5.6 million years of potential life lost each year," adding that, "Since the first Surgeon General's report on smoking and health in 1964, 27 reports have concluded that tobacco use is the single most avoidable cause of disease, disability, and death in the United States."[13] Take those three statistics and assess them proportionately to the region—even though health statistics cited in Chapter 1 indicate things are worse here than the rest of nation—and those numbers would be: 1467 deaths each year, $250 million in direct medical costs, and 18,667 years of potential life.

Tobacco use is a good example of a moral hazard. A moral hazard is a situation where an individual is separated from the consequences of his actions and therefore does not face incentives to change his behavior.[14] Smokers are separated from the consequences of their actions both temporally and financially. Because it takes so long for symptoms of respiratory diseases caused by smoking to exhibit themselves, they have no immediate feedback to change their behavior. In a society where the population in general is risk-ignorant, they worry more about low-probability shark attacks, lightning strikes, and plane crashes than they do about getting lung cancer or COPD from smoking, which is near certain. Once the symptoms do present themselves, treatment is required. The cost of that treatment is borne by society at large; the smoker does not bear the full cost of the consequences of their actions. Why should non-smokers pay for the unhealthy behaviors of smokers?

Another cause comes from something the region celebrates. Buffalo Niagara celebrates festivals where we binge on food. The CHA observes, "This area is also famous for its chicken wings. This could be considered a staple for many families. Many of the community events focus on food, including the Chicken Wing Festival and the Taste of Buffalo."[15] Such activities exacerbate obesity and related diseases.

The CHA presents ample evidence that the infrastructure for health and wellness care is here. The health indicator surveys cited in previous chapters also give the region high grades for infrastructure. Available resources, providers, and services are more numerous than they have ever been. Getting people to use them is another matter. It's a perfect example of the old adage about leading a horse to water. The Affordable Care Act prompts more individuals to use preventive services more often. Whether that succeeds or not remains to be seen, but clearly more needs to be done. The current mechanisms for persuading people toward healthy behaviors—such as vaccinations, losing weight, exercising more, quitting smoking—are insufficient. More and stronger behavioral mechanisms are needed. In response to rising costs of employer-provided health insurance, companies nationwide are currently pushing for something like this, something called "outcome-based incentives."

An example would be something like this: In the case of smoking, cigarette taxes are no solution: Despite having the highest cigarette taxes in the nation, New York State smoking rates are about average. Increasing taxes would be like pushing the string in the Eisenhower example earlier in this chapter. Identifying smoking behavior and linking patient investment in the consequences would be an outcome-based incentive. Patients who smoke currently self-report, and there are accuracy issues with that. If there were financial penalties for smoking, self reporting would be even less accurate. But physicians can, during routine blood tests on their patients, look for indicators present in blood and urine for active smoking. Once detected, the physician should notify the insurer and the insurer should raise the patient's premiums. Should pulmonary or cardiovascular disease present itself in the patient, that patient's co-pay for treating those disorders should increase as well, perhaps doubling or tripling. Such risk-dependent costs are not new to the insurance industry, nor even to the health insurance industry. Premiums for certain types of health insurance rise with age. Why not tie them to lifestyle choices known to cause poor health outcomes?

It begins with walking *Rarely! - no objections in item*

Figure 9.1: Wouldn't it be wonderful if Buffalo streets were filled with pedestrians more often, like they are in big cities?

The departments of health and many other community-based organizations provide a wealth of information on the benefits of walking, physical activity and healthy eating. A wealth of physical activity opportunities, technical assistance to groups establishing walking clubs, weight loss groups and worksite wellness policies are also present in our community. Despite that, the CHA reports," The federal Centers for Disease Control and Prevention (CDC) estimate that physical inactivity contributes to up to twenty-three percent of all deaths from major chronic diseases. Only one in five New York adults engage in the regular and sustained physical activity that is needed to reduce the risk of heart disease, high blood pressure and other health problems which lead to premature death or disability."[16]

Yet, there aren't many pedestrians on the streets in our region. Measurements of how many people walk and how much in this region are sparse. Wikipedia has a list of cities with the most pedestrian commuters and Buffalo ranks 37th with 5.43%, which

We rate in the lower-end BUT the problem is basically national

trails Syracuse, Rochester, and Erie, PA.[17] The website WalkScore.com measures and ranks metros for their walkability with an indicator that measures a variety of walking routes, distance to amenities, and pedestrian friendliness (not how many people walk). The city of Buffalo scores 64.9, which is described as "somewhat walkable: some errands can be accomplished on foot." This score does not take into account our suburbs, where walkability is worse. By comparison, New York City scores an 87.9 and Toronto scores 71.4.[18]

We take pride in the fact that it's easy to get around Buffalo Niagara, that commute times are short relative to the rest of the country, and our roads are seldom congested. That and the proliferation of parking lots make it too convenient to drive places instead of walk. Data on the One Region Forward website confirm this: Vehicle miles traveled daily per capita have more than doubled from 1970 to 2010.[19]

Community leaders should lead a movement to increase walking for commuting and recreation—organizing group walks with block clubs, organizations, neighborhoods, etc. Organizational retreats often end with a walk to sharpen the mind. Maybe public meetings should begin or end with a walk. Public walks would have ramifications far beyond health—the conversations that would take place among neighbors would build social capital and the crowds on the street would deter crime. It would have a positive effect on the environment as well, replacing some auto trips.

Education

Western New York has far fewer school districts today than it did a century ago, thanks to an intense thirty-year wave of consolidation, but it still has 97 districts over eight counties.[20]

A *Buffalo News* analysis of state education department data shows that:

> Erie County's public schools recorded the steepest percent decline in enrollment between 2007-08 and the 2012-13 school years among the state's counties and boroughs whose school districts enrolled 100,000 or more students in kindergarten through high school... Enrollment in school districts in Erie County decreased 8.5% during that five-year span, falling from 126,925 students to 116,104 students. Public school enrollment in the

other eight counties or boroughs with at least 100,000 students fell a combined 2%.... The decline was even steeper over 10 years. Enrollment in Erie County's public schools dropped 16% from 138,136 between 2002-03 and last school year. All but four school districts in Erie and Niagara counties have seen the number of students drop during the last two decades. Fourteen have lost more than a quarter of their student population in that time.[21]

Cheektowaga is a poster child for this inefficiency. The town's population is roughly 75,000 and declining, with, in 2012 a little over 10,000 children in grades kindergarten through 12. Cheektowaga has four school districts with four central administrations, four superintendents, four school boards, and four school board and budget elections. Is it working well? In a *Business First* ranking of the region's 97 school districts based on academic performance, Maryvale was ranked 41st and Cheektowaga Central 86th, out of 97, with the other two in between. For small districts, consolidation still offers the possibility of major efficiencies.[22] The reason this hasn't been done so far? As Paul Wolf pointed out in chapter 6, nobody likes to lose their job. People in administration and on the school boards want to preserve the status quo, putting their own interest in keeping things the way they are above the interest of doing what's best for their constituents. Another obstacle is voters who resist change for the sake of pride and nostalgia.

A policy brief from UB's Regional Institute states, "A challenge for all districts, and the region, lies in knowing when to centralize, when to localize and when to cooperate. As the Digital Age changes education and the meaning of location, networked governance may be the wave of the future."[23]

Kevin Gaughan has compared the number of school districts in Erie County versus five fast-growing regions in the United States. In his chart, Erie County had twenty-nine school districts while Fairfax County, VA had only two school districts; Montgomery County, MD had only one school district, and Glenn Burke County, NC, home to Charlotte, had only one school district. Each of these counties had a population in 2010 greater than Erie County. Gaughan's research shows that Erie County's property tax rankings are 12th highest of the 1824 U.S. counties because of it.[24]

[handwritten annotations in top margin]

School districts would be a good place to start regional consolidation. In a January report by the New York State Comptroller which analyzed the fiscal health of all of New York State school districts, it was reported that three of the region's school districts—Lewiston-Porter, Niagara Wheatfield, and West Seneca—are in significant fiscal distress, four of the region's school districts were labeled as facing moderate fiscal stress, and four districts were classified as susceptible to fiscal stress. The Western New York region had the third-highest percentage of stressed school districts of all the regions of the state and Buffalo Niagara metro had 25% of all the state's "significant fiscal stress" schools.[25]

Marlies Wesolowski once served on the Buffalo Public School's Board of Education and had a term as its president. An authoritative voice on the state of regional education, she says, "I'm not really sure that our educational system is doing what it should be doing. A lot of the people the Matt Urban Center serves are non-high school completers who, for whatever reason, have not stayed in school long enough to get their high school diplomas. This is a major problem because in order to be successful in employment, it not only takes a high school diploma but, in many cases, a college degree, even a masters."[26]

More money is not the solution. In 2012, New York State had the highest spending per pupil, $19,552, nearly double the USA average of $10,608. The state also had a better pupil/teacher ratio (12.91) than the USA average (15.96).[27] While spending varies by the school district, and per pupil spending data range widely over the Buffalo-Niagara region, the *Buffalo News*, quoted a study by the Center for Governmental Research in Rochester that claimed in 2012, the Buffalo public schools' spending per pupil, $26,903, was third-highest among large districts in the United States.[28] For all that spending, the National Assessment of Educational Progress shows that for grades four and eight in math, reading, science, and writing, New York State scores are about average with the U.S. So the quantity of money we pour into education is not the issue; it's how we spend that money. Having more school districts in the region than we need creates unnecessary overhead. The primary solution would be to consolidate school districts and reduce that overhead.

CHAPTER TEN

SOCIAL CAPITAL

America has civically reinvented itself before—approximately 100 years ago at the turn of the last century. And America can civicly reinvent itself again.[1]

– Robert Putnam

BetterTogether is an initiative of the Saguaro Seminar on civic engagement in America at Harvard University. That seminar issued a report, Better Together, "calling for a nationwide campaign to redirect a downward spiral of civic apathy. Warning that the national stockpile of 'social capital'—our reserve of personal bonds and fellowship— is seriously depleted, the report outlined the framework for sustained, broad-based social change to restore America's civic virtue."[2]

Co-chair Lew Feldstein wrote, "We must learn to view the world through a social capital lens....We need to look at front porches as crime fighting tools, treat picnics as public health efforts and see choral groups as occasions of democracy. We will become a better place when assessing social capital impact becomes a standard part of decision-making."[3]

Buffalo Niagara needs this kind of program

When activist filmmaker Annie Leonard calls us to action to develop our atrophied citizen muscle, she points to individual-level solutions to helping the environment— using canvas grocery bags, installing high efficiency light bulbs, riding your bike to work, and composting—as good things, but amounting to little more than modern adult hygiene. Leonard argues that these solutions are not sufficient for the magnitude of the problems that stand before us. For real change to occur, citizens must exercise their power by becoming active in the community and in the halls of government." What is important, she emphasizes, is thinking "about people beyond your household. Thinking about making change beyond your kitchen and into your broader community and into your country."[4] This would remedy the parochial thinking described in chapter 8.

Consolidation and Regionalism

If there were one "silver bullet", one simple remedy to the region's woes, it would be the consolidation of the region's 64 governments into one: One community working together, pooling resources, all on the same page; social capital unified and stronger for it. Imagine if Buffalo were to merge with Lackawanna, the national news would read, "Buffalo growing in population once again."

In her book, Diana Dillaway offers an historical overview of consolidation attempts: "In 1960, Erie County added the position of 'strong' executive to its County structure in an attempt to bring about a regional approach to governance in the delivery of services." As far back as 1935, the Kenefick Commission recommended this.[5]

Dillaway found another attempt: "In 1968 a private sector initiative again addressed local government inefficiencies in the delivery of services, pointing out areas where multiple levels of government had overlapping responsibilities throughout the region."[6] This group, the Citizens Committee on Inter-Municipal Affairs, wanted to consolidate local police forces countywide.

"This initiative was put to a referendum, which, in order to form new metropolitan structures under the state constitution, needed to garner a plurality in three different classes: cities, towns, and villages. The initiative passed in the city and the towns, but lost by five thousand votes in county villages. A handful of rural villages representing 9% of the total population sent the regional initiative down to defeat: 'The battle for regional approach...was lost there.'"[7] The incident, however, illustrates that this is a solution that has been proposed for a long time by many groups but has not yet been addressed.

A 1997 study published in the *Journal of Urban Affairs* found that "Buffalo had two anti-regional impulses. First, many citizens remain skeptical of consolidation," with city folk worried about a form of suburban plundering of city businesses and resources and suburban citizens worried about being saddled with the city's problems and bills."[8]

The history of regional consolidation goes back 70 years when Erie County took over most social welfare programs. Later, the county assumed responsibility for the library system, the public transportation system, cultural facilities, and in recent years, the operation of the downtown convention center.

Dillaway asserts, "Uncoordinated growth pits regional localities against one another and leads to inefficient, lopsided development. Regional approaches to all forms of services cut down on duplication and overlap of governmental services."[9]

She aims directly at "suburban leaders" who "need to recognize the value of revenue sharing throughout the region, including investing in Buffalo's downtown to reclaim its current architectural heritage, with the goal of making Buffalo once again a center of culture, entertainment, and banking."[10]

A paper looking at regional consolidation entitled "Regionalism revisited: the effort to streamline governance in Buffalo and Erie County, New York" is the product of research by David Rusk and Neal Peirce. They summarize their research by saying:

> In response to Buffalo's declining population and property tax rolls, the
> *Buffalo News*, along with key politicians, business leaders, and activists,
> promoted the city-county consolidation recommended by David Rusk, Neal
> Peirce, and the promoters of old substantive regionalism as the ultimate
> solution. However, Erie County's fiscal crisis of 2004 has stymied
> enthusiasm among residents for intermunicipal merger. In light of this
> setback, Buffalo and Erie County cannot wait idly for a revival in support
> for such a wholesale overhaul of local governance. Rather, citizens must
> devise strategies to bring about a new kind of regionalism in Western New
> York.... Above all, however, Erie County must continue to pursue every
> available opportunity for fostering intermunicipal cooperation, for reducing

the cost of government, and for encouraging new development at its urban center. Provided that residents and municipalities persevere by refusing to abandon ten years of regional progress, they may hope soon to earn a reputation for innovative governance that would exemplify the greatness and resourcefulness of Buffalo and Erie County.[11]

In light of the fact that there are 64 government agencies in the region, government expert Paul Wolf feels this way about local government consolidation: "I agree with it. I think it makes sense." He cites examples. "It seems crazy to me that within the town of Amherst, is the village of Williamsville which is literally one square mile. They have a town hall with a supervisor and town board. Right next to that is the village hall, the mayor and a village board. It seems insanity to me to have these two buildings next to each other that are completely separate entities for one square mile. The village of Kenmore is one square mile in the town of Tonawanda. It just doesn't seem like it makes sense, the town has a judge, the village has a judge, the village has a Police Department, the town has a Police Department." There have been efforts to eliminate the village of Williamsville, but the people overwhelmingly voted to keep it. Wolf's view on it is, "They understood it cost more taxes but [they feel] that 'my government is responsive, I'm a village of 6000 people, I like knowing who the mayor and the board members are, and it costs us a little more, so be it, we're willing to pay that price'."

So how do you convince them it would be better for them and they would get the same services as well? Wolf says, "That's the hard part. One of the biggest issues we have in government is trust." He quotes a recent statistic that only 37% of people trust their local government and it goes down from there when you go to the state and federal levels. Regarding the Williamsville vote, "That's what democracy is, they had a vote on it. Should we dissolve the village? The vote was no. So you don't get any more democratic than that. They had their say."[12]

Although Wolf believes "from an efficiency perspective, as far as running things, financially, consolidation makes sense," he does have some reservations about consolidation. He worries about excessive government, about people abusing their power and authority. Consolidation makes some offices and positions more powerful. "I see just how someone who is on a board, how arrogant they can become, how full of themselves they can become. Consolidation means making some people more powerful then they are already, and I don't know if everybody can handle that."[13] With attention to mitigating the downside, the net result is improvement.

Regional government consolidation is long overdue. The process should begin immediately with one big meeting including all the mayors and supervisors of municipal governments. The mayor of the city of Buffalo should have separate meetings with the mayor of the city of Lackawanna and the supervisors of West Seneca, Cheektowaga, and Tonawanda. The city of Tonawanda, the town of Tonawanda, and the village of Kenmore should all sit down and start talking. The mayor of the city of Niagara Falls should talk with the supervisor of the town of Niagara. Every village in the area should have consolidation meetings with their surrounding towns. If some legislative obstacle exists at the state level, our state legislative representatives should be charged to make the necessary changes in the immediate legislative session. Name changes are not necessary; identities can remain. Within the city of Buffalo, for instance, there are separate neighborhoods—South Buffalo, West side, Riverside, Lovejoy, they just don't have separate governments behind them. Likewise, the villages of Hamburg and East Aurora can still be called that without a separate government behind them. The unions that each municipality contracts should be protected and can remain as is. The construction industry is a good example of how contractors can work with different unions to get projects done. Just about the most serious challenge that would remain is changing the letterheads and stationery.

New leadership: Organizations

The current political structure is dysfunctional and not serving the residents of the region very well. Reform is needed, but how to do it? We can replace some of the functions that our current executive and legislative branches now exercise and hand them over to nonprofits.

Paul Wolf made this point in chapter 6, that it seems as though for elected legislators, the bulk of their work and interaction with their constituents involves reacting to the complaints and concerns of individuals. This is government by reaction, not action. To become more proactive instead of reactive, legislators can receive their agendas from local nonprofits who are the on-the-ground troops dealing with the public. An excellent model for this type of process comes from the Partnership for the Public Good (PPG). The PPG is a coalition consisting of over 150 community organizations. Each year, these partner organizations propose policy planks, and they then vote to prioritize the top ten, which become the community agenda. These agendas are thereafter given to elected leaders in the hopes that our electeds will use public resources to implement these planks. (To see examples of current and past community agendas, visit their website www.PPGBuffalo.org.)

Sam Magavern explained why the PPG started this: They saw decisions getting made without a lot of high quality research and small community groups lacking resources to do that. So the concept was for a community-based think tank to do research and advocacy. Another key part was to tap into resources among students and faculty who have to do research and writing for credit or for pay and would like it to be useful but aren't plugged in in a way that they can make it really useful for Buffalo. So PPG's intention was to have students produce work around Buffalo-based issues that people can actually use in the community. PPG also serves in a convening role and networking function to bring people together, sometimes on very specific issues. "Two of the main functions are to help draft the community agenda, so the partners come up with the proposed planks of that and then they vote on which ones end up in the top ten and become included in the agenda."[14]

A newer, better initiative is coming. Magavern explains, "Open Buffalo is part of a national initiative from the Open Society Foundation trying to create three laboratories for progressive change at a local level." Buffalo was in a group of sixteen communities the foundation winnowed down to three through a competitive process. The foundation chose the initial four local organizations to collaborate, unbeknownst to them. Now it's expanded to thirteen nonprofits to participate in Open Buffalo. This new collaboration of existing organizations will yield new resources in the form of national money coming into Buffalo to support it and yielding new efficiencies by allowing these groups to work together more efficiently. Why another new organization? Magavern says, "For now it's not a new 501(c)(3), but it might well turn into one just because that is the best way to do business." What can it do that PPG or other coalitions like Voice Buffalo cannot do? He replied, "One of the things it does is it allows us to combine the community organizing model and more grassroots groups with our research and policy focus. We've got these really small organizations and to be able to add more community organizers, more researchers, more communications people, it's going to be much bigger, a more sophisticated collaboration than we had before."[15]

As mentioned in chapter 6, Marlies Wesolowski suggested that nonprofits can often deliver services better than governments can. Dale Zuchlewski echoes that sentiment. He relates an incident when the Department of Social Services (DSS) was looking for standards for home shelters. His organization already did that because it was a HUD requirement. He was able to share that with DSS instead of their reinventing the wheel. Nonprofits working with government? He says, "Wow! I naturally agree with you."[16]

If this transfer of workload were to occur, nonprofits need be better funded than they are today. Phil Haberstro says, "I know they don't want to be always in the situation of asking for handouts, but they are smart places for investment in our community."[17]

From another perspective, Cara Matteliano now sees a change from "a community that's all about the silver bullet to a community that is embracing different but interrelated strategies and there is not someone up there who's controlling everything. It's okay for different groups of people to be working on the different parts knowing that the parts will hopefully fit together at some point. So I feel better about there being some hubs of effort that are driven by data largely, in some cases funded well, or resourced fairly well, or better than before, and that there are people earnestly working on it who weren't really a part of the picture before."[18]

Beginning in 1995 under the leadership of the Wellness Institute, a citizen-led civic project called Vision for Tomorrow commenced. Volunteers and citizen participants from Erie and Niagara counties participated in a series of community forums generating over 1500 ideas condensed into 39 goal statements. Their vision statement for the region:

> Citizens of the Erie Niagara community share in shaping the future of our thriving binational region. Safe and stable neighborhoods, respect for diversity, accessible cultural/recreation opportunities, healthy population and lifelong learning provide exceptional quality of life. Our dynamic business climate involves a competitive workforce, responsive governance and a

comprehensive transportation system. The balanced, sustainable environment ensures the prosperity and natural resources of our region.[19]

Paul Wolf doesn't have any problem with nonprofits taking on some of these things. He describes a Buffalo program to lend people money to rehab their homes. "It's been a disaster. People are on the waiting list for five years to get a loan to improve your home. What's amazing is this was the issue in the 80s, in the 90s, literally every ten years there's an article in the *Buffalo News* criticizing this loan program run by the city. It's completely inept, bureaucracy, part of it is patronage employees who aren't very well-qualified in doing what they're doing." People wait years and years to get their leaky roof fixed. Some are senior citizens and/or low income. The city started having this program partly run by Belmont Housing Resources—a non-profit dedicated to expanding affordable housing—and partly run by the city. Wolf feels strongly, "I would just as soon get the city out of that business. This is what Belmont does every day and they do it well. They have trained people who process loan paperwork to rehab homes. The city of Buffalo isn't very good at it.… I agree that nonprofits are more efficient, they are cheaper, they're more effective in a lot of ways."[20]

We have the beginnings of a regional plan. In the Framework for Regional Growth (FfRG), it states: "the Framework establishes basic policies and principles to guide the future growth and development of the Region" and lists some goals and a vision for how we wish the region to grow and redevelop over the next 15 years:

- Direction regarding growth and redevelopment matters to county decision-makers and other regional organizations linked to the two counties via funding, membership, or other relationships;

- Information on the ways local governments, private sector, and non-profit actions and initiatives can reinforce the overall regional vision; and

- Mechanisms to ensure that the goals, concepts, and recommendations of the Framework for Regional Growth are implemented in an efficient and accountable manner.[21]

These goals must be adhered to if the region has any chance of realizing its potential. Buffalo Niagara, let's begin with that and build on it.

We have the beginnings of a regional planning agency, UB's Regional Institute and One Region Forward.

For social capital, we already have many successful nonprofit organizations such as the Matt Urban Center and the Homeless Alliance. Wesolowski knows of many successful new programs for building social capital such as the Naturally Occurring Retirement Community Supportive Services Program (NORC SSP) paradigm, a community-based intervention designed to reduce service fragmentation and create healthy, integrated communities in which seniors living in NORCs are able to age-in-place with greater comfort and security in their own homes.

For the environment, we have the Buffalo Niagara Riverkeeper, the Clean Air Coalition, the Western New York Environmental Alliance and the Niagara River Greenway Commission. Regarding the Greenway Commission, Sierra Club's Schneekloth thinks it has potential:

> My sense is instead of being a reactive body it actually ought to be a planning body. It ought to start to develop its own plans for the Greenway and for things that should be happening along the Greenway. It's got access to a lot of money, it can do a lot of things, there's no reason it can't do things itself. So rather than sitting back and waiting for somebody to come up with a decent proposal to do something, there's no reason why they literally can't do it. If they take that more proactive role then we'll see a much faster transition of the waterfront into that image of a lake-to-lake Greenway.[22]

New Leadership: Individuals

Reacting to the famous 1901 quote about the city of Buffalo, and a point of the raised in chapter 6 about leadership, Robert Shibley of the University at Buffalo, School of Architecture and Planning compared the leaders from around 1900 who created the rising, dynamic city to the leaders of today. He said that times were different then but now,

> I would say to you we have some extraordinary leadership in our civic, not-for-profit sector of our community. They are activists, they don't accept the

idea that they are victims, and they solve the problems when they come at them... the aggressiveness, the "okay, I'm not going to be a victim—due to the lack of service here or the inability to be employed, or environmental circumstance I find, I'm going to work to fix it. I'm working it, and I'm going to make a difference." There are dozens, if not well over 100 that I would stand up and salute as powerful leaders in that capacity.[23]

These include all of the people interviewed for this book, and add to that list individuals such as Aaron Bartley of PUSH, Justin Booth of GObike Buffalo, Julie Barrett O'Neill of the Buffalo Sewer Authority, Peter Cammarata and Dave Stebbins of Buffalo Urban Development Corporation, Peg Overdorf of the Valley Community Association, Laura Kelly of the First Ward Association, Mark Zirnheld of the St. Vincent de Paul Society, Dave Speiring of Tifft Nature Preserve, Melissa Fratello of Grassroots Gardens, preservationist Tim Tielman, and many, many others. When talking about these new leaders, Tom DeSantis said, "I think there will be other people around responsible for continuing that momentum other than me or the people that are on the ground today."[24]

Phil Haberstro's idea of "stocking the pond": "For the community's well-being, the mentorship role, whether it's through internships or personal relationships, it becomes incumbent on leadership to mentor these young people. That very much has to be part of the fabric of our civic culture."[25]

Reducing segregation

On that note, one of the top priorities for improving our region social capital would to integrate all the people of the region into one community. As part of its strategic plan, the Community Foundation for Greater Buffalo adopted a vision of "a vibrant and inclusive greater Buffalo region with opportunity for all." They think the following strategies are needed to reduce racial and ethnic disparities:

1. increase educational attainment for low income children and adults;

2. improve the overall health status and school readiness of children living in communities of poverty;

3.increase the number of low income residents obtaining jobs that support economic self-sufficiency;

4. increase the financial assets for low income residents;

5. increase opportunities for residents to interact across racial/ethnic lines;

6. increase community understanding regarding racial/ethnic disparities;

7. increase grassroots leadership capacity.26

This would be, however, a long-term, ongoing process for growing the region's social capital—we also need something with more immediate results.

The city of good neighbors

Driving through the city of Buffalo on any given day, one would find examples of uncivil behavior at every turn. Many commentators in the mainstream media have bemoaned the loss of civility in American society at large, and it clearly is not just a regional problem. But in a city that prides itself on being "the city of good neighbors," it's especially ironic. Take red light runners: Someone who moved to Buffalo after having lived in Los Angeles and Chicago and other places in the country told me that when he first arrived here he was actually scared by the common practice of red light running in the city of Buffalo. Then there are the pedestrians who ignore signals; they regularly walk against the lights and cut off traffic that might have a green arrow to turn. Litter is everywhere. Recently while I was driving down the street in one of Buffalo's most exclusive neighborhoods, following an expensive SUV, a beer can with liquid still in it came flying out the passenger window. I pulled up next to the vehicle at a stop sign to see two teenagers, by all signs from the upper class. Graffiti mars the work of tradesmen and diligent property owners alike. "No Parking" signs are put up for a reason, but many drivers ignore the signs for their personal convenience without consideration to the consequences for others. Bar and restaurant noise disturbs neighbors nearby, especially from sound systems put on high volume so that people who don't want to hear it are forced to.

One of the most unneighborly behaviors is not shoveling sidewalks during the winter. Homeowners who commute by car seldom use their own sidewalks and therefore don't see the need to shovel it for themselves. Snowplow jockeys are too lazy to jump out of their heated cabs, shovel in hand, and do their customers' sidewalks, and the homeowners that contract them are too inconsiderate of their neighbors to demand that service.

One experiment in building social capital, beginning with the city of Buffalo and extending outward throughout the region, would be for our community leaders to demand, for the next winter season, that all sidewalks be shoveled promptly between 6 and 9 am. Announce before the winter season, on all public media, the "new" way we're going to be doing things. Then, for the first two or three storms, issue warning tickets to property owners who do not comply. Guidelines for snowplow operators should demand that sidewalks be included in their service. For rental properties where the landlord is not resident, tenants should be expected to do this. After the first three or four storms, those who do not comply should be fined. The municipality would hire a seasonal corps of workers to go out and do the work for the noncompliants and then property owners should be assessed costs. Laws need not be passed to back this up; this can be done by social networking. Of course, not everyone can shovel a sidewalk: there are elderly persons who are shut in during the winter and physically incapable of going out into cold weather, people for whom cold weather and doing the physical exertion could be dangerous. What are they to do? That's what neighbors are for. We should know our neighbors well enough to know if they can shovel their own sidewalks. If they can't, they should ask one of their neighbors; but able-bodied neighbors should know and do it without asking. On a block in North Buffalo, the first neighbor out with a snowblower does three or four houses. The next guy out does another three or four houses, and before you know it all the sidewalks are clear. Believe it or not, it happens. Our leaders should expect and demand it for public safety.

Buffalo News opinion letters suggest this is a service that should be provided by the public sector. No. One of the problems with that is that municipalities own properties with sidewalks themselves and very often are negligent on their own sidewalk clearing. The city of Buffalo is notorious for this as citizens have pointed out in Artvoice and the *Buffalo News*. Citizens should bear pressure on their public sector to clear their own sidewalks. Otherwise, no, this is something people can do for themselves and for their neighbors. This is an expression of social capital and, at the very minimum, it should be something that we see every winter.

CHAPTER ELEVEN

....

ECONOMIC CAPITAL

Many past proposals for rejuvenating the regional economy—a new Peace Bridge or a new Bills stadium, for example—are silver bullets. People might confuse this chapter's proposals with silver bullets, but these proposals will have a positive impact on the human, social, economic, and environmental capital of the region. There are qualitative differences between the proposals that follow and the typical silver bullet: They are comprehensive, sustainable, and synergistic, creating improvements across all capital throughout the region.

Densify

Densify: to make denser, condense.

Chapter 5 should convince the reader that the one factor with the greatest impact on human, social, economic, and environmental capital in this region is sprawl. The one initiative that will have the greatest impact on improving that capital would be to densify the region. This means to intensify urban land-use and to concentrate our capital within a smaller area of the region.

All the world's globally significant cities are denser than this region: (all numbers are people per square mile) New York City 26,402; Manhattan 69,467; Boston 13,321; Chicago 12,750; Toronto 10,747; Tokyo 16,000. Buffalo has 4,977.33. Densifying is an urban planning movement being considered or implemented elsewhere in this country, even in growing communities such as Silver Springs, MD; Raleigh, NC; and across the globe in the suburbs of London and Johannesburg, South Africa. There can be problems with density, but urban planners and architects are getting smarter about designs of buildings, open space, and streets to avoid those problems.

When many people think about density, they think crowding and congestion, and they fear it. But it doesn't have to be so; a dense place can be highly livable. The village of Kenmore is the densest incorporated place in the region, one of the few municipalities in the entire U.S. with a density exceeding 10,000 persons per square mile. Yet, it is a highly desirable place to live: In 2009 the American Planning Association named it one of the Top Ten Neighborhoods in the United States[1] and in 2011 *Buffalo Business First* named it the highest rated community in Western New York.[2] No one would characterize the village as being crowded or congested. The point is, higher density can be pleasant to live in.

Table 11.1: Comparing land-use in Buffalo and Kenmore

	City of Buffalo	Village of Kenmore
Land Area (square miles)	40.6	1.4
Population	261,310	15,423
Density (people/square mile)	6,436	11,016
% Agricultural Acreage, 2007	0%	0%
% Residential Acreage, 2007	57.1%	81.9%
% Commercial Acreage, 2007	11.5%	8.6%
% Industrial Acreage, 2007	7.7%	0.4%
% Vacant Acreage, 2007	20.5%	0.5%

Source: UB Regional Institute, Regional Knowledge Network, CommunityQuick Reports, http://rkn.buffalo.edu/reports/reports_choose.cfm?type=1&county=029 accessed January 6, 2014.

Vacant Land and the Blank Slate

This region has an excellent opportunity that few regions in the country have. While other metros were growing, largely in an unplanned fashion, resulting in many urban planning mistakes, this region was sprawling and the central cores of the two largest cities have been shrinking, leaving behind a patchwork of vacant land. In 2010, there were more than 36,000 vacant properties in Erie County, with more than 20,000 of them in the city of Buffalo. In some neighborhoods, these vacant parcels are contiguous and create very large open spaces.

Futurist and preeminent sci-fi writer William Gibson writes, "Cities, to survive, must be capable of extended fugues of retrofitting. Only the most pubescent of cities have never witnessed, to whatever extent, their own ruins. Berlin, has, Rome has, London has, Tokyo has, New York has. Relative ruin, relative desertion, is a common stage of complex and necessary urban growth. Successful (which is to say, ongoing) cities are built up in a lacquering of countless layers: of lives, choices encountered and made."[3]

Figure 11.1: Vacant land in the city of Buffalo, an increasingly common sight.

Even more land would be vacant if the city of Buffalo could catch up to the planned demolition of vacant, abandoned, and dangerous derelict structures. One of the major problems with these areas, such as the one above at Bradford and Elk, is that few residents remain on the block. The infrastructure in these areas was built for many more users and the costs are the same whether there is one, or two or three users on a block that was built for twenty, thirty, or more. The problem then is that these costs are spread out over the rest of the consumer base and those consumers are paying for unused capacity.

The solution is to clear the sparsely populated blocks and bank the land. Problem is, people are living on them, some of whom may be lifelong residents. The costs that allow them to live in these areas and receive services for which they do not pay their fair share ripple outward throughout the region. Utilities should calculate what it costs to provide services to only one house on a block, and municipalities should calculate what it costs to plow and salt the streets around it. These residents could be offered generous incentives to move elsewhere so that their properties can be acquired and cleared or they could be given the choice of paying the true cost of delivering services to their block. Once cleared, the community can create large contiguous areas, and then certain city services can be disconnected: water and sewer lines blocked off, electric power and telephone lines taken down, and even asphalt scraped off the streets. The fallow land would be left to go to seed and be banked for the day when there is demand for its development.

We have a new agency for it. "The Buffalo Erie Niagara Land Improvement Corporation (BENLIC) seeks to confront and alleviate the problems distressed properties cause to communities by supporting municipal and regional revitalization efforts and strategically acquiring, improving, assembling, and selling distressed, vacant, abandoned, and/or tax-delinquent properties."[4]

This is not a new idea. It's being considered in Cleveland and elsewhere. The *Buffalo News* reports Rochester and Detroit are deliberately downsizing their urban areas to reduce urban problems. Downsizing means closing down city blocks, relocating residents, tearing down vacant buildings, and turning the vacant land left behind into parks, greenways, gardens and farms. The organization NeighborWorks does this in

Rochester and in Detroit, Mayor Dave Bing supports this. In Buffalo, it does not have the support of City Hall, according to the *News* article quoting Brendan Mahaffey of the city's Office of Strategic Planning. But the idea does have its advocates, including councilmember Damone Smith and Michael Clarke of the Local Initiatives Support Corporation.[5] The fiscal benefits are important. By eliminating entire blocks of the city, taxpayer-funded services and utility costs are reduced. When fewer and fewer residents support aging infrastructure, the costs can soar beyond what is reasonable. A controversial documentary on the water system of Detroit's Highland Park neighborhood (waterfrontmovie.com) illustrates the crisis that this situation can go to in the extreme. Implementing an idea like this in Buffalo would reduce the cost of living for all residents.

Good bones: streets and infrastructure

Robert Shibley of University at Buffalo, School of Architecture and Planning regularly gives lectures about the City of Buffalo and the region. He describes the city as having "good bones," meaning that there is a skeleton of excellent features onto which to build the community. He says:

> The answer to the great bones/best planned city in America story is water: Niagara, Lake Erie, the Buffalo River. Turn of the 1800s, settlement patterns coming up perpendicularly from the water and colliding with the additional complexity of Main Street as high ground slicing at a diagonal through the grid. [Then] Joseph Ellicott came to survey for the Holland Land Company fresh from surveying Pierre L'Enfant's layout of the city of Washington. He thought about that in relationship to the grid collision of Main Street and thought "radial." He laid in the now-famous 1804 radial plan for the city.... It's an elegant and great infrastructure and plan, rationalizing historic settlement patterns, taking maximum advantage of access to the water and maximum advantage of first, carriage trade, then streetcar, from the neighborhoods to downtown. Olmsted comes along, looks at all that, and says, "Don't change a thing. In fact I'm going use those radials to bring those three parks to Delaware, Genesee, and downtown. I'm going to use the grid that grows up around those parks to take me to

the water." So now you've got Olmsted and Ellicott collaborating with this geological reality of the water placement and you got the best planned city in America. So the answer to your question of good bones, it's that.[6]

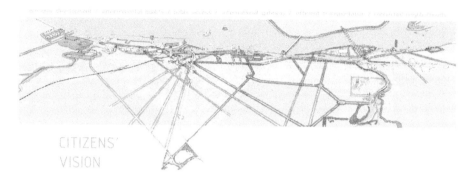

Figure 11.2: The City of Buffalo's "Good Bones"

Underneath it all is an infrastructure which, at one time, serviced 600,000 people and now is used by only 270,000. It could accommodate that 600,000 once again with some repair and replacement: It's estimated that the city's water system leaks half the water pumped into it before it reaches customers, for example.

The infrastructure should be green. The Sierra Club has a new campaign which calls for job-creating renewable energy in areas that could benefit from the transition away from fossil fuels.[7] Recent proposals to switch the coal plant in Dunkirk to gas and to begin dangerous fracking in the Southern Tier could mean an uncertain future for communities concerned about the economic and health impacts of volatile natural gas prices, air and water pollution associated with fracking, and the increasing risk of climate disasters.

Meeting the state's goal of 30% renewable energy by 2015 could create more than $6 billion in direct economic benefits to New York, according to a recently released study by the state's energy and research development agency, NYSERDA.[8]

A study by some scientists from Stanford examined the feasibility of converting New York State's energy infrastructure to renewable sources—wind, water, and sunlight—and concluded that:

- The conversion reduces NYS end-use power demand by 37%.

- The plan creates more jobs than it loses since most energy will be from in-state.

- The plan creates long-term energy price stability since fuel costs will be zero.

- The plan decreases air pollution deaths by 4000 per year ($33 billion/yr or 3% of NYS GDP).[9]

More about this in chapter 12.

Following the clearing of city blocks and reclaiming the land gives us a blank slate, one on which we can start from scratch and do it better. One way of doing it better would be to change some street patterns.

Figure 11.3: Comparing street patterns

STREET PATTERNS

The graphic above compares different street pattern configurations. On the left is the classic gridiron which was developed around 1900. On the right is a relatively new pattern called "lollipops on a stick," developed around 1980. The table below compares the efficiency in terms of land-use between the two patterns over 100 acres.

Table 11.2: Comparing efficiency of street patterns

	Gridiron (C. 1900)	Lollipops on a stick (C. 1980)
Lineal feet of streets	20,800	15,600
Number of blocks	28	8
Number of intersections	26	8

Source: Figure 19, Comparative Analysis Of Neighborhood Street Patterns, Florida Center For Transportation, Land Use And Sustainability, http://www.fccdr.usf.edu/upload/projects/tlushtml/tlus100.htm, accessed 7/18/14.

"Lollipops on a stick" is a type of cluster development. Cluster developments have been popular recently because the units are spread evenly across the property, preserving more open space. Shorter streets and utility lines which are possible with this configuration lower development costs. The open space that is preserved may be dedicated as public land.

Newer street patterns have 25% fewer lineal feet of pavement, which means lower costs for snowplowing and repaving, and less impervious area for storm runoff. What isn't paved can be green space, mitigating the effects of climate change. The newer pattern has only a quarter as many blocks, meaning far fewer intersections, which translates to far fewer opportunities for collisions and far less of a need for traffic signals and stop signs. Traffic would actually flow more freely. The bottom line is that newer street patterns "can help support a more time- and energy- efficient life style and can create more vital and diverse places to live."[10]

New residential patterns

The city of Buffalo has earnestly, with the best of intentions, filled in some of the vacant parcels that were created by demolition. In some cases, the infill is new residential development in a contemporary and popular style.

Figure 11.4a: Suburban-style infill on vacant city land.

This configuration, however, is more suited to the suburbs than the city because of its low density, comprised largely of single family, detached homes.

Single-family detached homes are the costliest, in terms of materials and energy usage, of residential configurations. "Detached houses according to one calculation, can use up to five times as much energy to build and live in as an apartment of comparable area."[11]

Figure 11.4b: The infill would be better for the region if it consisted of attached townhomes like this:

Figure 11.4c: Or even better still, multifamily housing like this:

Given the data from chapter 3, the region has fewer families and smaller households than is typical, and single-family detached homes may not be the best economic choice for them. The region has an unbalanced mix of single-family detached homes for the number of single person households, and that raises the cost of living here.

The American Planning Association, for instance, has explored mechanisms for realizing this goal. It includes a system of bonuses and dividends for developers to increase density.[12] Paul Wolf suggests land value taxation. This development can be gently guided by the area's Industrial Development Agencies (IDA's) and Regional Economic Development Council (REDC). Perhaps density could be factored in to real estate assessments, incentivizing high density and discouraging low density with a multiplier based on units per acre. It's justifiable: this would reflect real costs.

The city of Buffalo is in the process of completing a comprehensive and strategic plan for guiding the city's development, the Green Code.[13] It is a form-based code that is simpler and smarter than the previous version. Although this will surely result in better development outcomes, it must be a living document that is continuously improved by the results of ongoing development.

IDAs and REDC

For all their flaws and the mistaken decisions they've made, the IDAs and REDC centralized agencies for coordinating the development of economic capital. City planner Tom DeSantis said, "Regardless of what people think about Cuomo or his policies, the one policy that I would say by far that has been a clear success is the whole idea of regional economic development councils.... Whether people want to or not, it forced them to start at least talking as if there's a region out there."[14]

There's certainly room for improvement and, once improved, they could turn out to be the most efficient tool to guide the development of our economic capital. The first step toward improvement would be consolidation. Consolidation is necessary because IDAs currently think competitively intra-region. To do what's best for the region, they need to combine and their goal should to densify the central cores. They must identify the zones that are clearly low-density and sprawl and in those zones; new construction should be ineligible for incentives. IDAs don't have to prohibit new construction, just make developers pay the full costs. In inner ring suburbs, IDAs should be very selective with their incentives and limit them to only those projects which densify the suburbs. But the most incentives and the clear priority should be development within the cities of Buffalo and Niagara Falls, to a reasonable density with careful consideration toward smart design that would maximize all the capital: human, social, economic, and environmental.

One application for this process might be dealing with the excess of roads that Erie County maintains. County executive Mark Poloncarz recently said, "there is simply no reason for the County to maintain roads that have very little traffic and are residential in nature."[15] He proposes that ownership and responsibility for maintenance be transferred to the municipalities in which they're located. This could be a problem, however: If consolidation is implemented, there would be no lower level of government to transfer ownership and maintenance to. A cost-benefit analysis would determine which roads benefit few people and then transfer some of those costs in the form of special assessments to those people, perhaps by calculating road frontage per lot which would then be applied to property tax assessment. This would encourage density and discourage sprawl.

Another incentive to densify the cores and discourage sprawl is adjusted service charges. Infrastructure costs to reach individual properties in the town of Colden, for example, are greater than the same costs would be in the town of Cheektowaga, which are greater than they would be from home to home on Linwood Avenue in the city of Buffalo. This is due to the additional footage of pipe or wire to deliver services and the transmission losses caused by delivering over greater distances. But each of these consumers pays the same flat rate. Adjusting charges by road frontage and distance from service stations would result in consumers bearing a truer cost of delivering their services and would help to discourage sprawl.

Smart grid

One major project that would provide a powerful economic stimulus to the region and the state would be to build the "smart grid." This project would create jobs, lower the cost of electricity in New York State, provide the infrastructure that would make New York State more competitive in attracting new businesses, mitigate climate change, and improve the environment.

The energy infrastructure of the U.S. is old and inefficient, piecemeal and overtaxed. One of the major problems is political: three super grids—the Western interconnection, the Texas interconnection, and the Eastern inter-connection—and sub-regions serve the U.S. and Canada, which are joined by only a few weak links. The Eastern Interconnection is further subdivided by councils, and New York State falls under the Northeast Power Coordinating Council. The New York State grid is managed by the not-for-profit New York Independent System Operator. This corporation coordinates power generation and load among the regional utilities. Ideally the solution to this problem is at the federal level but is currently managed at the state level.

The other major problem with the U.S. energy infrastructure is the age of the transmission lines that carry electricity from generators to consumers. An upgrade to this transmission system could make electricity cheaper, reduce blackouts, and bring renewable power to cities far from where it's generated. One of the great benefits of upgrading the transmission system would be its ability to deliver more electricity—increasing capacity—without adding new generating capacity. Many of the existing transmission lines in this state are 230-, 345-, and 500-kV alternating current lines.

Technology has evolved to the point where high voltage direct current lines are the most efficient for carrying electricity over long—greater than 300 mile—distances. This is ironic because it was here in 1895 when an historic experiment proved the superiority of alternating current over direct current for the transmission and distribution of electricity from the generating plant to the consumer. This is still true for a local grid or even a regional grid where point-to-point distances are 300 miles or less. But these high voltage direct current lines lose less electricity over distances of 300 miles or more. Matthew Wald writes in *Scientific American* that using the "new 765-kV and HVDC lines could save billions of dollars a year, improve reliability, and supply ample wind and solar energy nationwide."[16]

Wald describes a system where "even when demand for electricity is low, certain power plants must run to keep voltage stable across the system, yet there is no demand for the actual power they are producing. At night, when winds are often high, there may be no place to send electricity they create." He concludes "this imbalance can make clean, renewable energy awfully expensive. Forcing wind turbines to stop producing when the wind is blowing can quickly make them uneconomical." The super grid would be an electric superhighway delivering this surplus "to customers who do need power but are far away. More lines can also help spread out voltage surges and dips across a larger area of suppliers and consumers, so the fluctuations can be absorbed without creating dangerous voltage spikes or meddlesome blackouts or brownouts."[17] His fourfold solution: erecting more transmission lines, transmitting power at higher voltages, putting high voltage direct current lines (HVDC) (which lose less than half the electricity during transmission than the highest voltage alternating current line) in the most heavily traveled corridors, and knitting regional systems into a continental super grid with short HVDC or even superconducting lines.

The benefits of this project are so numerous it could be considered a "win-win". According to a report from the federal government's national renewable energy laboratory,18 a national super grid could bring wind energy from the Midwest and solar energy from the Southwest to the East Coast and North Coast along the Great Lakes, eliminating the need for offshore wind turbines on the Atlantic Ocean and the Great Lakes. The billions of dollars of construction for the new grid would create far more jobs than the hydraulic fracturing of the Marcellus shale and be environmentally friendly as opposed to environmentally destructive. New York State already has surplus electric generation capacity so that the transmission increase will only add to that surplus and allow the state to close coal-fired power plants which are environmentally damaging. Workers at these plants would not have to worry about their future: there would be ample new jobs created by the construction of the super grid and the state and its power agencies should give priority retraining these workers to fill those jobs. NIMBYs needn't worry about the loss of forest land or new towers near their houses; the new grid can be overlaid on the top of the old grid.

The initiative for this construction should come from the U.S. and Canadian federal governments. But New York State could take the lead and get the project started on their own, perhaps creating the stimulus that might push federal government action. The Buffalo Niagara region can push the state to begin the work here at the regional level or at the western end of the state and push the federal government to allot stimulus funds for demonstration projects sited in Western New York.

The project is already begun. The New York Energy Highway Blueprint is "Governor Andrew M. Cuomo's bold proposal for a dynamic public-private partnership that will rebuild and rejuvenate New York State's electric power system and enable the state to meet the needs of a 21st century economy and society."19 This proposal calls for billions of dollars of investment. In February 2014, Gov. Cuomo announced $4.3 million in awards to researchers seeking to develop new techniques that would add resiliency and efficiency to the state's electric grid. The goal is to reengineer the grid to enhance performance, add clean energy, reduce environmental impacts and energy consumption, and lower costs. But $4.3 million is way too little for research and development. More money could be added from the New York Power Authority's annual budget surplus.

High-speed rail (HSR)

Passenger rail service in New York State is limited to Amtrak's Empire service, which currently offers four trains daily from Buffalo to New York City and three trains daily from Niagara Falls to New York City and only one on Sunday. A trip from Buffalo to New York City typically averages eight hours and the price of a one-way ticket ranges from $62-$119. For environmental and economic reasons, existing passenger rail service needs improvement. New York State currently has a plan for a high-speed rail system running from Niagara Falls to New York City, called the High-Speed Rail Empire Corridor Program.[20]

This proposal has five alternatives. The base alternative is a modest improvement in station facilities, rolling stock, and operating efficiency. The top alternative would include a maximum speed of 125 mph and an average speed of 77 mph, improving the Niagara Falls to New York City best time to six hours and two minutes, and would cost $14.71 billion. Alternatives would increase service to 19 daily trains. Higher-speed alternatives—160 and 220 mph maximum—were abandoned because of high costs and environmental impacts. But to put these speeds in perspective, the world records for conventional wheeled trains is TGV's 357.2 mph and for magnetic levitation (maglev) it's 361 mph. Japan's Shinkansen trains average 200 mph and France's TGV trains regularly operate at 200 mph.

The Empire Corridor proposal's high environmental costs for those higher speeds includes large land area consumption, parks and open space consumption, unpleasant aesthetics and hazards to wildlife. The rolling stock is a conventional wheeled train.

A better alternative would be an elevated rail system using magnetic levitation running the 490-mile distance between Toronto and New York City. Over much of that distance, it could be placed in the median of the QEW and New York State Thruway rights of way, significantly reducing land acquisition costs and not consuming any more land than is now used for transportation. Elevating it would allow wildlife to pass below and eliminate safety concerns at ground level with pedestrians and vehicles. Transparent shields on the side would mitigate crosswind forces on the vehicles and minimize wildlife collisions. A roof of solar panels over the rail structure would help generate the power necessary to run the system; not be sufficient by itself to power the entire system, especially at night, but it would go a long way toward reducing "fuel" costs.

The Buffalo-Toronto corridor is a natural for high-speed rail: densely populated; highly traveled; connecting a world-class city with an expensive airport to one of the world's scenic wonders with an underused airport and connected by a car-choked highway. A two-hour drive by car could be shortened to 30 minutes by the right transportation system. Imagine how many more trips, how much more activity could be generated by that.

Compared with conventional wheeled trains, maglev allows higher top speeds, much lower maintenance requirements, all-weather operations, faster acceleration and deceleration than wheels on wet rails, more energy-efficient at higher speeds, quieter the conventional trains at equivalent speeds, and fueled by renewable energy versus fossil fuels for conventional.

Maglev even has advantages over air travel. Although the speed of maglev is much less than aircraft, total travel time could be close to equal, due to the airport times required for departure and arrival. Also, maglev would not be vulnerable to weather delays, it would be safer, and would be more competitive over short routes, say between Rochester and Albany.

Figure 11.5: New high-speed rail concept.

New York State's High Speed Rail Empire Corridor will result in little change in the travel habits along the corridor, especially automobile traffic on the Thruway. The key is convenience. Four trains a day or even 19 trains a day, six or eight hours per trip, is not convenient for travel across the state. To really make an impact, the passenger rail system must be as convenient as hopping in your own car and driving on your schedule. The key to achieving that in a large passenger rail system is utilizing small vehicles—size of a typical urban bus—leaving at frequent intervals, such as every few minutes. High speed rail such as the high-speed (700 mph) transport system called Hyperloop proposed by PayPal, SpaceX, and Tesla motors genius Elon Musk would make travel between Tor-Buf-Chester as quick as a morning commute.[21] Musk also realizes the importance of frequent departures—he estimates departures every 30 seconds.

Now that would make a significant difference enough to replace automobile traffic on the state's interstate system in large numbers. Musk's proposal calls for capsules with passengers traveling in a tube in which the air has been evacuated. Some engineers have been critical of the proposal, citing several engineering hurdles. Regardless, one of the most important features of this proposal as it stands right now, is small—relative to large trains—capsules with fewer passengers and "with capsules departing as often as every thirty seconds from each terminal and carrying twenty-eight people each."

This project presents another opportunity for growth as well. The structure and vehicles of the system could be constructed in large part with the new supermaterial graphene. Since no large-scale graphene manufacturing facilities currently exist, a new facility could be built to construct the HSR system and it could be sited, if not in this region, then along the HSR corridor, creating jobs as well as economic activity and a brand-new high-tech industry.

Canada and Tor-Buf-Chester: The Mega Region

We could create America's first binational region: two countries—one region. In March 2000 at a forum held in Niagara Falls, New York and Niagara Falls, Ontario, 75 American and Canadian citizens talked about this very vision. This idea is already being implemented through heritage and cultural tourism, trade and transportation, brownfield redevelopment, and mutual efforts on the natural environment, but this concept has a much greater potential for improving the quality of life on both sides of the border. The forum's report concluded, "The region's potential is enormous. The situation, the assets, even the problems to be turned around are filled with opportunity.

Location, natural resources, local community assets, transportation infrastructure, the global economic context, history, culture, architecture, organizational capacity, and more, all bode well for the region if we can act appropriately."[22]

Urban studies theorist Richard Florida is known for his concept of the creative class and its potential for urban regeneration. Some of his work focuses on megaregions that concentrate economic development. The illustration below shows his megaregion stretching from Toronto to Rochester.

Figure 11.6: Tor-Buff-Chester the megaregion

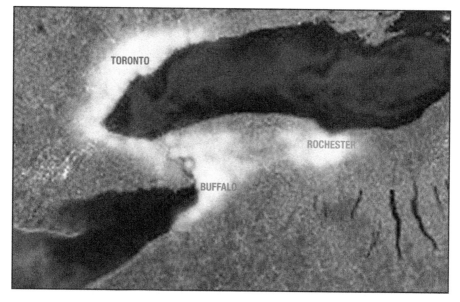

This is what Florida wrote in the Toronto Globe and Mail back in October 2007:

> Tor-Buff-Chester is bigger than the San Francisco-Silicon Valley mega-region, Greater Paris, Hong Kong and Shanghai, and more than twice the size of Cascadia, which stretches from Vancouver to Seattle and Portland. Its economic might is equivalent to more than half of all of Canada's. If it were its own country, it would number among the 16 biggest in the world, with economic output bigger than that of Sweden, the Netherlands, or Australia....Instead, we have two American cities that are in decline when they should be succeeding, and a border that gets harder to cross as new

security measures are imposed. It is so crazy and wasteful that in one city people are lining up on the street to pay $1500 a foot for condos and fifty miles away in another city they are demolishing 5,000 houses.[23]

A special report by BMO Capital Markets concluded that, "the Great Lakes region is a vital driver of the North American economic output." The Great Lakes region is comprised of the states Minnesota, Wisconsin, Michigan, Illinois, Indiana, Ohio, Pennsylvania, and New York and the province of Ontario, a region which accounts for 28% of the combined Canadian and U.S. economic activity and 28% of the Canadian-U.S. workforce. They conclude, "The region's output ranks ahead of Germany, France, Brazil and the UK, and it would rank as the fourth-largest economy in the world if it were a country, behind only the U.S., China and Japan." The growth in this regional economy is led by growth in education and health and professional services. Despite a recent uptick, levels of employment in construction and manufacturing are still well behind 2002 levels. The report states, "The good news is that economic activity in the region has bounced back, helped especially by a resurgent auto sector. North American car and truck production is back to pre-recession levels..." As for trade, "the Great Lakes region is a critically important North American trading hope, accounting for roughly a quarter of total U.S. merchandise exports in 2013." The report goes on to say, "the regions cross-border trade linkages are also immensely important. For example, the Great Lakes states are Ontario's single largest trading partner." Why then does a Brookings Institution study show population declining in the Great Lakes metro areas? According to the report one possible reason is, "union membership is in secular decline across the U.S., the Great Lakes region included, the region has well above average membership... A combined 16.1% of the workforce were union members in 2013, compared to 11.3% nationally... The broader challenge facing the region's factory sector is to ensure the productivity remains in line with labor costs."[24]

The Western New York Regional Economic Development Council has a strategy for leveraging our international border location "to expand our export base creating economic and employment opportunities for the region."[25] Their binational strategy, however, seems to be limited to a Canadian marketing campaign, and their regional destination brand development is limited to this side of the border. Binational tourism efforts are already underway, such as the Binational Doors Open Niagara.

Lastly

The proposals above are mostly regional in scope or can begin implementation at the regional level, but another, more important change needs to take place. New York State government has to reduce the cost of doing business in New York State. Currently ranked dead last among the 50 states, it needs to revise tax and regulation policies with the goal of, at the very minimum, being in the middle of the pack. This is hard for the people of Albany and New York City to see because their circumstances are special. But for the good of the rest of the state and for the state as a whole, it needs to grow its economic capital.

CHAPTER TWELVE
....

ENVIRONMENTAL CAPITAL

Phil Haberstro says, "I think it's an absolute blessing that we have a shared border with a whole different culture and a whole different country."[1]

What a border! This region has world-class assets: the Great Lakes and the Niagara River, an internationally designated, globally significant Important Bird Area. A coalition of local environmental groups is currently applying to the Ramsar Convention on Wetlands, an intergovernmental treaty that provides the framework for national action and international cooperation for the conservation and wise use of wetlands and their resources, for special designation for the Niagara River. What have we done with it? We dump our most toxic wastes in it, pollute the water that runs through it, divert the water that runs through it. Think about this: No one alive today has ever seen the full flow of the Niagara River over the falls. Since the 1800s, some portion of the Niagara River has been diverted for power generation. For some part of every day of the year, only 50% of the total river volume spills over the falls. Even at that, it is still magnificent.

Climate

As mentioned in Chapter 8, some people believe that our climate is a disadvantage. In truth, it's not that bad. For instance, from the shores of Lake Erie, you can watch the sun set over water, a phenomenon that you cannot experience in any other major city east of the Mississippi. From Memorial Day to Labor Day, this region has the highest percentage of sunshine and is one of the most temperate places in the U.S. Buffalo has the sixth coolest summer city in the U.S.[2]

In 2009, there were 237 consecutive days without snow between the last snowfall in spring and the first snowfall of the fall, the fourth-longest such drought since records were kept in 1884.[3] That represents almost two-thirds of a year without snow. And that's not even the record! The record of 277 days, set in 1947, represents just over three-quarters of the year. So much for the myth that "Buffalo has two seasons, Fourth of July and winter." In fact, about two thirds of the year there is no snow whatsoever.

The climate is changing. Jay Burney said, "Climate changes aren't only in the future. It's today, it's last week, it's last year."[4] As it progresses, it may work out to the advantage of our region.

The Oak Ridge National Laboratory did a study on future U.S. energy use for 2000-2025 computing a climate change prediction model by region and found that, with climate change, the region of the country with the least change in energy use would be New England (the region where they locate Buffalo Niagara) and "the East-North Central region (mainly the Great Lakes states) has the largest overall decrease in energy, because of... its relative climate."[5]

National Geographic did a cover story on "Rising Seas", climate change melting ice, resulting in rising sea levels putting the residents of coastal cities at risk. They projected that "136 large coastal cities are now at risk from sea-level rise, 40 million people at risk in those cities, $3 trillion value of assets at risk."[6] An article in the journal *Megacities* warns, "86% of urban residents in wealthy countries live on local coasts that risk flooding from rising sea levels."[7]

Bloomberg Businessweek reported how recent flooding caused a rewriting of flood maps by the federal government in East Coast and Gulf Coast communities (West Coast, Great Lakes, and Florida will follow), placing tens of thousands of homes in flood zones, raising flood insurance coverage under the national flood insurance program.[8] "New federal flood maps will force thousands of houses onto stilts" above sea level and storm surges, requiring investments into hundreds of thousands of dollars, an amount which could buy a nice house in Western New York. The Flood Insurance

Reform Act of 2012 was a result of opposition to spending national taxpayer dollars to rebuild homes for people who choose to live in high risk areas. The law gradually raises premiums closer to market rates. There are numerous problems with this change, including maps that are found to be inaccurate in many spots, but the bottom line is the new federal flood law will require thousands of homeowners to elevate their houses or pay very high insurance rates.

Those people will be looking for a place where they will not be put at risk. At more than 500 feet above sea level and on the coast of another kind, these people might find Buffalo Niagara an attractive place to relocate. UCLA environmental economist Matthew Kahn thinks so. In his recent book *Climatopolis*, he ranks Buffalo #3 in the top five most climate-resilient cities in the U.S. because of its inland coast.[9]

Cool summers have their advantages. *Scientific American* states, "The Internet's giant data centers generate heat which needs to be taken away by power-hungry air—and liquid—cooling systems to keep the Internet's engines from burning themselves out."[10] They are currently looking at increases in network energy efficiency, but "these data centers will need new approaches such as siting in cooler climes." One large data center in Western New York, for the internet giant Yahoo! cooled only by outside air and has no air conditioning. The project was heavily subsidized by tax breaks and low-cost power. The tax breaks, however, are expensive per job created and they are not going to create a lot of jobs.[11]

> Yahoo! Inc. has just opened a new data center in Lockport, New York. It is the company's first use of a new environmentally friendly design that relies in large part on Western New York's cooler climate. It makes use of the prevailing winds from Lake Ontario and low-cost hydropower from the New York Power Authority to keep the 120-foot by 60-foot server buildings cool. That significantly reduces its electricity use, so that its power usage rating is nearly half that of the industry average. According to the EPA, data centers across the U.S. account for about 1.5% of our country's electricity usage. The Lockport facility uses about 40% less energy and at least 95% less water than its competitors. It promises to be one of the most energy efficient structures of its kind.[12]

Another advantage of our region is that we have a relatively low risk of natural disasters such as earthquakes, hurricanes, storms and tornadoes, wildfires, and volcanoes. Buffalo Niagara is at the low end of the spectrum of risk for these disasters.[13]

Bloomberg Businessweek analyzed a ten-year survey of the damage caused by weather. Of all the fifteen causes—e.g. hurricane, flooding, coastal storm, drought, tornado—the least costly damage comes from winter storms, cold, and ice. In terms of fatalities, however, cold is sixth, winter storms are ninth, and ice is thirteenth. Significantly, heat is the highest cause of fatalities and second-largest cause of injuries in their survey, giving our region a significant advantage over the Sun Belt, one we have yet to capitalize on.[14]

But the damage continues—repairing the damage

Despite the assets and advantages that the natural capital of our region gives us, we continue to pollute the air, water, and land, and spew carbon into the atmosphere, exacerbating climate change. The first thing we have to do is stop our destructive practices. Erin Heaney has acknowledged that things are getting better because of the decline of industry, "but the narrative about Buffalo, that there's no industry here, is totally false. In Tonawanda it has a pretty thriving manufacturing sector, fifty-three plants in a two-mile radius."[15] Lynda Schneekloth reinforced that, "We have very high levels of waste continuing to come into our region [such as Niagara Falls] Covanta [which is] going to bring in tons of waste from New York City" for twenty years." She asks, "Why are [we] continuing the waste economy?"[16] The DEC's Doster says, "My activity [remediating brownfields] in Western New York is large because of all our problems and we still have problems."[17]

The Western New York Environmental Alliance's Working Group for Waste and Pollution produced an excellent report called "Mapping Waste" and a plan for action called Clean-Up Niagara. The report states:

> All of the issues of waste in WNY are not historic, but ongoing today. WNY continues to accumulate waste, hazardous and otherwise, in quantities beyond most communities. The ongoing struggle to stop the expansion of Chemical Waste Management's Model City hazardous waste

landfill (CWM), for example, highlights issues of ongoing pollution, and the designation of three rivers as Areas of Concern by the International Joint Commission as Great Lakes toxic hot spots. These are but two conditions that suggest that WNY is one of the 'toxic' hot spots in New York State, and perhaps in the United States.[18]

Ecological Intelligence author Daniel Goleman writes, "Our habits of consumption on a worldwide scale for creating an ecological deficit at a rate unparalleled in history."[19]

He goes on to say, "The old saying has it that 'what we don't know can hurt us.' But the truth today is just the reverse: But we do not know about what goes on backstage, out of sight, [that] harms us, others, and the planet."[20]

Will we be able to change? When Jay Burney talks about the in-migration of climate change refugees, he says we have to find ways to reconcile our economy and the environment that sustains it. Can we do that? He says, "I do not know." If we can conserve and protect our ecological resources, if we can take corporate profit and turn it into people profit and people capital, then we can survive and thrive. "But if we can't do that, then we have no hope. The economy will collapse. The ecology will collapse and climate change will end humanity."[21] He doesn't know if it's possible to do these things in ways that will really make a difference, but "there's hope."

What will it take for us to change?

Thinking a different way

Our population, collectively, needs to learn ecological intelligence. This phrase and concept were coined by Daniel Goleman.

> Ecological intelligence [is] our ability to adapt to our ecological niche. Ecological refers to an understanding of organisms and their ecosystems, and intelligence connotes the capacity to learn from experience and deal effectively with our environment.

> [E]cological intelligence, combined with marketplace transparency, can create a mechanism for positive change.[22]

He also says, "The business rule of thumb in the last century—cheaper is better—

is being supplemented by a new mantra for success: sustainable is better, healthier is better, and humane is better, too."[23]

How did we get to this point of damaging our environment? Goleman writes, "There remains a disconnect between our collective role in generating all those harmful particles and the damage they do."[25] Humanity has a blind spot about this damage.

Goleman adds, "Modern life diminishes such skills and wisdom (attuning ourselves to natural systems); at the beginning of the 21st century, society has lost touch with what may be the singular sensibility crucial to our survival as a species. The routines of our daily lives go on completely disconnected from their adverse impacts on the world around us; our collective mind harbors blind spots to disconnect our everyday activities in the crises those same activities create a natural systems."[26] And so we blithely go on about our business unaware of it all.

Sierra Club's Schneekloth agrees, "I'm a firm believer in the nature deficit disorder. That we as a species, especially in our modern cultures have lost contact with the natural world and so our not being able to actually access wildness."[26] Something important is missing in the quality of our lives.

The Buffalo Audubon Society is working on this problem now. Loren Smith explains, "Generally, we connect people with the natural world." Their focus has been grade school students.

> Buffalo Audubon believes that if we can get those students to understand and appreciate the natural world and not think that it's icky and gross or something to stay away from, but rather something that is interesting, fascinating, neat, messy in a good way, that those students will grow up to appreciate, enjoy, protect and care for the environment more than a student who has not had those experiences."[27]

That's the core of their educational work, but their "programs also extend more broadly to cradle-to-grave." They are part of a national organization that focuses on these issues as well, and collaborate with Audubon chapters in the state and the national organization, here in New York State, across the Great Lakes, throughout the Atlantic flyway, and throughout the Americas. That's the education part. They also conserve "a thousand acres that we own and we also see ourselves as stewards of the region's natural resources" They also work through advocacy with Audubon New York and national partners to ensure that regional and national policies protect our habitat and resources.

Beyond ecological intelligence, Goleman suggests other new ways of looking at things:

• A "green net national product" that, along with fiscal measures, takes into account depletion of natural resources and environmental degradation to replace the standard gross domestic product, the measure of a nation in common economic output, as the index of an economy's robustness.[28]

• Life Cycle Assessment, or LCA, [is] a method that allows us to systematically tear apart any manufactured item into its components and their subsidiary industrial processes, and measure with near-surgical precision their impacts on nature from the beginning of their production through their final disposal.[29]

Life Cycle Assessment shows virtually everything manufactured is linked to quantities of environmental toxins of one kind or another, somewhere back in the industrial supply chain.

Goleman draws attention to the "social dimension of products' LCAs. Human concerns like working conditions, forced labor or child labor, fair wages, health benefits, and the like are of increasing concern to companies that embrace ethical standards and take corporate swill social responsibility seriously."[30] This requires "systematic metrics for sorting out the myriad impacts of the things we produce."[31]

Around the world, work is already underway. Life Cycle Initiative is a joint organization between the United Nations Environmental Program (UNEP) and the Society of Environmental Toxicology and Chemistry (SETAC). They are looking for partners for demonstration projects. The Western New York Regional Economic Development Council should take the lead in introducing the LCA methodology to our region, especially the business community.

Measurements are being developed by the new science of ecological economics. One of the new centers for this field, the Concord Institute defines "Ecological economics is a transdisciplinary field of study that broadly examines the relationships between ecological and economic systems. Ecological economists understand that the economy is a subsystem of a larger ecological life support system, and they strive for an ecologically sustainable, socially equitable, and economically efficient future."[32] This is a calculus completely absent from local policy decision making.

On this topic too work is underway on a global scale. "The Natural Capital Project is a partnership among Stanford University, The Nature Conservancy, the World Wildlife Fund, and the University of Minnesota that works to develop and provide practical ecosystem services concepts and tools, apply these tools in select areas around the world, and engage influential leaders to advance change in policy and practice through mainstreaming the approaches."[33] They work with core partners, governments, corporations, universities, and other non-profit organizations "to integrate ecosystem services approaches into major natural resource decisions, and improve the state of biodiversity and human well-being by motivating greater and more cost-effective investments in both." Here too the Western New York Regional Economic Development Council can be the regional leader in implementing this process as a way of doing business.

Riverkeeper has a plan, as Jill Jedlicka explains: "Rust to Blue: It's a holistic approach. So it's not only repairing and restoring the damage from the past, but in the decisions that we're making now. Whether it's through the Regional Economic Development Council, the advanced manufacturing companies that we're attracting into Western New York, how are we setting the standards of excellence, new standards that are protective and create an environment and a resource that is healthy and protected?"[34]

RiverBend is a good example. After spending twenty years cleaning and restoring the Buffalo River and fifteen years working on the RiverBend brownfield site to clean up contamination, a new LED and solar manufacturing facility will be sited there. Jedlicka warns the production of solar photovoltaics can also be very toxic. She wonders, "How can we we ensure that the hundreds of millions of dollars of investment that's coming into Western New York come with a standard of excellence that we are not going to re-contaminate or repollute everything we've just spent a generation trying to clean up and restore?"[35]

Riverkeeper approaches environmental challenges with ecological intelligence. "It's how we engage the citizenry, how do we make them aware that there's a problem, make them understand that stewardship of this resource is of value. So there's environmental education and the outreach that goes with that."[36] Before sites can be shovel-ready to implement projects, there must be planning and assessments. Riverkeeper just wrapped up a three-year effort to map and identify the living infrastructure within the Niagara River watershed. Overall, they are guided by how this investment is going to benefit and protect our greatest natural asset, freshwater. Yet even after a project is built, the work is not done. "There always has to be a monitoring and stewardship component." When Jedlicka says "community", she includes residents and individual citizens, our elected leaders, our business developers, and the investors that are investing the funds in Western New York. She summarizes, "If we all have a shared and common approach that these investments are going to protect our freshwater resource or enhance them, or at the least not harm them, that's the model moving forward for rust to blue."[37]

Riverkeeper considers the economic impact assessment of the projects they undertake. One of the reasons, Jedlicka says, is to "communicate more than just the feel-good, bugs and bunnies type of stuff," to counter "the assumption that we only care about the natural environment, that we don't care about people or the economy or our neighborhood." An example of a rust to blue project is the Buffalo River cleanup, a "restoration effort which was a ten-year-long effort, multiple partners, public, private, nonprofit, all working together. That's a $50 million effort that looks to restore the river to its fullest ecological potential." Then the community can start to plan and invest up and down that river corridor, all the while protecting the ten-year investment to restore the actual waterway. Another example would be Riverkeeper's work with the Buffalo Sewer Authority in identifying alternatives to gray infrastructure using something called green infrastructure. She explains, "That green infrastructure investment in particular has tremendous potential to have a multiplier effect. Because when you start to implement green infrastructure projects, you do it at a neighborhood level and street level and improve the aesthetics and the quality of life."[38] These projects need "job-training programs because these systems have to be maintained, you've created an entire job market and job sector based on the premise of clean water. That is the blue economy."

Another organization can lead the way, the Western New York Environmental Alliance (WNYEA). Here is their shared agenda for action:

> We, the people of Western New York, are resolved to work collaboratively to improve our environment and our regional, international, community. We are a Great Lakes region and stewards of the world's largest supply of fresh water, vast forests, rich agricultural land, abundant wildlife, an incredible built heritage, historic park systems, the magnificent Niagara Falls and hundreds of wonderful communities. Unfortunately, much of our natural heritage has been lost and what remains is threatened. And, like the rest of the world, we face the prospects of climate change. We therefore establish this agenda to protect and restore our globally significant environment.[39]

They say our environmental resources are immeasurable assets which have direct impacts on our quality of life and our economy. Healthy ecosystems provide ecological as well as recreational and business opportunities. "The environment is a source of wealth for all of us."[40]

Our environmental community is strong and successful. The WNYEA states, "We are the birthplace of the environmental justice movement, a product of both our legacy of contamination and our determination to seek action through justice." The Alliance consists of hundreds of organizations and thousands of people working to improve the environment.

The Alliance laments that "our region and its people have suffered through the despoiling of our environment and the fragmentation of our collective efforts. Our dwindling population, declining health, vacant and contaminated land, and faltering economy are proof of this. Although some progress has been made, much more is needed." The Alliance commits to "collaboratively increase our region's environmental literacy, preserve its biodiversity, and ensure that our energy is sustainable, our air is clean, our water drinkable, our fish edible, and our forests, farms, and gardens plentiful."[41]

Their plan, "Our Shared Agenda for Action," is a regional vision for our future. It includes specific measurable actions that can be accomplished soon. Their aim is "to leave those who follow us a sustainable, thriving community where they can live healthfully, work productively, learn, teach, grow old, and choose their own path."[41]

One more project that would make a huge impact on the region is this: In 2012, a group of scientists and engineers from Stanford, Cornell, University of California at Davis, and some private consultants published a study that would:

Convert New York State's (NYS's) all-purpose (for electricity, transportation, heating/cooling, and industry) energy infrastructure to one derived entirely from wind, water, and sunlight (WWS) generating electricity and electrolytic hydrogen. Under the plan, NYS's 2030 all-purpose end-use power would be provided by 10% onshore wind (4020 5-MW turbines), 40% offshore wind (12,700 5-MW turbines), 10% concentrated solar (387 100-MW plants), 10% solar-PV plants (828 50-MW plants), 6% residential rooftop PV (5 million 5-kW systems), 12% commercial/government rooftop PV (500,000 100-kW systems), 5% geothermal (36 100-MW plants), 0.5% wave (1910 0.75-MW devices), 1% tidal (2600 1-MW turbines), and 5.5% hydroelectric (6.6 1300-MW plants, of which 89% exist). The conversion would reduce NYS's end-use power demand 37% and stabilize energy prices since fuel costs would be zero. It would create more jobs than lost because nearly all NYS energy would now be produced in-state. NYS air pollution mortality and its costs would decline by 4000 (1200–7600) deaths/yr, and $33 (10–76) billion/yr (3% of 2010 NYS GDP), respectively, alone repaying the 271 GW installed power needed within 17 years, before accounting for electricity sales. NYS's own emission decreases would reduce 2050 U.S. climate costs by $3.2 billion/yr.[42]

What are we waiting for?

Critics of renewables will complain that the energy from those sources is very expensive and heavily subsidized. This is currently true to some extent and with some exceptions but is largely the result of supply and demand—when demand increases, prices will come down. But more importantly, as pointed out by Jay Burney earlier, the costs of fossil fuels are often externalized and not factored into the end product, the energy that the consumer pays for. *Economist* magazine agrees, "Private insurers say that last year was the second most expensive in American history for disasters related to climate change, costing them $139 billion. The private insurance paid only a quarter of these costs, leaving taxpayers to cover the rest. By comparison, funding renewable energy properly seems rather cheap."[43]

Climate change will eventually force all the economies of the U.S. to convert to renewable sources. Imagine the competitive advantage it would give New York State to be the first? The advantages are not only environmental; the abstract above cites positive improvements in human health and economic capital. These scientists are certain such a project is practical, doable, and within reach. What are we waiting for? Say "no" to hydrofracking and let's move on to the future.

Another doable campaign would be to reforest our region: Increase the canopy cover to surpass the national urban average or even shoot for being first in the nation. Other options for greening our city as well:

- Vertical gardens or living walls are becoming more popular in Asia, Europe, and even Australia.

- Green roofs are taking off in cities like Chicago and Toronto.

The benefits of planting more trees are numerous: more trees equal cleaner air equals healthier people because trees catch airborne pollutants; trees increase property values by creating windbreaks which lower heating bills, summer shade which lowers cooling bills, privacy, and aesthetics which make properties more attractive. More trees equal cleaner water by retaining a great deal more rain than lawns and helping keep storm water from going down the sewers which result in overflows; plus, trees attract birds which eat insect pests. How can we do it? This could be another social capital experiment similar to what is being done by ReTree now. By asking landowners/homeowners to plant the maximum number of trees on their property; on public lands, having municipalities provide materials and citizens provide labor; and requiring this as community service for people convicted of minor crimes.

AFTERWARD

There's been some good news in Buffalo Niagara lately: unprecedented levels of construction resulting, in part, from unprecedented levels of support from the state's governor; the startup of high-tech, state-of-the-art industry on a former steel plant brownfield; consolidation of hospitals, research facilities, and medical school into a spanking new campus; construction of new buildings, hotels, and attractions in the Buffalo and Niagara Falls downtown cores; a downturn in unemployment and crime; an optimistic forecast for the region's population; and more. So much good news that it has community leaders caught up in an epidemic of self-congratulations and citizens euphoric about a renaissance, turnaround, and revival.

But the truth is that this good news only describes part of the whole community. The real story is that most of those developments apply only to one part, economic capital, of the whole community and the other parts—human, social, and environmental capital—are largely untouched:

• Our toxic waste sites continue to grow;

• Our Great Lakes freshwater supply continues to be polluted;

• The long-term trend for our population is to fail to attract new people to the area;

• The health of our population remains below average;

- Our education system is in considerable need of improvement; *at the least*

- As sprawl worsens it consumes farmland, increases costs of living, and weakens our economic power;

- And in virtually every indicator of social capital, "the city of good neighbors" is below average compared to the rest of the state and the nation.

The real story is that some of the positive developments fail to address or change the fundamental forces that have contributed to our decline and will continue to block us from reaching our potential.

One of these forces is sprawl and segregation, moving apart from our regional neighbors. The lines that we draw are arbitrary and artificial. The lines in our minds are paper barriers which are ignored by the flows of air, water, land, people, and economy. They reveal a population that has not learned the universal lesson of humanity best expressed by John Donne's Meditation XVII: "No man is an island, entire of it self; every man is a piece of the Continent, a part of the main…"

Yet the people continue to persist in this insular behavior and stubbornly defend their tiny boundaries. Twice in the last year a village voted to oppose a merger with the surrounding town. Other forces include traditional leadership that has failed to adapt to changing global conditions, whose primary purpose is to serve their self-interest, and whose major success is to perpetuate their own rule. Our economy idles, held back by burdensome state mandates, regulations, and taxation and by a population that collectively thinks small.

Do Western New York's leaders play like a team? No, it's the executives against the legislature; legislators vs. legislators; Democrats vs. Republicans. Self-righteous citizens are no better: talk show hosts vs. public figures, unions vs. non-unions, public-sector unions vs. the taxpayers, suburbs vs. suburbs vs. city, black vs. white, well-off vs. poor. When do we start behaving as a team and work as one?

There are fewer businesses today, fewer structures, and a smaller tax base. The population dwindles every day. Back to Donne again: Any man's leaving diminishes us because we are involved in mankind. Therefore do not wonder for whom the bell is tolling, it tolls for us.

Not to worry, folks. If we don't get together and act in a united way, we won't perish. Western New York won't die. We will muddle through, limp along, and wallow in mediocrity. We will survive. But surviving is not thriving. Do you know the difference? Wouldn't we all rather thrive? To grow, to thrive, we must unite. We must act as one community with all working in the same direction.

We have world-class assets: the Great Lakes, the Niagara River, Niagara Falls, fertile soil and a favorable growing climate; a climate that will grow increasingly attractive as the globe warms, seas rise, and weather events intensify. We have an unprecedented opportunity to create a new, innovatively built environment on a blank canvas. Global forces, such as climate change and its refugees, will work in our favor. We have what it takes right here, right now. We have the potential to take this mediocre metro and make it a world-class region again, all within a relatively short time. Keep in mind that in the 1950s, Toronto was smaller than metro Buffalo and, today, it has grown to the fourteenth most globally significant city in the world.

We can do better than that.

NOTES

PREFACE

1. Thomas DeSantis interview April 3, 2014

2. Cara Matteliano interview April 8, 2014

3. *Underperforming histories...* From: "Bigger cities do more with less: new science reveals why cities become more productive and efficient as they grow, by Luis M. A. Bettencourt and Geoffrey B. West, *Scientific American*, September 2011, page 52.

4. Sam Magavern interview May 7, 2014

5. Paul Wolf interview February 22, 2014

INTRODUCTION

1. The Niagara Book by W.D. Howells, Mark Twain, Nathaniel S. Shaler, and others; New and revised edition, New York : Doubleday, Page, c1901.

2. *A T Kearney's Global Cities Index...* http://www.atkearney.com/research-studies/global-cities-index/full-report, accessed 8/2/14.

3. *shrinking to greatness...* "Can Buffalo ever come back?", Edward Glaeser, http://www.city-journal.org/html/17_4_buffalo_ny.html, accessed 7/26/14.

4. Sam Magavern interview May 7, 2014

5. Ibid.

6. "While Western New York stands still, the world passes us by", Kevin Gaughan, *Buffalo News*, July 10, 2011, page G1

7. Sam Magavern interview May 7, 2014

PART ONE

1. Marlies Wesolowski interview February 5, 2014
2. Cara Matteliano interview April 8, 2014
3. *Sperlings Best Places to Live*, http://www.bestplaces.net/rankings/city/new_york/buffalo
4. *A healthy city is one that is continually...* From: the WHO document WHO/HPR/HEP/98.1, www.who.int/entity/healthpromotion/about/HPR%20Glossary%201998.pdf, accessed January 18, 2014.
5. Philip Haberstro interview January 17, 2014.
6. *Experts in 'alternative economics' have long suggested...* From: Building Community Capital, slide 5, a Powerpoint presentation by Dr. Trevor Hancock, which can be downloaded from: http://www.healthycities.ncku.edu.tw, accessed January 25, 2014.

Hancock as some

CHAPTER ONE

1. *Human capital—the end: educated...* From: Building Community Capital, slides 15 & 26, a Powerpoint presentation by Dr. Trevor Hancock, which can be downloaded from: http://www.healthycities.ncku.edu.tw, accessed January 25, 2014.
2. *City rankings can be found in* Statistical Abstracts of the United States, 1912, 1922, and 1931, census.gov.
3. *of the top 100 metro areas in the US, only 8 had lost population...* From: http://www.brookings.edu/about/programs/metro/stateofmetroamerica/profile?fips=15380#/?fips=15380&viewfips=15380&subject=7&ind=70&year=2010&geo=metro , accessed June 2, 2014.
4. *The situation is actually worse than first glance...* Births and deaths from: Vital Statistics for New York State 2009: http://www.health.ny.gov/statistics/vital_statistics/2009/table53.htm
5. *I find it very hard to read anything into it...* "Population Stabilizes after years of losses", Jay Rey, *Buffalo News*, 6/13/13, A1.
6. *"A brain drain or insufficient brain gain?"* Richard Deitz, *Upstate New York At-A-Glance*, No. 2, August 2007, http://www.newyorkfed.org/research/regional_economy/glance/upstate_glance1_07.pdf, accessed 5/19/14.
7. Ibid.
8. Ibid.
9. Ibid.
10. *A USA Today article which analyzed census data...* From: "Interstate Migration Still Sluggish," Greg Toppo and Paul Overberg, USA Today, 1/24/14, page 3A,

http://www.usatoday.com/story/news/nation/2014/01/23/census-deaths-births-population/4793105/, accessed 7/16/14.

11. *In a study on Americans interstate moves...* From: State Taxes Have Negligible Impact On Americans' Interstate Moves, Michael Mazerov, Center on Budget and Policy Priorities, 2014, http://www.cbpp.org/cms/index.cfm?fa=view&id=4141, accessed 7/16/14.

12. *an annual study performed by the Atlas Van lines...* From: 2013 migration patterns, Atlas Van lines, http://www.atlasvanlines.com/migration-patterns/, accessed 7/16/14.

13. "Bright lights, big cities win new grads", *USA Today*, May 15, 2013, 3B.

14. Sam Magavern interview May 7, 2014

15. Census Bureau, American Fact Finder, factfinder.census.gov

16. *A large percentage of these refugees...* United Way 2011-2012 Community Needs Assessment, http://www.uwbec.org/documents/needs%20assessment/2011-12%20needs%20assessment%20full.pdf, accessed 6/26/14, p. 15.

17. Ibid. p. 21.

18. Ibid. p. 22.

19. Ibid. p. 22.

20. Ibid. p. 22.

21. *Disability of the population is an issue...* From: 2009-2011 American Community Survey, census.gov, accessed 6/26/14.

22. Sam Magavern interview May 7, 2014.

23. *Can Buffalo ever come back?* Edward Glaeser, http://www.city-journal.org/html/17_4_buffalo_ny.html, accessed 7/26/14.

24. Sam Magavern interview May 7, 2014

25. *Gallup Healthways Well Being Index*, http://info.healthways.com/wbi2013

26. United Health Foundation's America's Health Rankings http://www.americashealthrankings.org/NY

27. Philip Haberstro interview January 17, 2014.

28. *Gallup Healthways Well Being Index*

29. *United Health Foundation's America's Health Rankings*

30. *The Robert Wood Johnson Foundation,* http://www.countyhealthrankings.org/app/new-york/2014/overview

31. *The Commonwealth Fund, a nonprofit that studies healthcare issues...* From: Healthy System Data Ctr., Commonwealth Fund, http://datacenter.commonwealthfund.org/#ind=529/sc=38, accessed 8/20/14.

32. *American Fitness Index* the detailed report on Buffalo can be found on pp. 26 & 27, http://americanfitnessindex.org/docs/reports/acsm_2014AFI_report_final.pdf

accessed June 12, 2014.]

33. *2014-2017 Community Health Assessment for Erie County, New York* (Accessed January 6, 2014. http://www2.erie.gov/health/sites/www2.erie.gov.health/files/uploads/pdfs/CHA.pdf. Statewide health statistics can also be found on the New York State Department of Health website, https://www.health.ny.gov/statistics/chac/indicators and from: http://cdn2.hubspot.net/hub/162029/file626890356pdf/WBI2013/New_York_2013_State_Report.pdf?t=1403550789331 accessed 6/23/14.

34. *Centers for Disease Control (CDC)...* From: http://www2.erie.gov/health/sites/www2. erie.gov.health/files/uploads/pdfs/CHA.pdf, p. 23, accessed 6/26/14.

35. Marlies Wesolowski interview February 15, 2014.

36. *There has been a decline in the overall death rate...* From: Community Health Assessment for Erie County, New York, page 119

37. *the number of children experiencing abuse or maltreatment* and *Senior women often live more than a decade...* From: United Way 2011-12 Community Needs Assessment

38. *2014 Community Health Needs Assessment for Charitable Hospitals* Niagara Falls Memorial Medical Center http://www.nfmmc.org/files/2014_Community_Health_Needs_Assessment_-Niagara_Falls_Memorial_Medical_Center.pdf, accessed 6/26/14.

39. *There is a shortage of health professionals in our area...* [to find out if where you live is underserved go to http://datawarehouse.hrsa.gov/geoAdvisor/ ShortageDesignationAdvisor .aspx and type in your address.]

40. *New York State's Medicaid spending...* From: The Henry J. Kaiser Family Foundation, http://kff.org/medicaid/state-indicator/total-medicaid-spending/ accessed June 5, 2014.

41. *The health care system has less impact on public health...* From: "Building Civic Health", Environmental Health Perspectives, volume 111, number seven, June 2003.

42. *the roots of the chronic conditions that are the leading causes of morbidity and mortality can be traced to lifestyle factors...* From: Co-Occurrence of Leading Lifestyle-Related Chronic Conditions Among Adults in the United States, 2002-2009, Earl S. Ford, MD, MPH; Janet B. Croft, PhD; Samuel F. Posner, PhD; Richard A. Goodman, MD, MPH; Wayne H. Giles, MD, MSc, http://www.cdc.gov/pcd/issues/2013/12_0316.htm, accessed 7/21/14.

43. *Human capital and local economic development: it has long been recognized...* from: "The Role of Colleges and Universities in Building Local Human Capital," Jaison R. Abel and Richard Deitz, *Current Issues in Economics and Finance*, V. 17, No. 6, http://www.newyorkfed.org/research/current_issues/ci17-6.pdf, accessed 5/19/14.

44. *High school graduation rate mirror assessment scores...* From: United Way 2011-12 Community Needs Assessment.

45. Richard Deitz interview June 27, 2014.

46. *top four in enrollment are all branches of the State University of New York system...*

Source: *Buffalo Business First Book Of Lists 2013*, American City Business Journals Inc., Charlotte North Carolina, 2012, pages 69 and 70.

47. *US News And World Report College Rankings And Lists*, 2014, htp://colleges.usnews. rankingsandreviews.com/best-colleges, accessed 7/8/14.

48. Cara Matteliano interview April 8, 2014.

CHAPTER TWO

1. *Social capital represents the degree of social cohesion...* from From: Health Promotion Glossary, World Health Organization, 1998, http://www.who.int/healthpromotion/about/HPR%20Glossary%201998.pdf , p. 29, accessed 6/17/14.

2. *For Dr. Trevor Hancock social capital is...* From: Building Community Capital, slide 13, a Powerpoint presentation by Dr. Trevor Hancock, which can be downloaded from: http://www.healthycities.ncku.edu.tw, accessed January 25, 2014.

3. Ibid. slide 16.

4. *Today, however, according to the bank...* From: " Expanding the Measure of Wealth: Indicators of Environmentally Sustainable Development", environment department, the World Bank, Washington, DC, http://info.worldbank.org/etools/docs/library/110128/measure.pdf, accessed 7/21/14.

5. Philip Haberstro interview January 17, 2014.

6. *In his pioneering book on social capital...* From: http://www.bowlingalone.org/ accessed January 6, 2014. Bowling Alone: The Collapse and Revival of American Community, Robert D. Putnam, Touchstone, New York, 2000.

7. *Annie Leonard, best known for her film "The Story Of Stuff...* From: Annie Leonard interview, http://www.postcarbon.org/blog-post/2001844-annie-leonard-on-stuff-citizen-muscle, accessed 7/29/14.

8. Phil Haberstro interview January 17, 2014.

9. Sam Magavern interview May 7, 2014.

10. *turnout for presidential elections has risen from the lowest point, 1996, since World War II...* From: presidential turnout rates chart, 1948 – 2012, United States elections project, http://elections.gmu.edu/voter_turnout.htm, accessed 7/30/14.

11. *comparing state turnout rates based on voter registration is not informative...* From: United States Elections Project, George Mason University, http://elections.gmu.edu/FAQ.html#VAP?, Accessed 7/30/14.

12. *According to data compiled...* From: Volunteering and Civic Life in America 2013, http://www.volunteeringinamerica.gov accessed January 6, 2014.

13. *the American Church research project...* From: http://www.theamericanchurch.org/metro/MetroList2.htm, accessed 7/30/14.

14. *The Religion Facts website...* From: http://www.religionfacts.com/religion_statistics/church_attendance_by_state.htm, accessed 7/30/14.

15. *A Pew Research Center survey...* From: what surveys say about worship attendance – and why some stay at home, Michael Lipka, September 13, 2013, http://www.pewresearch.org/fact-tank/2013/09/13/what-surveys-say-about-worship-attendance-and-why-some-stay-home/, accessed 7/30/14.

16. *Putnam's quotes on volunteering and philanthropy* come from: Bowling Alone, Robert Putnam, Chapter 7: Altruism, Volunteering and Philanthropy, in order, page 160, pages 116-117,

17. Ibid.

18. Loren Smith interview January 18, 2014.

19. Ibid.

20. Jill Jedlicka interview January 30, 2014.

21. Ibid.

22. Cara Matteliano interview April 8, 2014.

23. Ibid.

24. Ibid.

25. Loren Smith interview January 18, 2014.

26. Putnam, p. 118.

27. Loren Smith interview January 18, 2014.

28. *Here too the region is substantially behind the national average...* From: "the facts about organ donor registration and upstate New York", Univera Health Care, https://www.univerahealthcare.com, accessed 8/26/14.

29. Putnam p. 119.

30. Ibid.

31. *Robert Putnam finds that marriage can crimp social capital...* Putnam, page 278.

32. Coming Apart, Charles Murray, Crown Forum, New York, 2012, page 158.

33. *The United Way's Community Needs Assessment describes the importance of families...* http://www.uwbec.org/needsassessment, page 11, accessed 7/30/14.

34. Marlies Wesolowski interview February 5, 2014.

35. Ibid.

CHAPTER THREE

1. *Economic capital means creation of adequate wealth...* From: Building Community Capital, slide 7, a Powerpoint presentation by Dr. Trevor Hancock, which can be downloaded from: http://www.healthycities.ncku.edu.tw, accessed January 25, 2014.

2. *2014 Prospectus edition of the Buffalo News* is From: 21st Century Attitude, Buffalo News Editors, 1/26/14, p. H4, http://www.buffalonews.com/opinion/buffalo-news-editorials/buffalos-astounding-transformation-is-wiping-away-decades-of-gloom-20140126, accessed February 4, 2014.

3. *This time, it really does feel different....* From "Dreams of Revival looking like reality," David Robinson, 1/26/14, A1, http://www.buffalonews.com/feed/signs-of-economic-revival-finally-appear-20140125, accessed February 4, 2014.

4. *So what's different this time?* from "A new Buffalo? This time it's different," Grove Potter, 1/26/14, Prospectus 2014, http://www.buffalonews.com/business/prospectus/this-buffalo-renaissance-is-different-and-we-can-all-make-it-stick-20140126, accessed February 4, 2014.

5. *The Brookings Institution ranked the top 100 metros...* from Metro Monitor - June 2014, Alec Friedhoff and Siddharth Kulkarni, Brookings Institution, http://www.brookings.edu/research/interactives/metromonitor#/M15380, accessed 7/7/14.

6. Richard Deitz interview June 27, 2014.

7. *The Western New York regional Economic Development Council's 2013 state of the region...* From Progress Report 2013, Western New York Regional Economic Development Council, September 2013.

8. *In 2012, the per capita personal income of the metro area ranked...* From BEARFACTS, Bureau of Economic Analysis Regional Fact Sheet about personal income and gross domestic product, http://www.bea.gov/regional/bearfacts/action.cfm, accessed 7/24/14.

9. *When the Buffalo News wrote about the June 2014 unemployment report...* From "Buffalo area unemployment rate drops to six percent", David Robinson, *Buffalo News,* July 23, 2014, http://www.buffalonews.com/business/buffalo-area-unemployment-rate-drops-to-6-percent-20140722, accessed 7/23/14.

10. Marlies Wesolowski interview February 5, 2014.

11. Richard Deitz interview June 27, 2014.

12. *Buffalo Niagara, like many of the Great Lakes metros had long been a blue collar community with the steel...* From: 2014-2017 Community Health Assessment, Erie County Department of Health, page 3, http://www2.erie.gov/health/sites/www2.erie.gov.health/files/uploads/pdfs/CHA.pdf, accessed 8/11/14.

13. *UB's Regional Institute did an analysis of the breakdown of the regional...* From: Who's your economy? Buffalo Niagara Labor Market Assessment 2010, UB Regional Institute, 2010,

220

http://regional-institute.buffalo.edu/wp-content/uploads/sites/3/2014/06/Whos-Your-Economy-Buffalo-Niagara-Labor-Market-Assessment.pdf, accessed 8/20/14.
Prospectus: Health Care, *Buffalo News*, January 26, 2014.
14. *In 2011 STEM jobs account for 18.5%...* From: The Hidden Stem Economy, Brookings Institution, http://www.brookings.edu/~/media/Research/Files/Reports/2013/06/10%20stem%20economy%20rothwell/pdf/Buffalo_Niagara_Falls_NY.pdf accessed June 9, 2014.
15. *Since the 1980s, employment opportunities in both the United States and the New York...* From: "Job Polarization and Rising Inequality in the Nation and the New York–Northern New Jersey Region," Jaison R. Abel and Richard Deitz, *Current Issues in Economics and Finance*, V.18, No. 7, 2012, http://www.newyorkfed.org/research/current_issues/ci18-7.pdf, accessed 5/19/2014.
16. *Looking to the future, the New York State Department of Labor projects...* From: http://labor.ny.gov/stats/lsproj.shtm, accessed 7/7/14.
17. *The New York State Department of Labor employment projections for this decade...* From: http://www.labor.ny.gov/stats/2010-2020-Fastest-Growing-Western.xls, accessed 7/7/14.
18. Thomas DeSantis interview April 3, 2014.
19. *The American Society of Civil Engineers does do a rough survey of the state of the state's infrastructure...* 2013 report card for America's infrastructure, state facts: New York, http://www.infrastructurereportcard.org/a/#p/state-facts/new-york, accessed 7/24/14.
20. *In the past 20 years, the region has added...* From: One Region Forward, November 2013 Community Congress, Scenario Planning Workshops.
21. *July 2014 Investigative Post report...* From:"huge price tag for fixing Buffalo's buildings", Jim Haney and Pamela Cyran, July 14, 2014, http://www.investigativepost.org/2014/07/14/buffalos-costly-neglect-public-buildings, accessed 7/15/14.
22. *National Association of Homebuilders Housing Opportunity Index...* http://www.nahb.org/reference_list.aspx?sectionID=135, accessed 7/27/14.
23. *Sperling's Best Places Index...* http://www.bestplaces.net/rankings/city/new_york/buffalo, accessed September 2014.
24. *Forbes 2014 most affordable city...* http://www.forbes.com/sites/erincarlyle/2014/03/11/americas-most-affordable-cities/, accessed 11/18/14.
25. PPG position papers, http://www.ppgbuffalo.org/issues/housing/, accessed September 2014.
26. Dale Zuchlewski interview Mar. 3, 2014
27. Sam Magavern interview May 7, 2014.

28. *a recent feature in the Buffalo News...* from " Bidding wars and big prices: Buffalo real estate is red hot", Jonathan D Epstein, June 14, 2014, http://www.buffalonews.com/business/real-estate/bidding-wars-and-big-prices-buffalo-real-estate-is-red-hot-20140614, accessed 6/14/14.

29. *Buffalo-Niagara has the second oldest housing stock...* From: http://www.bizjournals.com/buffalo/news/2014/08/13/which-metro-has-americas-oldest-housing-stock-not.html?ana=e_du_wknd&s=article_du&ed=2014-08-16&u=qiSEv/3jXITC4P5lLdri5c8cRBt&t=1409658789 accessed 9/2/14.

30. *According to the 2010 census, the Metro region had 45,374 vacant housing units...* From: General Housing Characteristics: 2010 Census Summary File, table QT-H1, http://factfinder2.census.gov/faces/tableservices/jsf/pages/productview.xhtml?pid=DEC_10_SF1_QTH1&prodType=table, accessed 7/28/14.

31. *new housing increased 22% while vacant or banding housing units increased...* From: one region forward, November 2013 community Congress, scenario planning workshops.

32. Marlies Wesolowski interview February 5, 2014.

33. Ibid.

34. *The city has a unique program for urban pioneers – live NF...* http://live-nf.com/live.html, accessed 7/28/14.

35. Thomas DeSantis interview April 3, 2014.

36. Ibid.

37. Philip Haberstro interview January 17, 2014.

38. Cara Matteliano interview April 8, 2014.

39. *The Gini index a measure of income inequality,...* From: http://www.nyinequality.org/, accessed 9/2/14.

40. *A Business First analysis of The Census Bureau's American Community Survey...* http://www.bizjournals.com/buffalo/news/2014/08/18/rochester-and-buffalo-both-make-list-of-nations-20.html?ana=e_du_pub&s=article_du&ed=2014-08-18&u=qiSEv/3jXITC4P5lLdri5c8cRBt&t=1409658282, accessed 9/2/14.

41. *The city of Buffalo has long been near the top of the poorest large cities in the United States...* From: A *Business First* analysis, http://www.bizjournals.com/buffalo/news/2014/06/05/rochester-buffalo-rank-among-four-u-s-cities-with.html?ana=e_du_pub&s=article_du&ed=2014-06-05&u=qiSEv/3jXITC4P5lLdri5c8cRBt&t=1402339209 accessed June 9, 2014.

42. *But poverty is not confined to the cities...*From: Confronting Suburban Poverty, http://confrontingsuburbanpoverty.org/action-toolkit/top-100-us-metros/ and http://confrontingsuburbanpoverty.org/wp-content/uploads/metro-profiles/Buffalo-NY.pdf, accessed June 9, 2014.

43. Dale Zuchlewski interview March 3, 2014
44. Ibid.
45. Marlies Wesolowski interview February 5, 2014.

CHAPTER FOUR

1. "Natural Capital: Valuing goods and services from the natural environment,"
accessed July 31, 2014, http://www.iisd.org/natres/agriculture/capital.asp.
2. "About the Natural Capital Project", accessed July 31, 2014,
http://www.naturalcapitalproject.org/about.html#mission.
3. Erie County Environmental Management Council. "2013 State of the Environment
Report," accessed July 31, 2014. At the time of printing, the 2013 report was no longer
available online but the 2014 report (which was not available for research during writing)
can be found at: http://www2.erie.gov/environment/index.php?q=environmental-
management-council.
4. Jay Burney interview January 14, 2014.
5. Loren Smith interview January 18, 2014.
6. *The American Lung Association's State of the Air 2013 Report states...* From: State of the Air,
American Lung Association, http://www.lung.org/associations/states/california/assets/
pdfs/sota-2013/sota-2013-full-report.pdf, accessed 7/31/14.
7. *Erie County is fourth highest and Niagara County is 11th highest in New York State...*
From: Scorecard The Pollution Information Site, http://scorecard.goodguide.com/env-
releases/cap/rank-counties-risk.tcl?fips_state_code=36, accessed 8/19/14.
8. Erie County Environmental Management Council. "2013 State of the Environment
Report," accessed July 31, 2014,
9. Erin Heaney interview January 16, 2014.
10. Ibid.
11. Ibid.
12. Ibid.
13. Ibid.
14. Ibid.
15. Ibid.
16. Jill Jedlicka interview January 30, 2014.
17. Ibid.
18. Ibid.
19. Ibid.

20. Ibid.

21. Jay Burney interview January 14, 2014.

22. Ibid.

23. Ibid.

24. "Sustainability 101: Are we growing enough food in our region?", accessed 11/7/13, http://www.oneregionforward.org/datastory/arewegrowing-enough-food-in-our-region/.

25. *WNY is a rich agricultural region within one of the nation's top producing states...*
From: http://regionalcouncils.ny.gov/sites/default/files/regions/westernny/wny-2013-Progress%20Report.pdf, p.68, accessed 11/19/14.

26. *Data for Buffalo show the city's park acreage below the national averages...*
From: http://cloud.tpl.org/pubs/ccpe_Acreage_and_Employees_Data_2010.pdf

27. *More importantly than parkland is the amount of tree cover that our built environment has...*
http://www.systemecology.com/4_Past_Projects/AF_Buffalo.pdf, accessed 8/19/14.
Data on other cities comes from: http://www.deeproot.com/blog/blog-entries/tree-cover-how-does-your-city-measure-up, accessed 8/19/14.

28. Ibid.

29. *"Mapping Waste: Setting The Stage To Clean Up The Niagara"*, Prepared for the Community Foundation for Greater Buffalo and the Waste and Pollution Working Group of the Western New York Environmental Alliance by the Urban Design Project, UB, revised December, 2012, http://www.growwny.org/waste-pollution/, accessed 7/31/14.

30. Ibid.

31. Ibid.

32. Lynda Schneekloth interview February 6, 2014.

33. Ibid.

34. Martin Doster interview January 20, 2014.

35. Ibid.

36. Ibid.

37. Ibid.

38. Ibid.

39. Ibid.

40. Ibid.

41. Ibid.

42. Loren Smith interview January 18, 2014.

43. Ibid.

44. Ibid.

45. *Carbon footprint...* From: Blueprint for American Prosperity: Unleashing The Potential

Of A Metropolitan Nation, Brookings Institution, http://www.brookings.edu/~/media/research/files/reports/2008/6/metropolicy/06_metropolicy_100metroprofiles.pdf, accessed 7/7/14.

46. Jay Burney interview January 15, 2014.

47. Ibid.

48. Jill Jedlicka interview January 30, 2014.

49. Ibid.

50. Ibid.

51. Ibid.

52. Lynda Schneekloth interview February 6, 2014.

53. Ibid.

54. Ibid.

55. Erin Heaney interview January 16, 2014.

PART TWO

1. Musings of a Cigarette Smoking Man, X-Files, Season 4 (1996–97), written by Glen Morgan, original air date November 17, 1996.

2. "Buffalo and Bills get spook-proofed: the curse is lifted, is medium's message", by Harold McNeil and Matthew Spina, *Buffalo News*, January 27, 2008, B1.

3. *a kindly engineer from the Snowbelt made the Sunbelt boom....* from: "King of Cool: Willis Carrier", Molly Ivins, Time, V. 152, N. 23, December 7, 1998, p. 109.

4. *From 1950 to 1960, the population of the city itself dropped 8.2%, but the population of the region increased by 20% and the population outside the central city increased by 52.1%...* From: 1961 Statistical Abstract, 1961.02 pdf, p. 14/87, Table No. 10.

5. *An important provision of the G.I. Bill was low interest, zero-down-payment home loans for servicemen...* From: GI Bill: http://en.wikipedia.org/wiki/GI_bill, accessed June 12, 2014.

6. *Many Buffalonians attributed manufacturing's decline primarily to two events...* Power Failure, Diana Dillaway, pages 26 following.

7. *By September 1945 the 40,000 people working at Curtiss-Wright has been reduced to 5,500...* from:History of Buffalo website, Glenn Curtiss in Buffalo, NY, http://www.buffaloah.com/h/aero/curt/#Anchor accessed June 12, 2014

8. *freight carried on the Great Lakes waterways declined...* From:1991 Statistical Abstract, 1991-06.pdf, Section 22, table No. 1092 and 2012 statistical abstract, table 1084, freight carried on major US waterways, http://www.census.gov/compendia/statab/cats/transportation/water_transportation.html, accessed 8/1/14.

CHAPTER FIVE

1. *The world is undergoing the largest wave of urban growth in history...* From: "Urbanization: a majority in cities", United Nations Population Fund website, http://www.unfpa.org/pds/urbanization.htm, accessed 8/1/14.

2. *Many experts have come to realize that people are better off when they live in a city...* From: "Street savvy, meeting the biggest challenges starts with the city, by the editors, *Scientific American*, September 2011, page 39.

3. *Americans' growing love affair with cities shows few signs of abating...* From: "Will this be the 'Decade of the City'?", USA Today, 5/22/14, p. 4A.

4. *More than half of Metropolitan Seoul's (South Korea) 24 million residents live in high-rises...* from: The City Solution: Why cities are the best cure for our planet's growing pains, Robert Kunzig, *National Geographic*, December 2011, page 125

5. *A T Kearney's Global Cities Index...* http://www.atkearney.com/research-studies/global-cities-index/full-report, accessed 8/2/14.

6. *Why, then, do people throughout the world keep leaving the countryside for the town?...* From: "Bigger cities do more with less: new science reveals why cities become more productive and efficient as they grow", by Luis M. A. Bettencourt and Geoffrey B West, *Scientific American*, September 2011, page 52.

7. Ibid.

8. *Harvard economist Edward Glaeser has this point of view...* from: The City Solution: Why cities are the best cure for our planet's growing pains, Robert Kunzig, *National Geographic*, December 2011, page 133.

9. *National Geographic published an article arguing why cities...* Ibid. page 125

10. Ibid.

11. Ibid.

12. *Many people see social relationships is either private or public....* From: "Problems with mistaking community life for public life", Michael Brill, Places, 14:2, page 48.

13. Ibid.

14. *Robert Putnam considers mobility and sprawl...* Bowling Alone, Robert D. Putnam, page 205.

15. *Between 1980 and 2000, the Buffalo metro area consumed 4.03 acres of rural land...* From: Blueprint for American Prosperity: Unleashing The Potential Of A Metropolitan Nation, Brookings Institution, http://www.brookings.edu/~/media/research/files/reports/2008/6/metropolicy/06_metropolicy_100metroprofiles.pdf, accessed 7/7/14.

16. *One of the results of this sprawl is the fact that Erie County maintains more miles of road...* From: "Erie County paves the way to rid itself of some roads", Jay Rey, Buffalo News, 5/10/14, page A1.

17. *The organization Smart Growth America does an annual study...* From: Measuring Sprawl 2014, Smart Growth America, Washington, DC, http://www.smartgrowthamerica.org/measuring-sprawl, accessed 7/15/14.

18. Ibid.

19. *only one of 16 in the United States that has an incorporated place with a density of over 10,000...* http://en.wikipedia.org/wiki/List_of_United_States_cities_by_population_density, accessed January 11, 2014.

20. *Although they have their problems, urban areas continue to lure new residents...* From: "In Fairness To Cities: the US needs to level the playing field between city, suburb and countryside", by the Editors, *Scientific American*, September 2011, page 14.

21. *Well-run modern cities have demonstrated...* From: "Bigger cities do more with less: new science reveals why cities become more productive and efficient as they grow", by Luis M. A. Bettencourt and Geoffrey B West, *Scientific American*, September 2011, page 52.

22. *UB professor Uriel Halbreich expressed it well in a Buffalo News article...* "Growing Buffalo", Uriel Halbreich, *Buffalo News*, October 10, 2010, page G1.

23. Cara Matteliano interview April 8, 2014.

24. *The public life is morally deficient for three reasons...* From: "Problems with mistaking community life for public life", Michael Brill, Places, 14:2, page 48.

25. Ibid.

26. Sam Magavern interview

27. Ibid.

28. *Kevin Gaughan presented research comparing the number of school districts...* From: "while Western New York standstill, the world passes us by", Kevin Gaughan, *Buffalo News*, July 10, 2011, page G1.

29. *A total of 37,297 Erie County residents live in the Census Tracts considered to be food deserts...* http://www.uwbec.org/documents/needs%20assessment/2011-12%20needs%20assessment%20full.pdf, p. 144, accessed 6/26/14.

30. From: Western New York Regional Economic Development Council Progress Report 2013, http://regionalcouncils.ny.gov/sites/default/files/regions/westernny/wny-2013-Progress%20Report.pdf, accessed 7/15/14.

Chapter Six

1. Robert Shibley interview August 2012.

2. Ibid.

3. *The story at this point sounds like that of most other cities...* from: Power Failure: Politics, Patronage, and the Economic Future of Buffalo, New York, Diana Dillaway, Prometheus Books, Amherst, New York, 2006, page 16.

4. Ibid. p. 18.

5. Ibid. p. 15.

6. Ibid. p. 40.

7. Ibid. p. 14.

8. Ibid. p. 47.

9. Ibid. p. 152.

10. *Bankers are risk-averse and they have no imagination...* Rocco Termini speaking at an Entrepreneurship workshop, Medaille College, November 14, 2013.

11. Dillaway, p. 198.

12. Ibid. p. 15.

13. Ibid. p. 45.

14. Ibid. p. 138.

15. Ibid. p. 107

16. Ibid. p. 140.

17. Ibid. p. 140.

18. Ibid. p. 177.

19. Ibid. p. 33.

20. Ibid. p. 34.

21. Ibid. p. 107.

22. *Leadership takes courage and willingness to risk change...* Dillaway page 13.

23. Thomas DeSantis interview April 4, 2014.

24. Dillaway p. 13.

25. Ibid. p. 58

26. Ibid. p. 29.

27. Ibid. p. 54.

28. Ibid. p. 58.

29. Ibid. p. 97.

30. Ibid. p. 98.

31. Ibid. p. 98.

32. Ibid. p. 66.

33. Ibid. p. 69.

34. Ibid. p. 77.

35. Ibid. p. 77.

36. Paul Wolf interview February 22, 2014. Exposure of the failures of regional politics continues with the work of Paul Wolf on his excellent website, reinventinggov.org. There are many excellent essays and articles, and he also contributes occasionally to *Artvoice*. His essay, "Patronage and Corporate Welfare", Paul Wolf, *Artvoice*, issue v12n50, 12/12/2013, provides the reader with an investigation of how politics are currently conducted. All the following quotes attributed to Wolf come from that interview.

37. Philip Haberstro interview January 17, 2014.

38. Ibid.

39. Marlies Wesolowski interview February 5, 2014.

40. Ibid.

Chapter Seven

1. *When so many cities are booming, why are some in decline?...* From: "Brains over buildings: to rejuvenate urban centers, look to teachers and entrepreneurs, Edward Glaeser, *Scientific American*, September 2011, page 64.

2. Richard Deitz interview June 27, 2014.

3. *A Cornell University expert says state policies are making it harder for upstate...* From: "Are Albany policies starving upstate New York's cities", Ryan Delaney, http://www.northcountry-publicradio.org/news/story/24560/20140410/are-albany-policies-starving-upstate-ny-cities, accessed 7/15/14.

4. Ibid.

5. Paul Wolf interview February 22, 2014.

6. Ibid.

7. Delaney article.

8. *In a CNBC study, on the top states for doing business...* http://www.cnbc.com/id/101758236 http://www.cnbc.com/id/101723185 and http://money.msn.com/investing/americas-worst-states-for-business

9. *Forbes ranks the Buffalo metro area 75th out of 100...* http://www.forbes.com/best-places-for-business/#page:1_sort:0_direction:asc_search:buffalo%2C%20ny_filter:All%20states

10. *New York State has the highest state and local tax burden of all the states...* New York State taxes: state tax rankings, business tax climate data come from the Tax Foundation studies http://taxfoundation.org/state-tax-climate/new-york, http://taxfoundation.org/article/new-

yorks-state-and-local-tax-burden, http://taxfoundation.org/sites/taxfoundation.org/files
/docs/2014%20State%20Business%20Tax%20Climate%20Index.pdf, and
http://taxfoundation.org/article/2013-state-business-tax-climate-index-results accessed
June 12, 2014.

11. *In a study done by the Center for Budget and Policy Priorities...* "state taxes have a negligible
impact on Americans' interstate moves," Michael Nazarov, Center on Budget and Policy
Priorities, May 21, 2014, http://www.cbpp.org/cms/index.cfm?fa=view&id=4141, accessed
7/16/1412.

12. Ibid.

13. *The Tax Foundation's response:* From: The Facts on Interstate Migration, Lyman Stone,
Tax Foundation, May 13, 2014, http://taxfoundation.org/blog/facts-interstate-migration-
part-two, accessed 7/16/14.

14. Ibid.

15. Ibid.

16. Sam Magavern interview May 7, 2014.

17. Ibid.

18. Ibid.

19. *Research suggests that job opportunities and local amenities influence choice of location...*
From: "A brain drain or insufficient brain gain?", Upstate New York at a Glance, May 2007,
http://www.newyorkfed.org/research/regional_economy/glance/upstate_glance1_07.pdf,
accessed November 2014.

20. Marlies Wesolowski interview February 5, 2014.

21. *Similarly, strategic planning in the eight-county Western New York region proved difficult...*
From: Power Failure, Diana Dillaway, page 37.

22. *A 2007 study summarized their effect on the region...* "Sprawling by the Lake: How IDA-
Granted Property Tax Exemptions Undermine Older Parts of the Buffalo/Niagara Metro
Area", Allison Lack, Good Jobs First, funded by the Ford Foundation, May 2007,
http://www.goodjobsfirst.org/sites/default/files/docs/pdf/buffalosprawl.pdf, accessed 8/4/14.

23. *Architecture critic Jane Jacobs once wrote...* "Cities and the wealth of Nations: principles of
economic life, New York: Random House, 1984, p. 193.

24. *In her research and interviews, Diana Dillaway found...* Power Failure, Diana Dillaway,
p. 197.

25. Ibid. 165.

26. *The New York State Authorities Budget Office report...* Annual Report on Public
Authorities in New York State, New York State Authorities Budget Office, July 1, 2013,
http://www.abo.ny.gov/reports/annualreports/ABO2013AnnualReport.pdf, accessed 8/4/14.

27. *But reporting is not always accurate, and the two IDA's faulted the report...* "State audit goofed on counting of IDA jobs", David Robinson, Buffalo News, July 13, 2013, http://www.buffalonews.com/apps/pbcs.dll/article?AID=/20130713/BUSINESS/130719566, accessed 8/4/14.

28. *An excellent example of the IDA process gone bad can be found in a report...* From: "Delaware North's endless subsidies", Jim Heaney, Investigative Post, November 26, 2014, http://www.investigativepost.org/2013/11/26/delaware-norths-endless-subsidies/, accessed 8/20/14.

29. Ibid.

30. Paul Wolf interview February 22, 2014.

31. Sam Magavern interview May 7, 2014.

32. Ibid.

33. *Jonathan Epstein of the Buffalo News analyzed the effect of all the new construction downtown...* "New office demand creates vacancy woes", Jonathan D Epstein, *Buffalo News*, November 17, 2013, http://www.buffalonews.com/business/new-office-demand-creates-vacancy-woes-20131117, accessed 8/4/14.

34. Sam Magavern interview May 7, 2014.

35. Ibid.

36. *In a Buffalo News article, reporter Denise Jewell Gee...* "Private colleges get creative as pool of potential students shrinks", Denise Jewell Gee, *Buffalo News*, January 26, 2014, http://www.buffalonews.com/business/prospectus/private-colleges-get-creative-as-pool-of-potential-students-shrinks-20140126, accessed 7/14/14.

37. Ibid.

38. Ibid.

39. Ibid.

40. *In a special supplement before the school budget votes of May 2014...* From: "Special Report: Your Schools, Your Vote", *Buffalo News*, May 18, 2014, S1.

41. *The trend for college graduates to be unemployed or underemployed...* From: Regional Economic Press Briefing, Federal Reserve Bank of New York, June 27, 2013.

42. Richard Deitz interview June 27, 2014.

43. Thomas DeSantis interview April 3, 2014.

44. *The Buffalo Niagara Medical Campus has been the site of more than $1 billion...* From: "Measuring Success", Dan Miner, *Buffalo Business First*, January 25, 2013, http://www.bizjournals.com/buffalo/print-edition/2013/01/25/measuring-success.html?page=all, accessed 8/4/14.

45. Cara Matteliano interview April 8, 2014.

46. *Writer Aaron Renn...* From: "The end of the road for eds and meds", Aaron Renn, *New Geography*, 9/12/12, http://www.newgeography.com/content/003076-the-end-road-eds-and-meds, accessed 8/5/14.

47. *Duke economist Aaron Chatterji wrote...* From: "the bad news for local job markets", Aaron Chatterji, New York Times, October 24, 2013, http://www.nytimes.com/2013/10/25/opinion/the-bad-news-for-local-job-markets.html?_r=1&, accessed 8/5/14.

48. *Urbanist Richard Florida calls out Buffalo and Rochester...* From: "Where edge and meds industries could become a liability", Richard Florida, November 26, 2013, http://www.citylab.com/work/2013/11/where-reliance-eds-and-meds-industries-could-become-liability/7661/, accessed 8/5/14.

49. *Dr. Trevor Hancock agrees...* From: Building Community Capital, slide 28, a Powerpoint presentation by Dr. Trevor Hancock, which can be downloaded from: http://www.healthycities.ncku.edu.tw, accessed January 25, 2014.

CHAPTER EIGHT

1. *A T Kearney Global Cities Index...* http://www.atkearney.com/research-studies/global-cities-index/full-report#sthash.QxCihShJ.dpuf

2. Martin Doster interview January 20, 2014.

3. Lynda Schneekloth interview February 6, 2014.

4. Martin Doster interview January 20, 2014.

5. Ibid.

6. Ibid.

7. Jill Jedlicka interview January 30, 2014.

8. Erin Heaney interview January 16, 2014.

9. Lynda Schneekloth interview February 6, 2014.

10. Ibid.

11. Jill Jedlicka interview January 30, 2014.

12. The Future: Six Drivers Of Global Change, Al Gore, Random House, New York, 2013, p. 104.

13. Ibid. p. 314.

14. Ibid. p. 365.

15. That used to be us: how America fell behind in the world it invented and how we can come back", Thomas L Friedman and Michael Mandelbaum, Picador/Farrar, Straus and Giroux, New York, 2011.

16. *Many supporters of democratic self-governance are placing their hopes...* Gore, page 57.

17. Jay Burney interview January 15, 2014.

18. Ibid.
19. *In 2011, the US had eight climate-related disasters, each costing over $1 billion...* Gore, page 346.
20. *in every deliberation, we must consider the impact on the seventh generation...* I was unable to find a precise quotation so I had to paraphrase from several sources. The reader is encouraged to research it him or herself beginning with http://nativeinsight.blogspot.com/2012/11/seventh-generation.html, accessed 8/7/14.
21. Lynda Schneekloth interview February 6, 2014.
22. Erin Heaney interview January 16, 2014.
23. Ibid.
24. Lynda Schneekloth interview February 6, 2014.
25. Ibid.
26. Martin Doster interview January 20, 2014.
27. Ibid.
28. Jay Burney interview January 15, 2014.
29. Ibid.
30. Ibid.
31. Ibid.
32. Ibid.
33. Ibid.
34. Ibid.
35. Ibid.
36. Loren Smith interview January 18, 2014.
37. Richard Deitz interview June 27, 2014.

PART THREE

1. Thomas DeSantis interview April 4, 2014
2. Cara Matteliano interview April 8, 2014.
3. *Business First Journals did a study in 2011...* http://www.bizjournals.com/bizjournals/on-numbers/scott-thomas/2011/08/denver-is-most-overextended-market.html?appSession=244136768308876&RecordID=&PageID=2&PrevPageID=&cpipage=2&CPISortType=&CPIorderBy=, accessed 8/7/14.
4. *Sporting News used to rank the Best Sports Cities...* http://www.sportingnews.com/sport/vs-tory/2011-10-04/best-sports-cities-the-list-from-1-to-271

5. *Forbes ranks Buffalo fourth-most miserable sports city in America...* http://www.forbes.com/pictures/eddf45lhjf/where-they-let-the-fans-down-the-most/, accessed 8/7/14.

6. *The Buffalo News reported that, when it comes to revenue...* From: "Why the NFL wants a new stadium", Jerry Zremski, *Buffalo News*, August 24, 2014, page A1.

7. *the worst weather NFL city....* http://www.weather.com/sports-rec/5-best-worst-weather-nfl-cities-20130907?pageno=6, accessed 8/7/14.

8. *the list of notable cable-stayed bridges....* From: http://en.wikipedia.org/wiki/Cable-stayed_bridge, accessed 8/7/14.

9. Sam Magavern interview May 7, 2014.

10. *about the regional plan for sustainable development...* From: http://uploads.oneregionforward.org/content/uploads/2014/04/Session1_Toolkit_Handout.pdf, pp. 1 & 2.

11. *In presenting "A New Capitalism for the 21st Century...* From: Building Community Capital, slide 28, a Powerpoint presentation by Dr. Trevor Hancock, which can be downloaded from: http://www.healthycities.ncku.edu.tw, accessed January 25, 2014.

12. Sam Magavern interview May 7, 2014.

13. Phil Haberstro interview January 17, 2014.

CHAPTER NINE

1. *In July 1905, Negro-American members of the conference known as the Niagara movement...* From: From: http: www.Yale.edu/GLC/archive/1152.htm.

2. *Activist filmmaker Annie Leonard explains how we can do it....* From: http://www.postcarbon.org/blog-post/2001844-annie-leonard-on-stuff-citizen-muscle, accessed 8/8/14.

3. Ibid.

4. Ibid.

5. *we, the people of Western New York, are resolved to work...* From: Enhancing And Leveraging Significant Natural Resources, Community Impact Report, Community Foundation For Greater Buffalo, fall 2009, page 3.

6. Marlies Wesolowski interview February 5, 2014.

7. Ibid.

8. *Experts predict that the sea level along the USA's east coast...* from: "Storm of the Century Every Two Years", *Scientific American*, Mark Fischetti, June 2013, p. 59.

9. Jay Burney interview January, 2014.

10. *With poor diet and physical inactivity fast becoming two of the leading preventable causes of death in America...* From: 2014-2017 Community Health Assessment, Erie County Depart-

ment of Health, p. 37, http://www2.erie.gov/health/sites/www2.erie.gov.health/files/
uploads/pdfs/CHA.pdf, accessed 8/11/14.

11. *Reduction in teen pregnancy is critical as for every dollar spent in family planning, four dollars are saved...* Ibid. p. 35,

12. *Teen pregnancy can have serious consequences...* Ibid. page 33.

13. *Since the first Surgeon General's report and causing more than 440,000 deaths each year...* Ibid. page 107

14. *This area is also famous for its chicken wings. This could be considered a staple for many families....* Ibid. page 130.

15. *The federal Centers for Disease Control and Prevention...* Ibid. page 45.

16. *Wikipedia has a list of the cities with the most pedestrian commuters...* From: http://en.wikipedia.org/wiki/List_of_U.S._cities_with_most_pedestrian_commuters, accessed 8/8/14.

17. *The website WalkScore.com...* http://www.walkscore.com/NY/Buffalo, accessed 8/8/14.

18. *Data on the One Region Forward website confirm this...* http://www.oneregionforward.org/datastory/what-would-buffalo-niagara-look-like-if-we-stay-on-the-current-path/, accessed 8/8/14.

19. *Western New York has far fewer school districts today than it did a century ago...* In a UB Regional Institute Policy Brief, June 2009, "School Limits: Probing the Boundaries of Public Education", From: http://regional-institute.buffalo.edu/research/series.cfm? ID=63 &Series=19 , accessed January 6, 2014.

20. *A Buffalo News analysis of state Education Department data show...* From: "School districts studying options: Merge or close?", Denise Jewell Gee, *Buffalo News*, March 9, 2014. Cheektowaga census data from American Fact Finder.

21. *In a Business First ranking of the region's 97 school districts...* From: http://www.bizjournals.com/buffalo/feature/schools/2013-wnyschools/2013/06/western-new-york-school-district.html?page=all, accessed 8/11/14.

22. *A challenge for all districts, and the region, lies in knowing when to centralize...* Policy Brief, June 2009, University at Buffalo Regional Institute.

23. *Kevin Gaughan presented a chart comparing the number of school districts...* From his website letpeopledecide.org, http://www.letpeopledecide.org/KPG.school.district. consolidation. chart.2.5.9.pdf, accessed 8/11/14.

24. *it was reported that three of the regions school districts...* From: Fiscal Stress Monitoring System CY 2013, Office of the New York State Comptroller, http://osc.state.ny.us/localgov/fiscalmonitoring/pdf/schools/schools_summary_lists.pdf, accessed 7/21/14.

25. Marlies Wesolowski interview February 5, 2014.

26. *New York State had the highest spending per pupil...*
http://www2.census.gov/govs/school/current_spending.pdf, accessed 8/10/14.

27. *Buffalo public schools spending per pupil, $26,903, was third-highest...* From: Center for Governmental Research, http://www.cgr.org/docs/PressReleaseLargeSchoolDistricts Spending2010.pdf, accessed 8/10/14.

28. Pupil/teacher ratio and National Assessment of Educational Progress,
http://nces.ed.gov/programs/stateprofiles/sresult.asp?mode=short&s1=36, accessed 8/10/14.

CHAPTER TEN

1. *America has civically reinvented itself before...* From: http://www.bowlingalone.org/ accessed January 6, 2014.

2. *BetterTogether is an initiative of the Saguaro Seminar...*
From: http://www.bettertogether.org/ accessed January 6, 2014.

3. Ibid.

4. *Annie Leonard: our "citizen muscle,"...* From: "Annie Leonard's Story of Change", Daniel Noll, Triple Pundit, October 19, 2012, http://www.triplepundit.com/2012/10/annie-leonards-story-change/, accessed 7/29/14.

5. Diana Dillaway, Power Failure, p. 211.

6. Ibid. p. 212.

7. Ibid. p. 212.

8. Ibid. p. 212.

9. Ibid. p. 26.

10. Ibid. p. 217.

11. *A paper looking at regional consolidation...* From: " Regionalism revisited: the effort to streamline governance in Buffalo and Erie County, New York",
http://www.thefreelibrary.com/Regionalism+revisited%3a+the+effort+to+streamline+governance+in+Buffalo...-a0176204448, accessed 8/20/14.

12. Paul Wolf interview February 22, 2014.

13. Ibid.

14. Sam Magavern interview May 7, 2014.

15. Ibid.

16. Dale Zuchlewski interview March 3, 2014.

17. Philip Haberstro interview January 17, 2014.

18. Cara Mattleliasno interview April 8, 2014.

19. Citizens' Vision Statement for the Erie-Niagara Region, Wellness Institute of Greater Buffalo, http://healthycommunitynetwork.com/vision-statements.html.
20. Paul Wolf interview February 22, 2014.
21. *Erie-Niagara Framework for Regional Growth*, http://www2.erie.gov/regionalframework/.
22. Lynda Schneekloth interview February 6, 2014.
23. Robert Shibley interview August 2012.
24. Thomas DeSantis interview April 3, 2014.
25. Philip Haberstro interview January 17, 2014.
26. *As part of its strategic plan, the Community Foundation for Greater Buffalo...* From: Reducing Racial and Ethnic Disparities: Community Impact Report, Community Foundation for Greater Buffalo, Winter 2009.

CHAPTER ELEVEN

1. *Top Ten Neighborhoods in the United States...* From: American Planning Association, http://www.planning.org/greatplaces/neighborhoods/2009 accessed January 11, 2014.
2. *highest rated community...* http://villageofkenmore.org/.
3. *Cities, to survive, must be capable of extended fugues of retrofitting...* From: "Life in the meta city", by William Gibson, *Scientific American*, September 2011, page 88.
4. *The Buffalo Erie Niagara Land Improvement Corporation (BENLIC) seeks to confront...* From: http://www.benlic.org/#!about/cjn9, accessed 8/13/14.
5. *The Buffalo News reports Rochester and Detroit...* From: From: "Shrinking of cities catches traction," Phil Fairbanks, *Buffalo News*, June 14, 2010, page A1.
6. *The answer to the great bones/best planned city in America story is water...* From: Robert Shibley interview August, 2012.
7. *The Sierra Club has new campaign which calls for job-creating renewable energy...* From: http://content.sierraclub.org/press-releases/2013/04/new-renewable-energy-campaign-calls-ny-gov-cuomo-lets-turn-not-burn accessed June 12, 2014
8. *Meeting the state's goal of 30% renewable energy by 2015...* NYSERDA 2013 Renewable Portfolio Standard Evaluation Report: http://www.nyserda.ny.gov/Publications/Program-Planning-Status-and-Evaluation-Reports/Renewable-Portfolio-Standard-Reports.aspx
9. *A study by some scientists from Stanford examined...* From: Examining the feasibility of converting New York State's all-purpose energy infrastructure to one using wind, water, and sunlight, Mark Z. Jacobson, Robert W. Howarth, Mark A. Delucchi, Stan R. Scobie, Jannette M. Barth, Michael J. Dvorak, Megan Klevze, Hind Katkhuda, Brian Miranda, Navid A. Chowdhury, Rick Jones, Larsen Plano, Anthony R. Ingraffea,

http://www.stanford.edu/group/efmh/jacobson/Articles/I/NewYorkWWSEnPolicy.pdf accessed June 9, 2014.

10. From: Encyclopedia of Community Planning and Environmental Management, Schultz and Kasen.

11. *Detached houses according to one calculation, can use up to five times as much energy to build and live in as an apartment of comparable area.*, from: Sustainable Cities: Concepts and Strategies for Eco-City Development, edited by Bob Walter, Lois Arkin, Richard Crenshaw, Eco-Home Media, Los Angeles, 1992, page 12.

12. *The American Planning Association...system of bonuses and dividends...* From: PAS quick notes number 12, https://www.planning.org/pas/quicknotes/pdf/QN12.pdf, accessed 8/13/14.

13. *The city of Buffalo is in the process of completing a comprehensive and strategic plan...* http://www.buffalogreencode.com/, accessed 9/4/14.

14. Thomas DeSantis interview April 3, 2014.

15. *One application for this process might be dealing with the excess of roads...* From: "Erie County paves the way to rid itself of some roads", Jay Rey, *Buffalo News*, 5/10/14, page A1.

16. "How to Build the Super Grid", Matthew L. Wald, *Scientific American*, November 2010, page 57.

17. Ibid.

18. Eastern Wind Integration and Transmission Study: Executive Summary and Project Overview, prepared by enernex Corporation, National Renewable Energy Laboratory, Golden, Colorado, February 2011, http://www.nrel.gov/docs/fy11osti/47086.pdf, accessed 7/14/14.

19. New York Energy Highway Blueprint can be found at http://www.nyenergyhighway.com/, accessed 7/14/14.

20. *High-speed rail: New York State high-speed rail Empire corridor* can be found at https://www.dot.ny.gov/empire-corridor, accessed 7/14/14. Elon Musk's proposal can be found on http://www.spacex.com/sites/spacex/files/hyperloop_alpha-20130812.pdf.

21. *High Speed Rail such as the Hyperloop proposed by Elon Musk...* From: *Popular Science*, "What would a Hyperloop nation look like?", November 2013, p. 31.

22. *75 American and Canadian citizens talked about this...* From: From: rethinking the Niagara frontier: a report on the binational forum, March 30 and 31, 2000 the Urban Design Project, School of Architecture and Planning, University at Buffalo and the Waterfront Regeneration Trust, Toronto, Ontario.

23. *TorBuffChester*: http://www.creativeclass.com/_v3/whos_your_city/. Richard Florida http://en.wikipedia.org/wiki/Richard_Florida. Quote from *Globe and Mail*, http://www.buffaloniagara.org/About_BNE/PressRoom/2008Archive/February/TheBuffalo-

TorontoCorridor, accessed 7/14/14. http://www.creativeclass.com/_v3/whos_your _city/ maps/#The_Human_Capital_Map http://urbantoronto.ca/forum/showthread.php/3358-Tor-Buff-Chester-One-of-20-New-Megalopolis Tor-Buff-Chester is bigger than the San Francisco-Silicon Valley mega-region from: http://www.treehugger.com/sustainable-product-design/richard-florida-on-tor-buf-chester.html accessed April 21, 2014.

24. *In a special report by BMO Capital Markets...* BMO Capital Market special report, April 2014, entitled "North America's Economic Engine", by Robert Kavcic, Senior Economist, http://www.bmonesbittburns.com/economics/reports/20140425/GreatLakes1404.pdf, accessed 7/15/2014.

25. *Western New York Regional Economic Development Council binational strategy,* Progress Report 2013, http://regionalcouncils.ny.gov/sites/default/files/regions/westernny/wny-2013-Progress%20Report.pdf, accessed 7/15/14.

CHAPTER TWELVE

1. Phil Haberstro interview January 17, 2014.

2. *Buffalo is the sixth coolest summer city in the USA...* From: Bert Sperling, Sperling heat index, best places.net

3. *In 2009, there were 237 consecutive days without snow between the last snowfall...* Buffalo *News,* 11/28/09, "Buffalo, where's the snow?", Gene Warner.

4. Jay Burney interview January 15, 2014.

5. *The Oak Ridge national laboratory did a study...* From: Future U.S. Energy Use for 2000-2025 as Computed with Temperatures from a Global Climate Prediction Model and Energy Demand Model, Stanton W. Hadley, David J. Erickson III and Jose Luis Hernandez; S. L. Thompson, Oak Ridge National Laboratory; Lawrence Livermore National Laboratory

6. *National Geographic magazine did a cover story on "Rising Seas"...* From: "Rising Seas", *National Geographic,* September 2013, page 31.

7. *86% of urban residents in wealthy countries...* Source: Looming Disaster And Endless Opportunity: Our Worlds Megacities, by Saskia Sassoon, Megacities, number 2:2009.

8. *Recent flooding caused a rewriting of flood maps...* From:"Up in the air", Annie Linskey, *Bloomberg Businessweek,* 8/26 – 9/1/13, page 29.

9. *Matthew Kahn Climatopolis...* from "Will Detroit Become The San Diego of the 22nd Century?", Alan Stamm, Deadline Detroit, September 25th, 2014, http://www.deadlinedetroit.com/articles/10498/will_detroit_be_the_san_diego_of_the_22nd _century#.VFeJgMnp_xE

10. *The Internet's giant data centers generate heat...* From "Cool it," Larry Greenemeier, *Scientific American,* June 2013, page 23.

11. *There is one large data center in Western New York Yahoo....* "data centers are driving spending, not jobs" Matt Glynn, *Buffalo News,* 9/1/13, G1.

12. *Yahoo Inc. has just opened a new data center in Lockport, New York...* From: "Yahoo!'s New Lockport, New York Data Center Provides Jobs in a Depressed Area
Its Environmentally Friendly Design Relies on Western New York's Cooler Climate", Mary Carol Herwood, September 20, 2010, http://voices.yahoo.com/yahoos-lockport-york-data-center-provides-6823638.html, accessed 7/15/14.

13. *Another advantage of our region is that we have a relatively low risk of natural disasters...* From: "Where Disasters Hit Us Hardest," Erin Biba, *Popular Science,* August 2014, page 40.

14. *Bloomberg Businessweek magazine did an analysis of a ten year survey...* From: "Disaster Zones", *Bloomberg Businessweek,* May 9-May 15, 2011, page 74.

15. Erin Heaney interview January 16, 2014.

16. Lynda Schneekloth interview February 6, 2014.

17. Martin Doster interview January 20, 2014.

18. *All of the issues of waste in WNY are not historic...* Mapping Waste: Setting The Stage To Clean-Up Niagara, Waste and Pollution Working Group of the Western New York Environmental Alliance and the UB Urban Design Project, revised December 2012, page 8.

19. *Our habits of consumption on a worldwide scale...* Ecological Intelligence: How Knowing the Hidden Impacts of What We Buy Can Change Everything, Daniel Goleman, Broadway books, New York, 2009, page 4.

20. Ibid., page 30.

21. Jay Burney interview January 15, 2014.

22. *Ecological intelligence [is] our ability to adapt to our ecological niche...* Goleman, page 43.

23. *The business rule of thumb in the last century...* Ibid., page 11.

24. *There remains a disconnect between our collective role...* Ibid., page 32.

25. *Modern life diminishes such skills and wisdom...* Ibid., page 42.

26. Lynda Schneekloth interview February 6, 2014.

27. Loren Smith interview January 18, 2014.

28. *A "green net national product"...* Goleman, page 237.

29. *Life cycle assessment, or LCA...* Goleman, page 14.

30. *There is a "social dimension to products' LCA's...* Goleman, page 65.

31. *We need systematic metrics for sorting out...* Goleman, page 56.

32. *Ecological economics is a transdisciplinary field of study...* From the Gund Institute for ecological economics at the University of Vermont, http://www.uvm.edu/giee/?Page=purpose.html, accessed 8/14/14.

33. *The Natural Capital Project is a partnership...* http://www.naturalcapitalproject.org/people/collaborators.html, accessed 8/14/14.

34. Jill Jedlicka interview January 30, 2014.

35. Ibid.

36. Ibid.

37. Ibid.

38. Ibid.

39. *Western New York Environmental Alliance which has a shared agenda...* From: Mapping Waste: Setting The Stage To Clean-Up Niagara, Waste and Pollution Working Group of the Western New York Environmental Alliance and the UB Urban Design Project, revised December 2012, page 9.

40. Ibid.

41. Ibid.

42. *a group of scientists and engineers from Stanford...* From: Examining the feasibility of converting New York State's all-purpose energy infrastructure to one using wind, water, and sunlight, Mark Z. Jacobson, Robert W. Howarth, Mark A. Delucchi, Stan R. Scobie, Jannette M. Barth, Michael J. Dvorak, Megan Klevze, Hind Katkhuda, Brian Miranda, Navid A. Chowdhury, Rick Jones, Larsen Plano, Anthony R. Ingraffea, http://www.stanford.edu/group/efmh/jacobson/Articles/I/NewYorkWWSEnPolicy.pdf accessed June 9, 2014.

43. *private insurers say that last year was the second most expensive...* From: "Blown away", The Economist, 6/8/13, page 36

LIST OF ILLUSTRATIONS

COVER:
Demolition of Father Baker Bridge, Photo by author

TIMELINE:
Graphic by Robert E. Hochberg, REH Design

CHAPTER ONE:
Figure 1.1: Population trajectories for the nation, state, and region;
    Graphic by Robert E. Hochberg, REH Design
Figure 1.2: City of Buffalo ranking among US cities;
    Graphic by Robert E. Hochberg, REH Design

CHAPTER THREE:
Figure 3.1: Metropolitan area laborforce and employment;
Graphic by Robert E. Hochberg, REH Design

PART TWO:
Figure II-1: Speaking of curses, what's with Dallas? Photo by author
Figure II-2: Showing the growth of inner ring suburbs 1950 to 1960;
Graphics by University at Buffalo Regional Institute
Figure II-3a: Erie Canal 1950;
    Photo courtesy Lower Lakes MarineHistorical Society
Figure II-3b: I-190 2005; Photo by author

CHAPTER FIVE:
Figure 5.1: Metropolitan expansion in Buffalo and Erie County;
    Graphic by University at Buffalo Regional Institute

CHAPTER NINE:
Figure 9.1: wouldn't it be wonderful if Buffalo streets were filled with pedestrians like they are in big cities? Photo by author

CHAPTER ELEVEN:
Figure 11.1: Vacant land in the city of Buffalo; Photo by author
Figure 11.2: the City of Buffalo's "Good bones";
Graphic by University at Buffalo Regional Institute
Figure 11.3: Comparing street patterns;
　　Graphic by Robert E. Hochberg, REH Design
Figure 11.4a: Suburban-style infill on vacant city land; Photo by author
Figure 11.4b: Attached townhouses; Photo by author
Figure 11.4c: Multiunit, multifamily housing; Photo by author
Figure 11.5: New high-speed rail concept;
　　Graphic by Robert E. Hochberg, REH Design
Figure 11.6: Tor-Buff-Chester the megaregion;
　　Graphic by Robert E. Hochberg, REH Design

INDEX

256

ABOUT THE AUTHOR

Larry Brooks is a lifelong resident of Western New York. He was born in Lackawanna, raised in Cheektowaga, and for the last 40 years has been a homeowner in North Buffalo, where he lives with his wife of 43 years. His children, their spouses, and grandchildren all live in Buffalo.

Larry is now retired after several years in real estate, thirty years in industrial construction, and seven years working for a nonprofit environmental organization. His professional, volunteer, and social life has taken him through every town in Western New York, from Lake Ontario to the state line.

He wrote this book with the hope that it can help make Buffalo Niagara a better place.

CPSIA information can be obtained at www.ICGtesting.com
Printed in the USA
BVOW11s1347151015

422498BV00003B/4/P